CONTROLLING
WEEDS
WITH FEWER
CHEMICALS

*How to cut your herbicide costs
and protect the environment*

**Edited by Craig Cramer
and the staff of
The New Farm**

Greg Bowman

Mike Brusko

Karen Cicero

Bob Hofstetter

Christopher Shirley

Acknowledgements

Special thanks to former *New Farm* staffers Lesa Ayers, George DeVault, David Kendall, Michael Traupman and Fred Zahradnik, who contributed to this book; and to the farmers featured herein, many of whom painstakingly reviewed the manuscript to ensure its timeliness and accuracy.

Some of those talented, pioneering farmers and other experts also took time to write first-person accounts of their successes and failures with low-chemical weed control: Jim Bender, Tom Culp, Don Elston, Carmen Fernholz, Gene Logsdon, Russell S. Moomaw, Ralph Moore, Tom Morris, Steve Peters, and Dick and Sharon Thompson.

Finally, we extend our gratitude to all of the courageous individuals who continue to test alternative weed-management strategies on farms and at research sites around the globe.

Cover Design: Ed Courrier
Text Design & Page Layout: Karen Bleiker & Jim Redcay, Rodale Press
Production Coordinator: Helen Clogston, Rodale Press
Photo Research: Ramona Neidig & Rose Reichl, Rodale Press

RODALE INSTITUTE
Chairman: Ardath Rodale
President: John Haberern
Managing Director: Richard O. Wheeler, Ph.D.
Vice President: James O. Morgan

Published in the United States of America by Rodale Institute, 222 Main St., Emmaus, PA 18098

Library of Congress Cataloging-in-Publication Data

Controlling weeds with fewer chemicals: how to cut your herbicide costs and protect the environment/edited by Craig Cramer and the staff of The New Farm, Greg Bowman ... [et al.].
      p.   cm.
      Includes index.
      ISBN 0-913107-15-8 : $19.95
        1. Weeds — Control. 2. Weeds — Cultural control. 3. Conservation tillage.
4. Herbicides. I. Cramer, Craig. II. New farm.
SB611.C595 1991
632'.58 — dc20

91-28688
CIP

Table of Contents

◆ Chapter 5: Tools Of The Trade 91

Foreword
Why This Is The First Book Of Its Kind

In survey after survey, farmers rank "Weeds" as one of the top challenges to higher yields and better income.

Yet herbicides, which are by far the most commonly used tools for controlling weeds, have become increasingly risky to use.
◆ They're showing up in groundwater.
◆ They're getting more expensive to buy.
◆ They can limit your choice of crops in a rotation.
◆ They're undergoing intense legal scrutiny.
◆ And they're becoming less effective on several weed species.

Given all of that, you may wonder why it's so tough to find current, practical information on how to *reduce* herbicides.

One reason may be that you're looking in the wrong place.

If you're like most farmers, you typically get much of your crop production information from a chemical dealer. He's not likely to spend a lot of time telling you how to make the most of your rotary hoe, or how to use cover crops to smother weeds, or where to get beneficial insects that devour weeds.

Alternatives Are Risky, Too

But maybe you're relying on a more objective source of information — say, your county Extension agent or an expert at the local land grant university.

If that's the case, then there's an even bigger reason you have such a tough time getting information on alternatives to herbicides: There is very little scientific data on the use and cost-effectiveness of mechanical, cultural and biological weed controls.

For that reason, the "alternatives" may be just as risky as herbicides, themselves.

Granted, there are herbicide-cutting systems in place on thousands of farms all over the country. But none of those methods works the same way every year. And no one can say whether they'll work for you, no matter how closely your soils, weather, crop mix and equipment resemble those of the farms where alternatives have proved successful.

So, if you think you're about to read a recipe book for eliminating herbicides — a step-by-step blueprint that you can follow without relying on your own insight and experiments — you're going to be disappointed. That book hasn't been written, yet. And it probably never will be.

Learn From Your Peers

On the other hand, if you learn best by watching and listening to other farmers, and by using their experiences to help you test and fine-tune ideas for yourself, this book is for you. It features the most practical, innovative weed-management strategies uncovered by the staff of *The New Farm* magazine over the past several years.

All of the material has been newly updated, organized and edited with one goal in mind: to help you benefit from the collective wisdom of farmers and researchers who are pioneering low-chemical weed control by trial and error.

You'll read about their successes, so that you can apply the principles behind them (if not the actual techniques) to your own operation.

You'll read about their failures, too. It won't guarantee that all of your attempts to cut herbicides will be foolproof. But it can help ensure that your mistakes will be fewer, farther between and less costly than those endured by other farmers.

What you *won't* read is a glowing, varnished endorsement of low-chemical weed control. As any knowledgeable farmer will tell you, these techniques require a great deal of planning and precision. They're also subject to cooperation from Mother Nature. And they rarely provide the quick-fix solution that herbicides can offer.

Can those barriers be overcome? Are they worth overcoming?

We hope this book will help you answer both of those questions for yourself.

— *Craig Cramer and Mike Brusko*
August 20, 1991

Dedicated to the memory of

Robert Rodale
1930-1990

Chapter 1

HOW TO CUT HERBICIDES, AND WHY YOU SHOULD

Before you spray, take a close look at the real risks and benefits of herbicides.

The purpose of this book is pure and simple: to help you control weeds while reducing — or possibly even eliminating — herbicides.

But the first question you should ask yourself isn't, "How do I cut back?" It's "Why?"

Most obviously, there are health concerns. Studies have linked herbicide exposure to certain cancers in farmers and farmworkers. As a result, many farmers have turned dangerous application chores over to co-ops and custom sprayers.

But that won't keep herbicides out of your groundwater, and many chemical weed-killers are showing up in rural wells with alarming regularity.

Nonfarmers — both urban and rural — are concerned too. They want groundwater, lakes and rivers that are untainted by herbicides. They want food free of chemical residues — and they're willing to pay more for it. It doesn't take a think-tank policy study to predict that nonfarmers will play an increasingly powerful role in determining how you'll farm in the years to come.

But there are even more compelling reasons to cut herbicides — reasons that hit you right in the pocketbook.

Farmers spend more than $1 billion each year on corn herbicides alone, according to one USDA estimate. Much of the money is spent to control low-level weed populations that stand little or no chance of reducing yields or profits.

The USDA estimate is based on an experimental computer program that links weed-killing costs to profits in irrigated corn. In '89 and '90, 15 Colorado farmers tested the Corn-Weed Bioeconomic Model developed by USDA-ARS scientists. The farmers cut preplant herbicides by 40 percent — and saved about $15 per acre — *without reducing yields.*

"We can stop rating a farmer's ability to make money with how weed-free his fields are," says Dr.

Edward Schweizer, a USDA-ARS plant physiologist who helped develop the program. "Sometimes weedier fields are more profitable."

Once refined, the program could help corn growers reduce herbicide use by 45 million pounds nationwide. "With research like this, we can reduce the threat of chemicals accidentally seeping into our groundwater," adds Schweizer.

Banks and insurance companies are becoming increasingly concerned about farm-chemical liability. Add to that the fact that herbicides don't always work the way they're supposed to (either failing to control weeds or carrying over to damage sensitive crops) and you can see the writing on the wall.

The good news is, you *can* control weeds with fewer herbicides — or maybe even with none at all. University research from the Carolinas to the Dakotas has shown that it's not only possible, it's profitable. And farmers across the country have proved it.

In the next several chapters, you'll learn how they do it. We'll give you a preview toward the end of this chapter, too.

But first, you'll learn *why* cutting herbicide use is becoming such an important goal for many farmers.

You'll discover that herbicides aren't as convenient as you thought, and that mechanical and cultural weed controls offer flexibility that you simply can't get from a chemical-intensive program.

You'll also get a banker's-eye view of the potential risks posed by herbicides and other farm chemicals.

And finally, you'll learn why you should fight the urge to wipe out every last weed in a field.

We guarantee you'll find something in these pages that will help you farm in a more profitable and environmentally sound way. And we'd like to hear about your experiences. Tell us what works for you — and what doesn't. Write: Weed Control, *The New Farm*, 222 Main St., Emmaus, PA 18098.

How Convenient *Are* Herbicides?

They're no more convenient than non-chemical weed control, says this Nebraska farmer.

JIM BENDER

Is chemical weed control in row crops more convenient than non-chemical weed control? Does it solve more problems or create fewer problems than the non-chemical alternative?

Convenience is usually assumed to be the strong point of chemical weed control. I challenge this assumption. Here are some of the issues and problems of alternative systems of weed control in the context of a complete planting season. The force of my challenge will be the *sum* of considerations interspersed through four stages of a planting season.

Early Spring

Machinery requirements are central to weed control decisions prior to the beginning of spring work. Non-chemical weed control requires none of the machinery associated with herbicide application.

Chemical weed control occasionally requires all the weed control machinery of non-chemical control. A rotary hoe and a row-crop cultivator are minimally sufficient weed control machinery for non-chemical control. Chemical control requires some combination of the following spraying equipment: booms on tillage equipment, tanks on tractors, a general sprayer and liquid-handling equipment.

In addition, almost all chemical control systems include a row-crop cultivator to manage uncertainties in chemical control and a rotary hoe to cope with crusting problems and herbicide failure. Whether the rotary hoe is owned, rented or custom-hired, it must be taken into account when planning a chemical control system.

Another decision at this time of year concerns the location of crops. A chemical control system is much more restrictive because of herbicide carryover. Issues include compatibility between this year's crop and last year's herbicide, living with herbicide-stressed crops when compatibility is misjudged and sometimes being prevented from planting a particular crop in a field. One example is the incompatibility of oats with triazine herbicides. Non-chemical control faces no such problems.

Middle Spring

Primary concerns in spring tillage are weed

Having to find and wear protective clothing during one of the busiest, warmest times of the year is just one of the many "conveniences" that herbicides offer.

control and seedbed preparation. Chemical control systems with preplant herbicides add the need for herbicide incorporation. The problem from the perspective of convenience is that herbicide incorporation cannot always be combined with another tillage operation. For example, farmers sometimes till a field just to incorporate the herbicide, and sometimes till a field twice to enhance the incorporation. Nothing is gained by extra tillage except incorporation.

How much attention to detail in tillage do the alternative systems require? For non-chemical control, the final tillage prior to planting must be thorough, both to control weeds and to enhance uniform germination. Requirements of preplant herbicide incorporation include completely uni-

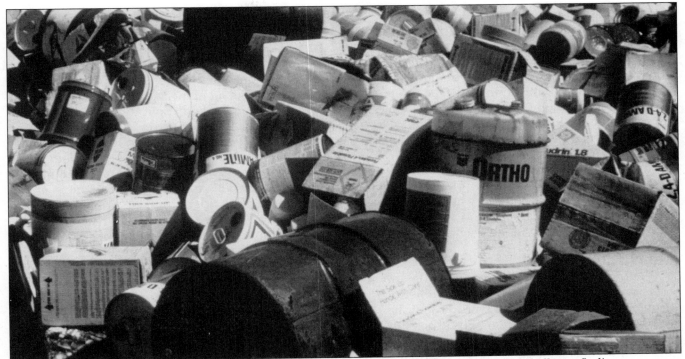

After you've enjoyed all the convenience of their contents, herbicide containers present an additional challenge: finding a convenient method of disposal.

form application. Missed spots result in no weed control. Overlaps increase herbicide costs and can increase herbicide stress on the crop. Uniform application also requires accurate tank mixes and correctly calibrated sprayer nozzles. Chemical control is more complicated and less convenient than non-chemical control at this stage of the planting season.

Planting Time

Each method of weed control can place stress on the crops. With non-chemical control the potential for stress is rotary hoeing, which tears out some of the crop seedlings. For chemical control the potential problem is herbicide stress. Only non-chemical control, however, permits compensatory measures. A farmer can increase the planting rate to compensate for thinning by the rotary hoe. In contrast, chemical control permits no way to compensate.

Planting places demands on a farmer's resources, and farming at this time of year is complicated by chemical control. Most chemical systems involve application of herbicides at some stage of planting, whether it is preplant incorporation by the tillage tractor, application with the planter unit or pre-emergence applications. In addition, the herbicide applicator who rigorously follows label and EPA instructions bears the burden of cumbersome protective clothing and other measures. Non-chemical systems are free of all these concerns at this acutely busy time.

After Planting

Shortly after planting, the fine-tuned weed control of non-chemical systems must begin. The inherent advantage of this method is that it can be applied *as needed*. Non-chemical control can capitalize on favorable conditions to reduce costs, work and management. For example, if rainfall is delayed after planting, conditions have permitted me to complete effective weed control with one rotary hoeing and one cultivation. In contrast, chemical systems are committed to the cost of herbicide before post-planting conditions are known. Chemical control has no flexibility to capitalize on cost-saving opportunities.

Crusting is one problem after planting. For chemical systems, breaking the crust with a rotary hoe is a wholly additional cost. For non-chemical systems, the crust-breaking tillage can be an additional benefit of the first scheduled rotary hoeing, so that its cost can be disregarded.

Another threat is early crop failure from many causes, such as heavy rain, hail, lost weed control or plant diseases. Crop failure can create two problems peculiar to chemical control. The first is the inflexibility of herbicides discussed above. For non-chemical control, crop failure means that some weed control costs can be avoided.

The other potential problem after crop failure is herbicide incompatibility between the lost crop and the replacement crop. Suppose that a field of milo is destroyed by hail in mid-June. The most obvious planting option available would be soybeans. There is a good possibility that soybeans will be incompatible with the milo herbicide. Even if the damaged crop is replaced with the same crop, it is difficult to determine whether enough of the original herbicide remains or whether a second application would be too much.

Two additional notorious problems of chemical control are herbicide drift and weed resistance to herbicides. Herbicide drift can damage the applicator's other crops as well as those of neighbors. Non-chemical control has no potential problem to harm other crops. The fast-developing problem of weed resistance to herbicides continues to include more kinds of weeds and expand to more areas of the U.S., another problem unique to chemical systems.

Conclusion

Chemical weed control generates problems at every stage of the growing season. Problems peculiar to this system include crop rotation restrictions, greater machinery costs, possibly extra preplant tillage, a small margin of error in application, herbicide-stressed crops, application demands at the busy planting time, inflexibility in coping with various crop conditions after planting and weed resistance to herbicides.

Non-chemical weed control is beset with its own significant challenges. Concerns include diversified crop rotation, lengthened planting dates to coordinate the workload of mechanical weed control and meticulous timing and application of mechanical weed control. Further, extremely wet growing seasons challenge non-chemical control and reduce the farmer's options. It is important to note, however, that these special concerns are surmounted by learning new skills and better management, not by additional cash outlays.

It is not clear how to tally which system "wins" the competition. I have described how chemical weed control — advertised as convenient in making weed control easier — causes numerous complications, inefficiencies and unresolvable problems that do not plague chemical-free weed control approaches.

Editor's Note: *This article originally appeared in* The American Journal of Alternative Agriculture. *Reprinted with permission of the Institute for Alternative Agriculture.*

The Trouble With Herbicides

Here's how to avoid herbicide failure, carryover, leaching and water pollution.

The trouble with herbicides is that they don't always work the way they're supposed to.

If it's too dry, some won't activate. If drought is prolonged, some persistent herbicides may carryover to the next season and damage sensitive crops.

Too much rain will leach other herbicides out of the weed-seed zone, and possibly into groundwater. Some that aren't prone to leaching bind tightly to soil. They can hitch a ride into surface water on particles of eroding soil.

How a herbicide behaves depends on not only on the weather, but also on its chemical makeup, soil type, application methods and other factors. (See sidebar, "How Safe Is Your Herbicide?") Predicting how effective a herbicide will be can get complicated. And guessing its ultimate fate in the environment is even harder. But there are still steps you can take to make sure you get good weed control — even when herbicides fail — and to avoid carryover and pollution.

Prepare For Failure

If soils are dry — like many were after the '88

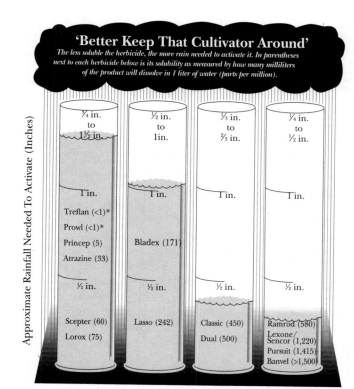

'Better Keep That Cultivator Around'

The less soluble the herbicide, the more rain needed to activate it. In parentheses next to each herbicide below is its solubility as measured by how many milliliters of the product will dissolve in 1 liter of water (parts per million).

Approximate Rainfall Needed To Activate (Inches)

¾ in. to 1½ in.	½ in. to 1in.	⅓ in. to ⅔ in.	¼ in. to ½ in.
1 in.	1 in.	1 in.	1 in.
Treflan (<1)*			
Prowl (<1)*			
Princep (5)	Bladex (171)		
Atrazine (33)			
½ in.	½ in.	½ in.	½ in.
Scepter (60)	Lasso (242)	Classic (450)	Ramrod (580)
Lorox (75)	Dual (500)	Dual (500)	Lexone/Sencor (1,220)
			Pursuit (1,415)
			Banvel (>1,500)

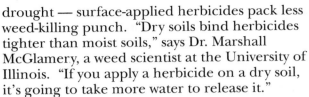

drought — surface-applied herbicides pack less weed-killing punch. "Dry soils bind herbicides tighter than moist soils," says Dr. Marshall McGlamery, a weed scientist at the University of Illinois. "If you apply a herbicide on a dry soil, it's going to take more water to release it."

Timely rainfall can activate herbicides in even the driest conditions, says Dr. Jeffrey Gonsolus, a weed scientist at the University of Minnesota. "A rough rule of thumb is that it takes about ½ to ¾ of an inch of rain within a week or so of application to move the herbicide down into the top couple inches of soil," he explains.

But some herbicides require more rainfall than others, observes McGlamery. In general, the less soluble the herbicide, the more rain needed to activate it (see chart).

How can you be sure dry weather doesn't confound your weed-control program? First, says Gonsolus, "Better keep that cultivator around. The herbicide is really just a labor-saving tool to buy you some time. You get the idea that it will do everything. But it's really just a complement to the cultivator and rotary hoe."

While dry weather can cause herbicide failure, it increases the effectiveness of mechanical weed control, notes Gonsolus. Weed populations are reduced, and drought-stressed weeds are more likely to dry up and die after cultivating, he explains. It's also easier to be timely when the soil is dry.

If you use herbicides, check labels carefully to match products and rates to your conditions, suggests Gonsolus. Crop residues, organic matter and clay can also bind herbicides. "In a wet year, you can get by with lower rates. But that won't work in a dry year," he cautions. Also, herbicide manufacturers are less likely to stand behind their product if you reduce rates.

Incorporating herbicides is a good way to reduce weather worries. Double-incorporation paid off during the '88 drought, says Gonsolus. "You could see the difference; there was a lot less streaking. But that won't show up in a wet year," he observes.

Another option is to incorporate herbicides lightly by rotary hoeing — and get some mechanical weed control in the process, he suggests.

In dry seasons, timing is critical if you rely on post-emerge herbicides. Weeds "harden off" in response to drought stress, says Gonsolus. Some develop tough waxy coats that herbicides have difficulty penetrating. For best results, select post-emerge herbicides that are most effective on the specific weed species that escape, suggests Gonsolus.

Herbicides Haunt Crops

Another dry-weather concern is damage to

How Safe Is Your Herbicide?

It's no problem finding out what a pesticide is supposed to control and how to mix it. All you have to do is read the label. But the label isn't as much help if you want to know how dangerous a pesticide is to you — or to the environment.

Fortunately, there's the Minnesota Extension Service's 34-page booklet, "Pesticides: Surface Runoff, Leaching, and Exposure Concerns." This guide provides the information you need to assess pesticide risks. The text clearly explains pesticide properties, such as the difference between LD50 (a measure of lethal toxicity when ingested, or when absorbed through skin) and LC50 (a measure of lethal toxicity when inhaled). Tables allow you to compare the toxicity of different products.

Using the tables, you can also compare:
◆ **Solubility** — How likely a pesticide is to leach from the soil.
◆ **Adsorption** — How tightly a pesticide clings to soil, influencing how likely it is to run off into surface water with eroded soil.
◆ **Persistence** — How long it takes the pesticide to break down.

Then, with information about your soil type, you can choose the "greenest" pesticide that will do the job.

To order a postage-paid copy, specify Extension publication AG-BU-3911 and send $2 (plus 6 percent sales tax if you live in Minnesota) to: University of Minnesota, Distribution Center, 3 Coffey Hall, 1420 Eckles Ave., St. Paul, MN 55108-1030.

crops from herbicides that carryover from the previous season. Perhaps the most widely publicized problem concerned Scepter, a soybean herbicide manufactured by American Cyanamid. The firm's officials acknowledged that carryover from '87 applications damaged 50,000 acres of corn in Iowa and Illinois, alone, during the '88 drought.

But Scepter isn't the only herbicide that can cause carryover damage. Others include:
◆ **Corn herbicides** — atrazine (alone and in mixes), Princep
◆ **Soybean herbicides** — Classic, Command, Commence, Lorox Plus, Preview, Prowl, Scepter, Sonalan, Treflan
◆ **Small-grain herbicides** — Assert, Curtail, Glean

There are steps you can take to reduce damage from herbicide carryover. First, pray for a warm, moist spring. If it's dry the spring following drought, herbicide residues in the soil will break down at a snail's pace. Even a cool, moist spring could pose problems by slowing early crop growth and reducing a crop's ability to overcome carryover injury.

If your prayers go unanswered, there is still plenty you can do to minimize crop injury — and to prevent it in the future. First step is to be careful which, if any, herbicide you use. "Read the label and see what it says about recropping problems," says Gonsolus. Plus, he adds, "A lot of people forget that a herbicide is just one part of weed management. You shouldn't let it dictate your whole strategy. You owe it to yourself to keep in mind it's just one tool."

'Easy Trouble'

The factors that increase herbicide carryover — like persistent chemicals, alkaline soil and reduced tillage — are the same anywhere. But label restrictions and growing conditions vary by state. If you spot a problem, contact your Extension agent or herbicide dealer for local advice.

Most of the questions they get concern atrazine. In areas affected by the '88 drought, corn and sorghum were the only crops farmers could plant in '89 if they applied 3 or more pounds of atrazine per acre in '88, or if they applied atrazine later than June 10, 1988.

If you use atrazine at 1.5 pounds or less, it's normally OK to plant soybeans the following year, provided soil pH is below 7.0. But if drought is severe, even those modest rates may be too much for the following year's soybeans, and you should test soil for herbicide residue. (See sidebar, "Test Herbicide Carryover For Yourself.")

Minnesota's Gonsolus is even more cautious. In '89, he suggested planting soybeans only in fields that received no more than 0.75 pounds of atrazine per acre in '88. "But we always find exceptions," he cautions. Again, the best way to find out if you're the exception is to test for carryover, yourself.

Sencor or Lexone can aggravate atrazine carryover, because all of these products have a similar chemical makeup, says Gonsolus. He also notes that wheat and alfalfa are even more sensitive to atrazine than beans are.

Many weed scientists say problems with Scepter and other new herbicides could have been avoided if researchers had had more time to evaluate how these products affect rotations. Scepter was first labeled in the South, where the warmer, wetter climate made carryover less of a concern. It marched north across the Missouri-Iowa border for the first time in '87. Scepter carryover posed less of a problem in Minnesota, where it was labeled only for reduced-rate, post-emerge applications.

The DuPont herbicides Classic, Preview and Lorox Plus could be a problem if soil pH is 6.8 or higher. And it's common to see oats damaged by Treflan and Prowl. Glean is the wheat herbicide most likely to cause carryover problems, says Gonsolus.

Don't Quit Rotating!

Your first reaction to drought-induced carryover might be to abandon your rotation. But planting corn on corn or beans on beans should only be a last resort. "First, you lose the demonstrated 5- to 10-percent yield increase due to the rotation effect," warns Illinois' McGlamery. You also lose the roughly 1-pound-per-bushel N contribution from soybeans. Add the cost of rootworm insecticide and the greater risk of root rot and cyst nematodes in second-year beans, and the cost of not rotating may be more than carryover damage, he notes.

Tillage is one way to reduce damage. That's bad news if you're trying to reduce tillage to prevent erosion. But the good news is there's little difference in the rate of herbicide breakdown whether you plow in spring or fall. And both practices remove herbicide residues from the "sprouting zone" equally well. Ridge-tilling has fewer worries, because the planter throws soil out of the row area.

Even disking or chisel plowing can help dilute "hot spots" where overlapping has left double rates of herbicide on strips of ground. On the other hand, cultivating after crops are up won't help much. By that time, the carryover damage is done.

Another alternative is to select a more herbicide-tolerant crop. For example, spring wheat is more tolerant than corn to the soybean herbicides Classic, Lorox Plus and Preview. Crop sensitivity varies depending on the herbicide, so, again, consult Extension or your chemical dealer for local advice.

Also, seek cold-hardy crop varieties. Plants with good early-season vigor are best able to outgrow damage. Some herbicide companies conduct trials to see if certain hybrids or varieties are more tolerant to carryover than others. Check with seed or chemical dealers for results.

Quality seed is an important safeguard against carryover damage, too. Quiz your seed corn dealer and check tags to make sure seed was properly stored, suggests Gonsolus.

Finally, do all you can to eliminate early-season crop stress from cold. Plant suspect fields last to give them a chance to warm up. That may reduce herbicide residues a bit and give crops a better chance to grow out of chemical injury. Some microbial and biological products claim to accelerate herbicide breakdown. But researchers say there is little evidence to support such claims. If you try them, experiment on a few acres first.

Document Problems Early

If you follow label directions and still have carryover injury, most herbicide manufacturers will provide reimbursement in cash or products, says Gonsolus. But it's important to document injury early in the season. Most carryover problems can be diagnosed before corn reaches the four- to eight-leaf stage. "As the season goes on, more things happen that can be blamed for losses," says Gonsolus. "Often you see physical injury without hurting yield. So you'll have to do a yield check, too."

There is a silver lining to the carryover cloud: Bad experiences might inspire some farmers to take another look at persistent pre-plant herbicides to rely more on prescription post-emerge applications and mechanical control only where they're needed. Some farmers aren't ready for the extra management that will take — mapping specific weed problems, planning rotations and tillage carefully to minimize infestations, and matching control measures to soil type and other considerations.

If you continue to rely largely on chemical weed killers, you will need to become a careful reader — and be ready to change herbicides as readily as a chameleon changes colors. As new products come and go, label restrictions change and regulation becomes more stringent, you'll have to keep up with all the new information.

Pollution-Prone Pesticides

A good place to start looking for herbicides that might soon face more stringent regulation is a list of pesticides the EPA tested for in its comprehensive nationwide study of drinking-water well contamination. (See sidebar, "55 Pollution-Prone Pesticides.") "These are the pesticides we're looking for because we think they have the greatest potential for ending up in groundwater," says Al Heier, a spokesman from the EPA press office.

"These pesticides are of particular concern because they are likely to leach, *even under normal agricultural use*," adds Mary O'Brien, information coordinator for the Northwest Coalition for Alternatives to Pesticides. "This list should make farmers pause to consider how vulnerable their groundwater is, and what they're putting into it."

Should farmers start looking for alternatives to these chemicals? "Sure," says EPA's Heier. "They should be taking precautionary measures. They're the ones drinking the water."

Test Herbicide Carryover For Yourself

Bioassay is a 50-cent word for planting a crop indoors in suspect soil to see if it's damaged by herbicide carryover. Bioassays beat lab residue tests two ways. They're cheaper. And, while they don't tell you the exact concentration of residues, they *can* tell you if it's risky to grow sensitive crops. Here's how to do your own bioassay:

1. Collect soil samples 3 inches deep from at least six different parts of the field.

The final sample should weigh about 10 pounds and represent no more than 10 to 15 acres. Take separate samples of "hot spots" where you expect higher herbicide residue levels — for example, headlands, overlaps, eroded knolls and terrace channels.

2. Start your bioassay within two days of sampling, or herbicide residues may start breaking down.

If you're delayed, freeze the samples until you are ready to start. Wet samples should be air-dried until they're workable. Crush clods, but do not pulverize.

3. Divide the 10-pound sample in half.

Add 1 teaspoon of activated (finely ground) charcoal to one half and mix thoroughly. Charcoal will bind herbicides and serve as a control. If you don't have charcoal, you can use a similar soil to the one you're testing — provided you're sure it has no herbicide residue — as your control.

4. Punch drainage holes in quart or pint containers; label and fill with "herbicide" and "control" soils.

Plant six bean seeds or 15 grass or grain seeds ½ inch deep in each container. Water thoroughly and place in a warm (72 F) spot that receives direct sunlight. Thin to three beans or 10 grasses or grains after emergence (otherwise, competition could be confused with herbicide injury).

5. Direct sunlight is needed for triazine herbicides (atrazine, Princep) injury to develop.

Look for yellowing on older leaf tips 14 to 21 days after planting. Yellowing progresses from tips and margins to center of leaf. High residues cause more rapid dieback and "burned" appearance. Symptoms of dinitroaniline herbicide injury (Treflan, Sonalan, Prowl) appear at emergence. Look for stunted plants, unrolled leaves and poorly developed roots compared with plants in the charcoal-treated sample.

6. If you want to make sure your residue-reading is accurate, do a separate bioassay using a more sensitive crop than the one you actually intend to plant.

The Minnesota Extension Service has developed the following chart showing sensitivity of crops to different herbicides.

◆ **Triazine herbicides** (atrazine, Princep)
Very sensitive — ryegrass, bluegrass
Sensitive — oats, alfalfa, wheat, sunflowers, sugar beets, potatoes
Moderately sensitive — soybeans, edible beans, barley
Tolerant — corn, sorghum, sudangrass, proso millet

◆ **Dinitroaniline herbicides** (Treflan, Sonalan, Prowl)
Very sensitive — ryegrass, bluegrass
Sensitive — sorghum, sudangrass, sugar beets, potatoes
Moderately sensitive — corn, wheat, alfalfa
Tolerant — soybeans, sunflowers, edible beans

55 Pollution-Prone Pesticides

The EPA's full list contains 70 pollution-prone pesticides, some of which are closely related to or are breakdown products of, other chemicals on this list. We've combined those under one name (trade names are in parentheses).

acifluorfen (Blazer, Tackle)
alachlor (Lasso)
aldicarb (Temik, Standak)
ametryn (Ametrex, Evik)
atrazine (AAtrex)
bromacil (Borea, Bromax)
butylate (Sutan)
carbaryl (Sevin)
carbofuran (Furadan)
carboxin (Kemikar, Vitavax)
chloramben (Amiben)
chlordane
chlorothalonil (Bravo)
cyanazine (Bladex)
cycloate (Ro-Neet)
2,4-D
dalapon (Basfapon, Revenge)
dibromochloropropane (Nemaset)
DCPA (Dacthal)
diazinon

dicamba (Banvel)
3,5-dichlorobenzoic acid
1,2-dichloropropane
dieldrin
dinoseb (Premerge)
diphenamid (Dymid, Enide)
disulfoton (Disyston)
diuron (Dailton)
endrin
ethylene dibromide (EDB)
ETU
fenamiphos (Nemacur)
fluometuron (Cotoran, Cottonex)
heptachlor
hexachlorobenzene (No Bunt, Ceku C.B.)
hexazinone (Velpar)
methomyl (Nudrin, Lannate)
methoxychlor (Marlate)
methyl paraoxon

metolachlor (Bicep)
metribuzin (Lexone, Sencor)
nitrates
oxamyl (Vydate)
pentachlorophenol (PCP, penta)
picloram (Tordon)
pronamide (Kerb)
propachlor (Ramrod)
propazine (Gesamil, Milo-Pro)
propham (IPC, Ban-Hoe, Chem-Hoe)
propoxur (Baygon)
simazine (Princep)
2,4,5-T
tebuthiuron (Graslan, Spike)
terbacil (Sinbar)
trifluralin (Treflan)

Ag Bankers Shun Chemical Risks

They don't want to get stuck with the cost of cleaning up environmental pollution.

GENE LOGSDON

OK, make a guess. If and when society's head-long rush to a toxic, unsustainable agriculture is stopped, which fearless group of dedicated environmentalists will get the credit? Greenpeace? The Organic Food Production Association of North America? The Amish? The Audubon Society? The Rodale Institute? The Sierra Club? The no-till marijuana growers of Meigs County, Ohio? Nope. Sit down and take a deep breath. How about the American Bankers Association (ABA)?

In the lunatic world of modern agriculture, it is difficult to think of *anything* so preposterous that it might not be true. This, remember, is the country where a hard-working, lower-middle-class family may pay more income taxes than a Texas oil company and then see its money go to subsidize millionaire Non-Farmers for Non-Farming. This is the country where old Mrs. Moneybags, who inherited 3,000 acres of prime farmland in Ohio that she has never set foot on, receives tens of thousands of dollars in farm subsidies — on top of a plush income from other investments left by her late husband that make her a millionaire three times over without counting the farmland at all. And as the richest citizen in her county, her accountants, God bless their pointy little pencils, have figured out a way for her to collect the largest Social Security check in town, even though she paid nothing into the retirement fund during her entire working life, which consisted of nothing more than fixing breakfast on Sunday mornings when the maid was off.

So it really doesn't push one's sense of propriety too far to envisage another manic scenario: Ag bankers may very well be the force that puts an end to the exploitive toxic farming methods that have helped make them rich.

Covering Their Assets

This change is not of the bankers' own free wills, to be sure. The real motive force is that mouthful of legal alphabet soup known as the Comprehensive Environmental Response, Compensation and Liability Act of 1980 (CERCLA) and the Superfund Amendments and Reauthorization Act of 1986 (SARA). To boil the fat of that legalese down to good clear lard, these two laws make anyone financially involved in a farm, however remotely, possibly liable for cleaning up any hazardous waste that is found there contaminating soil or groundwater.

It should be unthinkable that the farm, that once-mythic bastion of fresh air, clean water and good food — a safe place to raise children — is now a potential hazardous-waste site. But alas, in a lunatic world, such is the case. And not just because the back 40 might harbor some canisters of evil crud squirrelled away there years ago by the likes of Daddy Warbucks, or a long-forgotten underground tank with gasoline seeping into the soil. Or even because of a dump full of asbestos or PCB insulators which good old Jes Jimdandy, as president of the school board in 1955, allowed the school district to dump in his woods when the perfectly good township high school building was torn down in lieu of a consolidated in-town school — the new school that has had two new roofs in 15 years, the school where 80 percent of the graduates can't read. No, the main source of concern, because it is so tenuous and ubiquitous, is possible contamination from overuse or misuse of farm chemicals.

And why should this suddenly alarm the ABA, the national trade and professional association for banks of all sizes that, together, account for about 95 percent of all banking assets? Who do you think owns much of the farmland of America? You don't think farmers have been making enough money to finance all those new illiteracy schools plus the chemical companies and still pay off their mortgages, do you?

The law so states, or at least has been explicitly interpreted by judges to state, that a bank which assists in the conduct of the farm business it has financed, or forecloses on its mortgage, can in either case be liable for the cleanup cost of hazardous wastes found there. Doesn't matter that the bank or even the mortgagee may have had nothing to do with the waste problem. The liability may even extend to hazardous waste seepage or runoff from surrounding properties if your pockets are deep enough.

'Expensive Lessons'

"The courts have taught lenders expensive lessons about the amount of responsibility that can be placed on a bank that has financed or foreclosed on a property that is environmentally contaminated," says Michael E. Grove, chairman of ABA's Agricultural Banking Division. "Today we must analyze the lending risks from this problem just as thoroughly as the risks a banker might face from a drought or a significant downtrend in the market."

It was in the early '80s — hardly 10 years ago — when a common complaint of organic farmers was that they could not get bank credit. The standard banker position went something like this: *"Son, we've got our depositors' money invested in that corn, too, you know, and we strongly suggest* (you'll never get another cent from us otherwise) *that you spray for rootworms, even if you don't see any, just in case."* The Just-In-Case-Ass-Covering Policy was, in fact, the leading cause of farms turning into potential toxic waste sites in the first place.

But that was then and this is now, and keeping one's derriere clothed in silk and satin requires a total 180-degree turn today. ABA's new bombshell handbook, "Agricultural Lenders Guide To Environmental Liability," leads the way. Big red flags leap out of almost every carefully worded page.

"Although a lender is not liable as an 'owner' under CERCLA and SARA simply because it has a lien or security interest on the property contaminated by a hazardous substance," the book intones, "the lender can still be affected by the broad legislative reach of CERCLA and SARA. The value of any collateral securing loan may be significantly impaired or destroyed by contamination ... (or) the borrower may default because it cannot afford the cost of cleanup or regulatory compliance. The lender may incur cleanup liability either by exercising sufficient control over the borrower or the property to be determined an 'operator,' or by acquiring ownership of the contaminated property through foreclosure."

Therefore, to keep lenders clear of cleanup costs that can far exceed the value of the mortgage, the ABA is advising bankers to make a move that could do, in one deft stroke, what Sir Albert Howard and his legion of ecological followers have failed to accomplish in nearly a century. The bankers intend to turn off the credit spigot for chemicals if a farm enterprise reveals any significant risk of hazardous waste.

The ABA handbook advises bankers to make a thorough examination for hazardous waste before, during and after approving a loan. And when bankers, the epitome of caution, decide to do something thoroughly, you know what that means: No empty drum will be left unturned, no sprayer head left unobserved, no supporting legal document left unprepared, no expert opinion left unrecorded.

Although Grove insists that "with proper bank policies, bankers can continue to place quality loans in their ag loan portfolios," the upshot of ABA's new position will inevitably slow down the process — if not actually reduce the number of ag loans. "Well, yes, I'm sure some local chemical companies will find it harder to get credit," says John Blanchfield, manager of the ABA's Agricultural Bankers Division. "So will operators of intensive livestock operations where manure runoff has been a problem."

Thus, lenders will come full circle from 10 years ago: *"Son, we've got our depositors' interests to protect, you know, and we strongly suggest* (otherwise, you will never get another cent from us) *that you find a non-toxic way to control rootworms."*

Feds Pass The Buck

"We feel that we have been put in an extremely embarrassing role," says Blanchfield. "The courts have come down with decisions that they want us to enforce. The government is passing the buck. This should be the EPA's duty, not ours. But we're the deep pocket in this issue, and so we must protect ourselves. This policy doesn't really emanate from us. We are bankers, not chemists. If 10 years ago we seemed to advocate more chemical usage and now we advocate less, we are simply trying to follow the best expertise available at the time."

Wherever the blame (or praise, depending on your point of view) belongs for putting the kibosh on environmentally risky credit, the "Agricultural Lenders Guide To Environmental Liability" sends a strong message to agribusiness and to the public. Dow, Ciba-Geigy, *et al*, may *say* there's nothing to worry about with farm chemicals, with the Council for Agricultural Science and Technology (CAST), the Farm Bureau and the aerial sprayers chiming in with a rousing chorus of support, but the money lenders *are* worried and they don't intend to be left holding the environmental cleanup bag. It's enough to make even Tenneco tremble.

"He who has his thumb on the purse has the power," Bismark observed a century ago. That is even truer today when a large-scale corn dodger can hardly drive his Cadillac to town to play church bingo without a loan from his banker. Can you imagine multi-million-dollar Tyson Farms (shucks, with all the Tysons that work here, we're just a family farm, you know) announcing that it has just bought the state of Arkansas to use as free range for its organic chickens? Or Earl Butz hobbling up to the podium and saying to his good ol' agribusiness buddies: "Sure, we can go back to farming with chemicals, but which 500,000 of you want to starve to death?"

Borrowers To Pay More

The sticky part of all this is just how bankers will determine which farms they will consider to be environmentally at risk. "Some experts consider any type of agricultural property to be at risk environmentally," the handbook says, almost balefully. But it does not address that dilemma directly. A cotton planter and a certified-organic farmer are going to define risk-free in quite different ways. Whose standards are going to apply? How much chemical use is misuse?

"What we have to do is exercise enough 'due diligence' in a search for possible contaminants that will satisfy a court of law that we have done everything in our power to determine that a farm is not contaminated," answers Blanchfield. "We will rely on expert opinion from mainstream agriculture, and on regulatory standards. The EPA has set standards of allowable content, as for example nitrates in water. Label directions on chemicals give guidelines we can follow in judging misuse."

As it stands now, ABA wants its members to go through a risk-assessment process before approving a loan. The assessment begins with a detailed questionnaire, then proceeds to a review of public records about the farm, followed by a visual and sub-surface inspection of the property and, finally, a calculated estimate of any costs and changes in operations needed to make the property environmentally sound. Then a farm is classified in one of three categories: low-, medium- or high-risk. And God help the mediums and the highs. The lender may demand of them yet more environmental auditing from outside experts, in addition to its own detective work, the cost of which the handbook instructs bankers to pass on to the borrower whenever possible.

Chemical Conservatives

How much "due diligence" is necessary to give the bank innocent-party status according to the law is not known. "To date there is very little judicial guidance as to what should constitute a 'due diligence' inquiry," complains the handbook.

"The EPA guidance on landowner liability did not address questions of how to avoid such liability!" laments Ed Alwood, a spokesman for the ABA's Agricultural Bankers Division.

Obviously, in the absence of clear guidelines, banks will have to err on the side of caution when evaluating a property for possible environmental risks. The handbook then directs the lender to compare the value of the property with an estimate of the costs of curing any existing or potential hazard. If the latter is significant, "the lender should consider not extending the loan," according to the handbook.

Even if *"the risk requires no immediate action or can be cured inexpensively, the lender nonetheless should exercise caution if the real estate at risk is to be the primary collateral for the loan. Experience has demonstrated that environmental hazards tend to be understated upon discovery because of the difficulty inherent in making generalizations from the limited data afforded by inspections and resource sampling. In addition, public concern about environmental issues is continuing to prompt new laws and more stringent regulations which are likely to be retroactive,"* the handbook continues.

In other words, it is going to be as difficult to get credit for chemical-intensive farming as it once was for organic farming, even when the farmer is doing his best to follow the label exactly and calibrate the sprayer precisely. A sudden air inversion can carry drift from the most correctly calibrated aerial spray tank to the wrong location. The added hassle and red tape of determining risk classification will draw not only on the temper but the pocketbook. Just one water test for nitrates and pesticides costs more than $100, says the handbook. In addition, in today's phobic climate of eco-asscovering, any evidence of environmental damage, however slight, is going to reflect negatively on the value of the property. Lastly, the new oligarchy of deep-pocket agribusiness corporations, accustomed to gobbling up small farms at will, may just decide to go into something safer, like gambling casinos.

Farmers who have gone to the expense of having their land legally certified as organic are going to be smiling, yes, all the way to the bank. Sustainable farming practices will be able to compete financially with short-term exploitive farming. If you want to practice Chemical-Soak Tillage, be prepared to bring a whole bunch of your own money. Or get organized crime to finance you.

The bankers aren't going to give up without a fight, though. ABA President Kelly Holthus says one of ABA's top legislative priorities is to "seek changes in lender liability laws to ensure credit availability for American business and agriculture."

But that will not be easy, even for an organization as powerful as the ABA. There is good reason why CERCLA makes it difficult for a bank or anyone else to claim innocent-party status in hazardous-waste liability cases. Without the law, any owner of any property could sell it, perhaps in collusion with the buyer, and escape responsibility for the cleanup. The new owner, without the law, could argue that he did not cause the contamination, did not know about it and so does not have to pay for the cleanup, either. Not even in the lunatic world are the courts ever going to allow that kind of subterfuge ... are they?

Editor's Note: *Gene Logsdon is a free-lance writer in Upper Sandusky, Ohio. He is a frequent contributor to* The New Farm, Farm Journal *and other publications. "Agricultural Lenders Guide To Environmental Liability" costs $112 ($74.50 for ABA members). Phone: (202) 663-5399.*

Can You Afford 'Perfect' Weed Control?

Probably not. But here are some effective weed control tips you can afford.

RUSSELL S. MOOMAW

CONCORD, Neb. — We've all seen photographs of weed-free fields in herbicide ads, and we know about the "satisfied performance guarantees" that some chemical companies offer. These pictures and promises create unrealistic expectations of perfect weed control.

True, too many weeds will reduce crop yields. That principle won't change. But farmers need to take a closer look at their weed control programs to make sure they get maximum returns from the dollars they spend.

Here are some practical, research-based rules of thumb that can help you achieve that goal.

1. Total, full-season weed control is seldom economical.

We all take pride in keeping fields clean all season long, and multiple herbicide applications make that possible. The only problem is the cost of the chemicals usually exceeds the return from increased yields.

We learned that with an experiment on irrigated corn several years ago. On some plots, we applied a standard Lasso-atrazine mix at planting. Other plots received the same pre-emerge herbicide treatment; plus $7 to $11 worth of either Prowl, Bladex, Lasso or atrazine per acre at lay-by to control late-germinating crabgrass. The post-emergence applications provided excellent full-season weed control, but they didn't increase yields.

Weeds that come on in mid-season rarely cause yield reductions. Competition between weeds and crops is most critical about three to six weeks after planting. Before then, crops and weeds have relatively low demands for light and moisture. A good example is velvetleaf. It won't reduce soybean yields until it starts shading the beans.

The factors that influence weed-crop competition — like moisture — vary from year to year. But your crop is most likely to reach its yield potential if you keep weeds in check during that critical three- to six-week period after planting, by removing them before they're 3 to 4 inches tall.

2. Herbicides aren't perfect.

When using herbicides, don't be spoiled by the occasional good year when they really do the job. Be willing to accept less-than-perfect control due to poor weather conditions, and focus on controlling the effect weeds have on yields.

Researchers in Arkansas, North Carolina, Colorado and Minnesota have developed sophisticated computer programs to determine economic thresholds for weed competition. But you don't need a computer to know that moderate populations of many weeds can be tolerated without reducing profits.

Grass weeds, for example, are generally less competitive than broadleaves with row crops. The exceptions are tall-growing grasses like shattercane.

Pigweed escapes in soybeans can be unsightly, but spending money to control them isn't always justified. A good example of that is a 1986 study conducted in Lincoln, Neb., in which one pigweed every 20 feet in 30-inch rows reduced soybean yields by 5 percent. We seldom see infestations that heavy in farmers' fields, but most growers would intuitively decide that such weed pressure justifies additional control measures.

That may or may not be true. In this experiment, the 5-percent yield loss meant 1.75 fewer bushels per acre, compared with the 35-bushel yield in the control plot. So at $5 per bushel, you'd lose about $8.75 per acre by not controlling those weeds. If most of the weeds were between the rows, one cultivation would likely have been cost-effective. But if they were in the rows, cultivation wouldn't have worked as well, and the cost of a post-emerge band-application might be justified.

The effects of weed competition aren't the same under all conditions. For example, research in Nebraska and other states indicates that the same level of weed infestation will cause greater yield reduction in irrigated soybeans than in dryland beans.

Sandbur is another pesky weed that starts germinating around corn-planting time and continues into early summer. You can apply Treflan through a center-pivot system to control late-germinating sandbur at minimal cost. That will reduce new seed production, but it won't necessarily increase corn yields or profits.

During the '80s, herbicides clearly became the most popular way to control weeds. More than 90 percent of Nebraska's corn, soybean and sorghum acres were treated with herbicides in '82. Overall, the state's pastures, rangeland and major cash crops received more than 24 million pounds of weed control chemicals that year.

But environmental concerns and escalating costs have encouraged many producers to look at supplemental weed control practices. And that brings us to our next rule:

3. Since herbicide performance varies from year to year, supplement chemical weed control with good cultural practices.

Make sure you use clean seed with good germination. And if possible, try planting a little later. That will allow you to mechanically destroy one more set of germinating weeds, and the warmer soil will help crops germinate quickly to get a jump on weeds. However, conservation compliance on highly erodible lands limits the amount of tillage you can do and still receive government payments. Many farmers simply don't have as much flexibility to substitute tillage for herbicides that they once had.

Of course, there are risks to late planting. Unless you switch to a shorter-season hybrid or variety, an early fall freeze could damage your crops before they mature.

But with early planting, you will almost always have to rely more on herbicides. In northeastern Nebraska, for example, farmers may have more problems controlling weeds in soybeans if they plant in mid-May than if they wait until early June. Herbicides sometimes don't work as well in cooler soil, and crop vigor isn't as good with the earlier planting.

Crop rotation is another good cultural weed control. Crops suffer most from weeds that share the same life cycle. That's why winter annuals like downy brome and mustards thrive in winter wheat.

Rotating wheat with corn helps control these winter annuals, because spring tillage destroys the weeds before they mature. Even a corn-soybean rotation can help you reduce herbicide costs, since grasses like shattercane are less expensive to control in soybeans, and broadleaves like velvetleaf are often easier to control in corn.

Most small grains in our area are spring-planted and require very little, if any, herbicides. Oats compete very well with weeds, and the few weeds that survive in oats usually don't reduce yields. Winter wheat in the rotation would break up weed cycles even better, but it often winterkills here.

Finally, rotary hoe and cultivate at least once. We estimate total operating and ownership costs for rotary hoeing at $3.50 per acre, and row-crop cultivating at $4.50 per acre. That's pretty reasonable, compared with the estimated $14 per acre for broadcasting pre-emerge herbicides in corn, and $19 per acre in beans (not including application costs). Of course, those are averages, and herbicide costs vary depending on the products and rates you use.

Our research shows you can get maximum yields by applying a 14-inch herbicide band over the row, and cultivating between the rows. Hot, sunny weather and dry, mellow soil are ideal for successful mechanical weed control. But remember, extended rainfall can prevent timely cultivation, and larger weeds may be more difficult to kill when wet weather ends.

4. Some midseason weed controls may be worthwhile in the long run, even though they don't pay this year.

Soybean yields may not be increased right away by using wick applicators, bean buggies, bean bars or hand weeding to control escapes. But such practices can help reduce the weed seed reservoir in the soil over the long term. That's especially important with tough weeds like cocklebur, shattercane and velvetleaf. You have to decide if the cost of midseason control is warranted.

You can develop the best weed control strategy by knowing your fields and anticipating weed problems. Record weed outbreaks when you see them, and draw maps so you won't forget them next season.

Plan ahead to customize your weed control field-by-field, rather than using a costly, uniform program for the whole farm. If you expect grass problems but no broadleaves, use a grass herbicide, then wait to see if a post-emerge broadleaf treatment is really necessary. Be sure to get back into the fields where you expect problems, and take care of them before it's too late.

The challenge is to achieve the best possible weed control at an affordable cost. Recently, herbicides have been the cornerstone. Perhaps we can add more cultural practices and mechanical weed control to reduce input costs.

Editor's Note: *Russell S. Moomaw is an Extension crops and weeds specialist at the University of Nebraska's Northeast Research and Extension Center, Concord, Neb.*

Spray Less, Make More
Beef up your weed-control program with these farmer-proven tips.

Weed control is more like negotiating a treaty than waging a war. And lately, with herbicide costs rising and farm chemicals showing up in a growing number of wells, farmers are starting to think more like even-tempered diplomats and less like trigger-happy infantrymen.

"I've had to sit on my hands bad, sometimes. But I don't spray unless it's economical to do so," says Arkansas farmer Glenn Brown, who grows 1,200 acres of soybeans, milo and wheat.

Brown is one of thousands of farmers across the country who are saving $10, $20, even $30 or more per acre on herbicides. They're also helping keep chemicals out of groundwater, without sacrificing yields.

How can you do the same? By recognizing that total annihilation of weeds isn't always necessary for profitable yields, and that effective weed control involves every aspect of your farm — from crop rotation and tillage to equipment inventory and labor constraints.

Here are some field-proven tips to get you started.

Rotate Crops
It doesn't matter if you depend mostly on herbicides or mechanical weed control. Crop rotation is still one of the best ways to put weeds on the defensive. The trick is to disrupt their life cycles by alternating close-growing, cool-season small grains and forages with warm-season row crops.

Crops suffer most from weeds that share the same life cycle. That's why winter annual weeds thrive in winter wheat and other cool-season crops. Rotating wheat with corn helps control winter annuals, because spring tillage destroys them before they can set seed. Even a corn-soybean rotation can help cut herbicide costs, since grasses like shattercane are cheaper to control chemically in soybeans, and broadleaves like velvetleaf are often easier to control in corn.

The effect can be even more dramatic with ridge-till, where a corn-bean rotation can reduce potential weed pressure by up to 75 percent and cut herbicide costs in half. "If you want good weed control with ridge-till, you should rotate corn and beans. It just doesn't work as well with continuous corn," says Dr. Frank Forcella, a USDA weed scientist. Soybean roots tend to break up soil clods and keep weed seeds near the surface, so the ridge planter's sweeps can remove them from the row more effectively, he explains.

After seven years of good weed control, ridge-tillers who rotate corn and beans can rely exclusively on cultivation with little or no yield loss, according to Forcella's research. Farmers growing continuous corn can expect a 10- to 27-percent yield loss if they don't spray.

Cultivate, Even If You Spray
Cultivation pays off even with effective chemical weed control, land grant studies show. Just one pass increased yields as much as 24 bushels per acre for corn and 9 bushels for soybeans, according to a three-year study at the University of Illinois.

Row-crop cultivation costs about $4 per acre ($6 for ridge-till), agronomists say. "In contrast, many of the newer, broadcast post-emergence herbicides are selling at $15 to $20 for a single chemical," says Richard Johnson, an agronomist for Deere and Company.

Some herbicides make cultivation more effective. Farmers can save $14 per acre, get one-third better weed control and have up to three weeks longer to cultivate by combining cultivation with growth-inhibiting herbicides such as Classic, Gemini and Scepter, says Frank Webb, an Extension

New Farm Photo by Mike Brusko

A $150 herbicide-banding kit paid for itself after just 10 acres of spraying on Donn Klor's cash-grain farm in Buffalo, Ill.

weed specialist at the University of Delaware. That's because even though the active ingredients in those herbicides may not kill all weeds, they can suppress weed growth longer than products that block photosynthesis. "Weeds might stand but they won't grow, sometimes for two or three weeks." says Webb. "Any further injury will finish them off. That's where even a light cultivation comes in."

During drought, he adds, "Some herbicides are totally useless. But in many cases, cultivation paid out better than herbicides, alone." Still, he says, the two weed weapons together give farmers more flexibility. "I think they can have a happy marriage."

Band Herbicides

You can cut chemical costs by half or more simply by applying herbicides over the row and cultivating weeds between rows. Vic Madsen, who farms 600 acres in Audubon, Iowa, gets excellent weed control that way with just $5 worth of Bladex for corn and $7.50 worth of Dual and Preview for soybeans. Madsen's only warning: Make sure the band is wide enough to overlap slightly with the cultivator. "I had some escapes where they didn't overlap," he observes.

Before he eliminated herbicides completely, Vaughn Edwards of Terre Haute, Ind., banded herbicides only where they were needed, using a simple setup that let him turn his sprayer on and off from his tractor cab. One year, he received a post-emerge herbicide sample that the manufacturer said was enough for 5 acres of soybeans. Edwards covered *100 acres*, by banding it only where he saw weeds in the rows.

Put Nature's Herbicides To Work

When residues of many common crops — including sorghum, sunflowers and some small grains — decompose on the soil surface, they release natural herbicides called allelochemicals. Row crops no-tilled into fall-planted cereal grains can provide excellent allelopathic weed control, says Dr. Doug Worsham, a weed scientist at North Carolina State University. He cites good control for morning glory, sicklepod, prickly sida, cocklebur, pigweed, lambsquarters and ragweed when crops were no-tilled into a killed-back rye mulch.

Mike Strohm of West Union, Ill., used to spend $35 per acre on herbicides for no-till beans. But in '86, he spent just $5 to $8 per acre for weed control, due in part to the allelopathic effect of a grain rye cover crop.

Strohm established rye after corn harvest the previous fall. In early May, he no-tilled beans on 15-inch rows into the shoulder-high rye. Following his planter was a flail-type stalk shredder that reduced the rye to a weed-suppressing mulch. "We wanted to leave the rye on top, because when you incorporate it, you lose the weed control," says Strohm. Beans made 58 bushels per acre, about the same as his straight no-till beans. "The difference was I spent about $40 an acre on weed control in the straight no-till beans," he notes.

Plants in the sorghum family (including sorghum-sudan hybrids) are good at controlling annual weeds. Sunflowers — unlike many other allelopathic crops — don't appear to lose their weed-suppressing ability when incorporated into the soil.

Smother Weeds With Cover Crops

If you don't keep disturbed soil covered, weeds will cover it for you. That's why Michigan farmer Rudy Layher has been planting grain rye after row crops for 35 years. "We put it on any ground that would otherwise be bare over the winter," he says.

Layher broadcasts 2 bushels of rye per acre immediately after incorporating row crop residue with his fitting disk and harrow. "This seeding rate will compete well with the weeds," he observes. "There are very few weeds in the rye. It's a rugged crop that allows us to plow something down every year." As a result, Layher spends as little as $2 or $3 per acre for herbicides.

A cover crop of black medic can help farmers in the Northwest and Northern Plains cut herbicide bills, too, according to Washington State University (WSU) research. When managed as a reseeding annual replacing fallow in dryland rotations, this legume slows erosion, improves soil structure and water-holding capacity, reduces saline seep without pumping the soil profile dry, and disrupts weed and disease cycles. Although wheat following black medic had up to 47 percent more weed seedlings in WSU studies, wheat following barley had up to 30 times more weed biomass at harvest. Researchers think the medic minimized root disease, and helped wheat outcompete weeds.

Plan Ahead

You wouldn't use the same fertilizer rate on your whole farm. So why use the same weed-control program? The most profitable one is tailored to individual fields and — better yet — to different weed pressures in specific areas within fields. That means carefully scouting and mapping escapes during the season so you can plan ahead for next year. For example, an area with heavy perennial-weed pressure might be earmarked for extra tillage or a spot spray.

Land grant university weed scientists in several states have developed computer programs that allow farmers to scout weeds early in the growing season and decide if post-emerge applications are needed. Weed counts are fed into a computer program that factors in each weed species' competitiveness. For example, more than one cocklebur per 20 feet of row might be enough to reduce yields, while it may take 20 or more prickly sida plants (which are less aggressive) to do so.

Like IPM for insects, you spray only if herbicide costs will pay off with higher yields. "This takes the guesswork out of weed control and makes it more reliable," says Dr. Dick Oliver, an agronomist at the University of Arkansas who developed one such program.

Oliver's program saves Arkansas farmer Glenn Brown as much as $15 per acre in soybean herbicides.

Start Early, Plant Late

Fall is the perfect time to start thinking about low-cost weed control for next year — no matter how clean your fields look at harvest, and no matter what tillage system you use.

Do you have a hay or small-grain field that will be planted to corn or soybeans with conventional tillage next spring? Shallow tillage in early fall can awaken and kill many of next year's weeds without sacrificing erosion control, says Iowa farmer Dick Thompson. If you'll be ridge-planting next year's row crops into this year's sod, build ridges in early September so new weeds will germinate before a killing freeze, he notes. (That will force you to plan late grazing or hay harvest around weed control, of course.)

In both cases, seeding a cover crop after fall tillage will help control erosion and inhibit weed pressure even more, adds Thompson. Cover crops can offer many of the same benefits when overseeded into standing corn or soybeans or drilled after harvest in continuous row-crop systems.

On erosion-prone soils, avoid tilling pasture or hay crops until early spring. Then, use shallow tillage to incorporate the sod before planting row crops. That will expose weed seeds to the oxygen they need to germinate, and will let you destroy one more flush of weeds with tillage. You may have to plant row crops a little later than usual. That's OK. The warmer soil increases herbicide effectiveness and helps crops germinate quicker to get a jump on weeds.

But unless you switch to a shorter-season hybrid

or variety, an early fall freeze could damage crops before they mature. Delay planting too long, and yield losses can offset weed-control savings.

Cultivate Tough Perennials

Louis Riou uses his field cultivator to control Canada thistle without herbicides on his 300 acres of small grains near Arborfield, Sask. During fallow, Riou cultivates at weekly intervals, then uses a rod weeder at 10-day intervals. "The rod weeder tends to pull out, rather than sever, the thistle roots," he says. That slows root regrowth. Intensive cultivation is expensive, Riou adds. "But I got close to a 100-percent kill."

Fight Grasses With Fertilizer

Dairyman Larry Woolfrey of Brandy Station, Va., fertilizes and kills weeds at the same time in 135 acres of silage corn. He hires a custom operator with a high-boy to sidedress 75 pounds of liquid 30-percent N. The material costs about $18.75 an acre (including application). But in addition to providing enough N for a 15-ton silage crop, it also offers excellent grass control. "It definitely retards the grass. There's no other 'herbicide' I know of that will help grow a crop," says Woolfrey.

A new 'non-toxic' herbicide burns weeds much like liquid N. SharpShooter, from Safer Inc., is a broad-spectrum product registered for controlling weeds along fences, roads and barns. "It's a blend of naturally occurring fatty acids that penetrate plant cell walls and disrupt cell membranes, causing weeds to wilt and die," explains Fred DeFinis, Safer's marketing manager.

"It works fastest in warm, sunny weather," he continues. Depending on weed species and weather conditions, SharpShooter can deliver a complete knockout in anywhere from two hours to two days. It costs from 30 cents to $1.23 more per gallon, mixed, than does Roundup, but it biodegrades rapidly, DeFinis points out.

Customize Your Cultivator

Carl Pulvermacher has far fewer weed escapes since he equipped his four-row IH cultivator with a set of used disk hillers he bought for $80 in '86. They're one reason the Lone Rock, Wis., dairyman grows 160-bushel corn without purchased chemicals. "Two of the best-kept secrets in agriculture, if you're going to grow corn, are the rotary hoe and disk hillers," says Pulvermacher. Disk hillers are especially good at uprooting and covering late-season weeds like quackgrass.

One of Doug Wiley's secrets for growing 245-bushel corn without chemicals is his customized Alloway cultivator. "The most important thing is to have different tools that can be adjusted to do any job under every condition," says the Boone, Colo., farmer.

Wiley's bag of weed-killing tricks includes the spyders and spring-hoe weeders made by Bezzerides Brothers Inc. of Orosi, Calif., as well as S-tine furrow sweeps, L-shaped beet knives and platypus shovels for shaping irrigation furrows. He even attaches cultivation tools to his planter to control early weeds.

Says Wiley: "The most reliable and effective herbicide is cold, hard steel."

10 Years Without Herbicides
Weeds are still there, but crop yields keep rising.

STEVE PETERS

KUTZTOWN, Pa. — Weed-free fields may look attractive, but they cost you money. That's right. You needn't buy herbicides to eradicate weeds if you want to optimize yields in corn or soybeans, or even in small grains such as wheat or oats. A Rodale Institute Research Center (RIRC) study, the Farming Systems Trial (FST), has been proving this for more than a decade. In many fields, you can almost ignore weeds by using proper fertility practices.

The three FST cropping systems all use traditional tillage practices — moldboard plow, disk, harrow and cultipacker. The primary differences between systems are that the low-input ones use animal manures and/or legumes rather than synthetic nitrogen fertilizer, have more diverse rotations, and have more live plant cover throughout the year than the conventional cash-grain (corn-soybean) system. No herbicides are used in the low-input systems.

Although weed levels haven't changed significantly in any system, crop yields in the low-input plots have gone up tremendously. Low-input corn averaged about 80 bushels per year during the transition years (1981 to 1984), but since then has consistently matched or exceeded conventional yields of 140 bushels per acre. The county average for corn usually is 90 to 110 bushels per acre. For soybeans, we've matched or exceeded county average (anywhere from 30 to 50 bushels per acre) in all systems, despite weed levels in the low-input plots of two to three times that of conventional plots.

Weeds reduced yields in only two of 11 low-input corn treatments, when compared to plots kept weed-free by hand-pulling. In one of the two plots, a short-season hybrid produced a later canopy cover and enabled more weeds to take hold. In the other case, drought reduced the corn yield. Weeds reduced soybean yields in only two of seven low-input treatments since 1986, according to RIRC Agronomy Coordinator Rhonda Janke, who established the weed-free plots and helps with data analysis.

We see year-to-year shifts in weed species, as you would expect in most fields. You'll have variations over time, as cultivation, crop plantings, allelopathy, moisture levels and other factors affect weed populations.

Cultivation Confounds Perennials

Foxtail, pigweed, lambsquarters and bindweed have provided more than 50 percent of the weed biomass in almost all years of the trial. Other weeds include Canada thistle, dock, quackgrass, plantain and a few other perennials, plus some annuals such as ragweed, galinsoga and velvetleaf.

Bindweed has been the dominant weed in the conventional plots, accounting for anywhere from 30 to 55 percent of weed biomass. These plots receive 30 pounds of starter N per acre. We also sidedress 100 pounds of N in late June, and incorporate fertilizer with a shallow cultivation.

The conventionally treated soils usually crust over and pack down, reducing weed and crop vigor. Herbicides wipe out most annual weeds and a few of the perennials, but do a poor job of controlling pesky perennials such as dock, Canada thistle and bindweed.

Bindweed hasn't been a problem in the more friable soil found in the low-input plots. Two rotary hoeings and two cultivations with a ridge-till cultivator equipped with disk hillers (or old-fashioned shank or sweep cultivators before 1986) help keep bindweed and other weeds down. We typically rotary hoe seven days and 14 days after planting corn, before weeds have emerged. We

cultivate anywhere from 20 to 30 days after planting, when corn is 6 to 10 inches tall. Second cultivation is 30 to 45 days after planting, when corn is 18 to 20 inches tall.

Cultivation is the first line of defense for controlling weeds without herbicides. Cultivation timing, speed, disk-hiller settings, operator skill, soil conditions and weather all can influence weed levels. But even the best cultivation practices aren't enough to eliminate the effects of weeds on yields.

Long-term weed management, we've seen, requires the use of cultural controls such as crop rotations, cover cropping and, where suitable, intercropping or relay cropping. Well-designed cultural controls improve soil fertility and enhance biological processes at work in your soil, which in turn improves crop performance and enables crops to better withstand competition from weeds.

Rotations Keep Weeds On Defensive

Crop rotations are important for weed control in a number of ways. Good rotations limit buildup of weed populations and prevent major weed species shifts.

◆ **You can disrupt weed growth cycles by alternating:**

Clean-cultivated, warm-season annuals (such as corn and soybeans)
Densely planted, cool-season small grains
Mowed, untilled perennial forages

◆ **You can suppress weeds physically by:**

Selecting vigorous cultivars
Including a short-duration smother crop such as buckwheat, sorghum-sudangrass, or sweet clover in the rotation
Timing planting carefully
Overseeding a crop such as clover into wheat

We drill soybeans into small grains before their stems are elongated, to minimize tractor- and grain-drill damage to the small grain. We've had better results growing soybeans with winter wheat than with oats or spring barley. This is partly because fall establishment of wheat avoids spring soil disturbance and effectively suppresses weeds until soybean planting. Oats and spring barley require spring plowing, which stimulates many weeds that can interfere with soybean growth.

We've been getting county-average yields for wheat (40 to 45 bushels per acre). And our oats have produced 75 to 110 bushels, versus the 60-bushel county average. But we think we can do even better with small grains by using a modified rotation that will enhance nitrogen availability. Currently, the rotation calls for a small grain one or two years after corn, when nitrogen fertility is

New Farm Photo by Ed Landrock

Crop rotation and timely cultivation help corn produce profitable yields with no purchased chemicals at Rodale Institute Research Center.

on the low side. We'll be bringing more legumes into the rotation just before or closer to wheat. We'll continue to relay-crop soybeans into winter wheat but will simultaneously broadcast black medic or white clover to add more nitrogen. This will be followed by corn interseeded with ryegrass, and then spring oats planted with another legume green manure.

Any green-manure cover suitable for your area will provide balanced fertility and will improve soil structure. This should give the crop a competitive advantage over weeds. A big flush of nitrogen, as often occurs with commercial fertilizer or raw manure, will tend to encourage rapid weed growth and, therefore, likely will increase your reliance on herbicides. A slower-release nitrogen, whether from a legume green manure or composted manure, benefits the crop and the soil, our research shows. That helps reduce the need for herbicides.

Later Planting Pays Off

For corn that follows a legume, we delay spring planting until mid-May (more than two weeks past the conventional corn-planting date in our area) to allow the cover crop to put on as much biomass as possible. Just a few days difference can double biomass production, improving soil fertility and weed control. The corn quickly catches up to the conventional plots even without any starter fertilizer, thanks in part to warmer soil at planting.

Just before spring plowdown, we have almost weed-free stands of red clover, our primary legume green manure. Cutting the field with a flail mower the previous August stimulates clover regrowth and controls foxtail, the main weed present, before it goes to seed. We use a seeding rate of 10 pounds per acre for red clover, which provides 120 to 150 pounds of total N at plowdown. About 20 percent of this nitrogen is readily available to the crop, along with other nitrogen reserves from previous legume crops. We're considering adding to the cover a grass such as orchardgrass, brome or timothy. Our goal is to enhance nitrogen fixation, increase green-manure biomass and provide a higher-quality forage.

For the low-input plots that simulate a livestock operation, we apply aged steer manure in April, then plow immediately. An application of 8 to 12 tons (with straw and a moisture level of 70 percent) provides 150 to 200 pounds of N per acre. We're not sure how many weeds are being brought in with the manure. In recent years, we've seen more weeds in these plots than in the low-input plots not receiving manure, but this hasn't reduced yields.

To provide winter soil protection and to suppress weeds on some of our experimental fields, we've been trying to establish a cover crop in corn harvested for grain. We've had mixed success. The large amount of corn residue remaining after grain harvest suppresses growth of an overseeded cover crop. We've been experimenting with rye, ryegrass and various legumes broadcast in June at last cultivation or in late summer with a high-boy seeder.

Overseeding cover crops into soybeans at leaf yellowing (early September) has been very successful. We usually overseed hairy vetch, crimson clover or winter rye.

Weeds aren't all bad, I might add. They loosen the soil, reduce erosion from rain runoff and keep nutrients in the system for the following year's crop. You have to determine what weed levels you can permit without sacrificing yields. Economic weed threshold levels usually are a lot higher than visual comfort levels. In our study, we've probably had more weeds year to year than most farmers would. That's because they'll hand-pull weeds in trouble spots, do extra cultivation in problem fields or make other management decisions that a replicated study such as ours won't allow.

If you're thinking of adopting a lower-input system, you might not want to eliminate herbicides in one season. If a field has been pretty productive, and soil fertility and structure are good, then you probably can drop herbicides altogether. If it's a very weedy field or has low fertility, go a little slower until you're happy with your yields. In row crops, first do some testing, or banding or spot-spraying after cultivation. Your progress will depend on your cultivating skills, crop rotation and field conditions.

Based on our findings, you can minimize the effects of weeds on your yields by converting to a low-input system and keeping these recommendations in mind:

1. Begin with soybeans or a legume hay in a field with high nutrient status and good soil structure.

2. Include legume green manures in the new rotation; precede high N users with a legume.

3. Alternate cool-season crops (hay, small grains) with warm-season crops (corn, soybeans) to interrupt weed cycles.

4. Perform field operations such as plowing, cultivation and overseeding in a timely manner.

5. Experiment on a small scale so you can become familiar with practices such as rotary hoeing or overseeding without risking your entire operation.

6. Expect a three- to five-year transition period for yields to stabilize.

Over time, you'll find, as we did, that low-input management techniques reduce your weed worries and boost yields. They also reduce your *risk* — by decreasing year-to-year variations in your yields. That's something to bank on.

Editor's Note: *Steve Peters is project leader of the Farming Systems Trial at the Rodale Institute Research Center, Kutztown, Pa.*

Composting Kills Weeds

Composting manure before application will kill many — though not all — weed seeds found in manure, says Cyane Gresham, composting specialist at the Rodale Institute Research Center.

"A peak of 130 F followed by 120 F for most of the composting would be an ideal temperature range," says Gresham. "But don't be overly concerned about achieving a specific range. Some people think you have to maintain really high temperatures, but that can kill beneficial organisms. You'll have a range of temperatures in a compost pile, and it helps to turn the cooler outer edges into the middle periodically."

If you're adding pulled weeds to your compost pile, do so before they go to seed. Never add weeds with rhizomatous roots. "Many weeds that look really bad — chickweed, pigweed, foxtail and mustards or cresses, for example — compost really well, especially if you add them before they set seed," adds Gresham. "But avoid composting quackgrass, morning glory, nutsedge, thistles, dock, greenbriar and any really noxious weeds."

Chapter 2

DOWN ON THE FARM

*11 Midwestern growers share their best ideas
for cutting herbicide costs.*

You're about to meet a unique group of farmers. It's not their locations that makes them unique. They come from typical Farm Belt towns like Madison, Minn., West Union, Ill., and Easton, Kan.

Nor do they produce any off-beat commodities. Granted, most of them raise at least one type of livestock, which may be *somewhat* rare in today's world of specialized farming. But otherwise, their enterprise mixes are typical of their respective areas — small grains in the Plains, row crops in the Midwest.

What makes these farmers exceptional is *how they farm* — particularly their determination to solve problems such as weeds with more than just one type of production tool.

Many of them do use herbicides. But you won't find any of these farmers putting all of their weed-control eggs into the chemical basket. Before they even think of spraying, they use:
◆ Rotations that discourage weeds
◆ Planting schemes that help crops outrun the competition
◆ Cover crops that smother or suppress weeds
◆ Implements that uproot, chop out or cover unwanted plants
◆ And lots of other cultural, mechanical and biological weapons

Many of these techniques play multiple roles. For example, you'll read about crop rotations designed not just to manage weed pressure, but also to build soil fertility, reduce insect and disease problems, and control soil erosion.

Rather than omit such details and focus only on the weed-controlling elements, we've outlined each farmer's entire system. That way, you'll see

Cultivation is the cornerstone of most non-chemical weed-control programs. But the foundation is laid long before crops even emerge.

how all of the parts fit together. You'll also be able to identify the many general principles that these farmers make use of, no matter what they grow or where they farm.

We encourage you to look for these shared principles. They, more than the individual techniques themselves, are your real key to cutting herbicide costs.

Note how the farmers closely observe the life cycles of dominant weeds on their farms, and then how they design crop rotations to disrupt them. Study their use of early tillage — and of cover crops (including "weed" cover crops!) — to reduce the need for rescue measures later in the season.

And finally, read between the lines for the one thing that all of these farmers have in common: plenty of experience relying heavily on herbicides, and a commitment never to do so again.

How I Control Weeds Without Herbicides

It doesn't take a lot of special equipment. Just a good rotation, the right tillage and timing.

CARMEN FERNHOLZ

MADISON, Minn. — Weeds have been the proverbial burr under the saddle for farmers ever since we started tilling the soil. While I may never totally dominate weeds, I have reduced them to a manageable level on my 200-acre farm — with next to no herbicide.

In fact, I haven't used any chemicals since the early '70s — except for an occasional Banvel spot spray to control Canada thistle escapes on the portion of my farm that is *not* certified-organic. As my soils and skills have improved, my average yields have been inching up, too — corn from 100 to 110 bushels per acre, soybeans from 30 to 40 bushels and wheat from 35 to 40 bushels.

Those are respectable yields for western Minnesota. Plus, my crops cost a lot less to grow. The average farmer in my county spends about $40 per acre on fertilizer for corn. I depend on manure and legumes to supply my fertility. Their average herbicide bills run $15 to $20 or more per acre for corn and soybeans. I substitute a rotary hoeing or two, two cultivations and sometimes an extra preplant field cultivation on soybeans.

It doesn't take a lot of specialized equipment, either. My inventory isn't much different from my neighbors'. I use a chisel plow, a tandem disk, a field cultivator equipped with a mulcher, a rotary hoe and a row-crop cultivator. What it does take is some attention to detail, the right attitude and a carefully planned combination of rotation, timing, tillage and good management. Once you get that combination working together, non-chemical weed control gets easier every year.

Flexible Rotations

If I had to single out just one practice essential for weed control without herbicides, it would be crop rotation. Most farmers in this area rotate corn, soybeans and wheat. Normally, I add an extra year of small grains to that. It not only helps me control weeds better, it also fits the needs of the rest of our farm.

We keep our fields small. I don't have any fields larger than 30 acres. That, along with the longer rotation, gives us more flexibility to respond to the ever-changing provisions of federal commodity programs. It also gives us flexibility

putting together a balanced ration made up primarily of homegrown corn, barley and oats for our 60-sow farrow-to-finish operation. I also roast and feed my own soybeans, and occasionally feed some of my wheat, depending on market prices.

Livestock make sustainable farming much easier. But ours is a confinement hog operation, which doesn't really call for pasture or hay. To realize some of the benefits forages contribute to cropping systems, I'm experimenting with seeding non-dormant alfalfas — like NITRO — with small grains. I bale it and feed it free-choice to my hogs, and I sell any extra. Not only does it supply cover and help me control weeds, but it also provides extra N for my grain crops.

The best way to show you how I control weeds without herbicides is to run through the field operations for a four-year cycle, starting with the first year of small grains following soybeans. I usually plant oats or barley the first year, because they require less nitrogen than wheat. I leave the bean stubble untouched over winter to protect the soil, and I make just one shallow pass with the field cultivator and mulcher in spring. I've tried drilling the grains directly into the bean stubble without cultivating first. It worked OK except where the soybean trash was too thick and our press drill didn't get enough penetration. It would be no problem if we had a no-till drill.

One of the most effective ways to control grasses like foxtail in spring grains is to plant as early as possible. But to be successful, soil conditions must be perfect. If you work the soil too early, when it's still wet, the resulting compaction will create a perfect seedbed for grass weeds. The grains will get off to a slower start, too, and the entire strategy of early planting is negated. With the proper seedbed, spring grains will take off before weeds. They will tiller well and quickly dominate the field.

Another way to help grains outcompete grass is to avoid short-stemmed varieties. These varieties appear to tiller less. Coupled with their short stature, this makes them less effective at shading out weeds. I use PRESTON oats, which are medium in stature but high in protein — making them better for my hog ration. Most barleys are especially good at shading out weeds, because they

Clean beans without herbicides. Carmen Fernholz uses rotation, tillage and timing, instead.

have broader leaves. They also mature sooner and can be harvested before later weeds catch up and go to seed. Another way to increase competition is to experiment with increasing your seeding rate.

Broadleaf weeds such as wild sunflowers, pigweeds or lambsquarters are no problem if they've been adequately controlled in the previous soybean crop. They are warmer-season plants, so the spring grains mature well ahead of any of these weeds that happen to sprout.

Free Cover Crop

Weed control continues at harvest. I begin when the grain is still two or three percentage points above storable moisture levels. Then, I force air through the bin for several days to dry it down. Instead of windrowing grain, I direct combine. This reduces shattering losses in the field, and it lets me cut out weeds a few days earlier than if I windrowed. It also eliminates another trip across the field, and I don't risk having windrowed grain damaged by wet weather.

I disk grain stubble right after harvest to kill any weeds that may have survived *before they can go to seed.* Grass seed still in the soil seldom germinates this late in the season. But growing grasses have a tremendous drive to quickly go to seed after the grain comes off. So an immediate and

thorough job of tillage is necessary. This helps reduce weed pressure in following crops.

After cutting out the grasses with a disk, I chisel plow as soon as possible. This opens up the soil to soak up late summer and fall rains, and encourages shattered grain to germinate. The sprouted grain competes with late-germinating broadleaf weeds and provides an excellent — and "free" — cover crop before it winterkills. Some small grains, particularly oats, have been reported to have weed-suppressing (allelopathic) properties that also help control weeds.

Usually, I spread slurry from the hog house manure pit immediately after combining — roughly 4,000 gallons per acre (about 160 pounds of N, total). By immediately incorporating the slurry along with the high-carbon straw and stubble, I reduce nitrogen losses. As my shattered-grain cover germinates and grows, it takes up some of the soluble nitrogen that might otherwise leach. The soil is usually dry when I spread, so I avoid compaction. Chiseling right after spreading also helps reduce this problem.

In fields where I've experimented with the NITRO alfalfa, I broadcast about 10 pounds of alfalfa seed per acre (seed costs about $1.90 per pound). To sow the alfalfa, I use a Cyclone seeder mounted in front of the tractor when I plant grain. The grain drill presses the alfalfa seed into the soil. In '89, I didn't get a hay crop, because of the grasshoppers. But the alfalfa came back. I chisel plowed it in late November. I chiseled some strips twice and that gave me a better kill. These non-dormant alfalfas are supposed to winterkill this far north, but that hasn't always been the case. Still, they're easier to kill with the field cultivator and row cultivator than regular alfalfas are, because the non-dormants don't put as much energy into their root systems.

Since wheat requires more nitrogen than oats or barley, I usually plant it during the second small-grain year so it gets the benefit of the previous summer's manure application. Otherwise, my field operations and timing are the same as the first year. If I have an excellent soybean crop to provide lots of carryover legume nitrogen, I'll sometimes plant wheat after beans. Another reason I usually plant wheat the second year is that the varieties I use are shorter-stemmed than the other grains, and so are less competitive with grasses. But, hopefully, I've gained good grass control the previous season.

I depend on good weed control during those two years of small grain to reduce weed pressure going into corn. I've also built up a high reserve of soil nitrogen through manure applications and/or legumes. And, if the weather cooperates,

I've built up some moisture reserves, too. All of this is important, since corn is the foundation of my hog ration and I need abundant yields of high-quality grain.

Hoeing Hints

With row crops, the strategy is just the opposite of small grains: Instead of planting early to get a jump on the weeds, I delay planting and kill early weeds with tillage. But the reason is the same: You want to do all you can to get the corn and soybeans out of the ground fast to outcompete weeds.

Corn is very slow to germinate when soil temperatures are below 50 F. But cool-season weeds are well on their way when the soil is still 45 F. So if you plant corn in cold soil, the first thing to grow is weeds. That's why so many farmers rely on preplant herbicides.

As soon as my soil is dry in spring, I lightly work small grain stubble with my field cultivator. This helps warm the soil, forcing early weeds to germinate. Ideally, some rain and warm weather help speed the flush. I field cultivate a second time, 24 hours or less before planting, to kill the weeds that sprouted. Remember, weeds start growing right after you cultivate. Corn can't get started until you get it into the ground.

This second pass leaves a good, firm seedbed which aids in uniform planting depth and prompt germination. It's important never to work the seedbed more than 3 to 4 inches deep. You want to go just deep enough to kill weeds without bringing up a lot of new weed seed to germinate or waste moisture.

I usually plant around May 15, a week to 10 days later than usual for this area. I plant the same 95- to 100-day corn hybrids as other farmers do at the same rate of about 23,000 plants per acre. I may increase my planting rate slightly to make up for plants lost during rotary hoeing and cultivating close to the row. I know the rule of thumb is that I lose 1 bushel of yield a day for every day I'm late planting. But I don't think it applies to my timing. My corn is often up at the same time as others, despite later planting. And in a good year, I can still grow 150-bushel corn in my better fields.

Most years, early tillage and late planting are very effective. The corn germinates quickly and competes well with any weeds that come up simultaneously. If the weather is dry, I won't rotary hoe until the sixth or seventh day after planting. But if there is adequate to surplus subsoil moisture, I automatically rotary hoe within three to four days. If it rains anytime that first week, I'll hoe just as soon as I can get into the field. I also take advan-

tage of the more accurate weather forecasting we have these days. If rain is predicted on day six or seven, I'll hoe on day five. If a half-inch or less of rain briefly delays planting after I field cultivate, I'll plant shallower and definitely rotary hoe within three or four days.

I travel about 9 miles per hour when I hoe, and I look for occasional corn plants rooted out to make sure I'm using the proper speed and depth. With all row crops, I double hoe in opposite directions on the first rotary hoeing. This works so well, the corn often is tall enough to cultivate before a second hoeing is needed.

Timing is just as critical if a second hoeing is called for. You need to be out in the fields daily, scratching the ground and looking for the fine white roots of germinating weeds — *before* they break the surface. As soon as you see those roots, it's time to hoe.

Kill Weeds, Save Moisture

Since I use no herbicides — not even a band — I rely heavily on my six-row John Deere row-crop cultivator. It's equipped with half sweeps next to the row, full sweeps in the middle and Danish-tine spikes following the wheeltracks to reduce compaction. It's critical to set the sweeps next to the row as close as possible. I set mine just 8 to 9 inches apart on first cultivation, and I travel about 3 mph. I don't use shields, because I *want* to roll some soil into the rows. I open up the half-sweeps slightly on the second pass to avoid root pruning, and I speed up to about 6 mph.

To make it easier to cultivate close, I've returned to a front-mount cultivator. It makes it easier to negotiate the contours, and I can see all six rows. I also have dual-hydraulics, so I can raise one side of the cultivator and still keep the other side in the ground. That way, I can do a better job keeping point rows clean. This is very important, because one of my long-term goals is to reduce the source of weed seeds. And dirty point rows are a *very* good source.

Cultivating also helps keep the top 1 to 2 inches of soil loose and fluffy — one of the best ways I know for controlling weeds. That layer dries out quickly and prevents new weeds from germinating. It also forms a layer of insulation that prevents further moisture loss and helps rain soak in.

Weed control in soybeans is similar to corn, except I sometimes add a third preplant field cultivation, depending on weather and weed pressure. I'm trying to reduce the number of tillage passes by letting weeds grow as long as possible in spring, and hitting them with the tandem disk and then the field cultivator just before planting. Leaving all that trash intact prevents erosion and

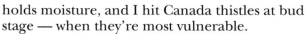

holds moisture, and I hit Canada thistles at bud stage — when they're most vulnerable.

I usually delay planting until June 10 to June 15, about two weeks later than most. I plant 12 seeds per foot at a depth of 1½ inches in this warm, moist seedbed. My beans germinate quickly — usually five to seven days after planting.

I use the same rotary hoeing guidelines in beans as I do in corn. First cultivation is usually just three weeks after planting. By cultivating this early, we can dig out or cover many hard-to-control weeds before they are well-established. Even Canada thistles have a hard time regrouping, because their prime growing season has peaked and the soybeans can overtake the thistles and shade them out. I also plant soybeans in rows running east to west whenever possible. This helps them shade the row middles faster. It's good for moisture retention, too.

Unfortunately, I can't keep weeds from going to seed in other farmers' fields. And those seeds get blown all over the place with snow and soil during winter. That's one reason why we, as sustainable farmers, also need to do all we can to keep windbreaks, grassed fence lines, pastures and hay land around to slow the spread of weeds from field to field.

Editor's Note: *Carmen Fernholz is a Rodale Institute On-Farm Research Cooperator in Madison, Minn. He is also Board Chair of the Minnesota Organic Growers and Buyers Association, and a member of the Sustainable Agriculture Working Group. He has farmed since 1972, and has been a certified-organic grower since 1975.*

Ridge-Till Without Herbicides
Cover crops and careful cultivation help save $45/A.

BOONE, Iowa — Half a dozen hay racks are overflowing with curious farmers, scientists and lawmakers. Dick and Sharon Thompson's annual field day is ready to begin. And if you count the contingent from the People's Republic of China, some have come literally halfway around the world to see how the Thompsons control weeds without herbicides.

A TV camera crew scrambles for a better angle, and the bullhorn crackles to life as Dick welcomes the crowd. "We don't have all the answers," he proclaims. "We're always looking for something better, so we reserve the right to change our minds. The last chapter hasn't been written."

Some visitors may be disappointed by the caution in Dick's opening remarks. But their concern will be short-lived. In about two hours, when the convoy of hay racks returns from touring the 300-acre farm, clusters of folks will be discussing passionately how the Thompsons:
◆ Grow 150-bushel corn without herbicides for $45 less per acre than conventional farmers
◆ Grow 50- to 60-bushel soybeans for $48 less
◆ Overseed cover crops to protect soil, suppress weeds and reduce purchased N
◆ Raise healthy cattle and hogs without antibiotics
◆ Store and handle manure to make the most of its nutrients
◆ Plant more than 200 research plots that satisfy the needs of both researchers and farmers, while helping the Thompsons fine-tune their own management methods

Still, it takes more than research plots to make a model regenerative farm. The heart of the Thompsons' message is that farmers can adapt — not adopt — their techniques. Test new practices on your own farm and let Nature teach you how to improve your bottom line, they stress. "There are no simple recipes," says Dick. "Farmers have got to think for themselves instead of letting everyone else do their thinking for them."

The Thompsons have been thinking for themselves for more than two decades, now. And while they've changed their production methods often during that period, they have never changed their original goal: "Profitable and environmentally sound farming — pure and simple," says Sharon. "It's got to sustain the land, the soil, the people, the communities and the pocketbook. It all has to fit together."

Whipping Weeds Naturally
Several practices work together to help the Thompsons grow ridge-till corn and beans without herbicides. "We've been doing it for more than a decade now, and have it to the point where we can write down how we do it without having an eraser handy," quips Dick.

Weed control begins in fall, when the Thompsons sow weed-suppressing cover crops (more about these later). In spring, their modified Buffalo ridge-till planter skims the top 2 inches of soil off the ridge, taking the cover crop, weed seed and manure out of the row. In '91, they tried removing the planter coulter and depth band on top of the ridge, replacing them with depth bands on each side of the ridge. "So far, it looks good," says Dick.

The Thompsons spread about 15 tons of manure-sludge mix per acre just ahead of the planter. The planter's sweeps throw soil off the ridge, covering manure between rows to help reduce N volatilization. "You can lose a quarter to a third of your N in 36 hours if you don't incorporate the manure," observes Dick. The only drawback is that spreading slows down planting.

The Thompsons are testing different starter fertilizers, carefully placing them next to the row where they'll give corn a quick boost instead of feeding weeds. "And no spring tillage on the ridges," stresses Dick. "All that does is wake up weeds in the row."

In '89 and '90 test plots, the Thompsons tried pre-cultivating cover crops before planting, either to kill rye in the valleys between ridges or to speed N release from hairy vetch. In both cases, weed pressure increased dramatically. "Pre-cultivation to remove cover crops in spring is not a good practice," says Dick.

High plant populations help shade weeds. The Thompsons plant 12 soybeans per foot (175,000 plants per acre) and corn at 7-inch spacings (26,000 plants per acre) in 36-inch rows. They choose varieties that emerge quickly, have good early growth and perform well at high populations. They also prefer tall corn hybrids and bushy, high-podding beans that fill in quickly between rows.

With no herbicides, weed control in the row is the toughest job. "The row area must be kept clean," stresses Dick. The couple rotary hoe corn about one week after planting (before crop emergence), and soybeans about three days after planting. A second hoeing and two cultivations follow at roughly one-week intervals.

The Thompsons set disk hillers just 5 inches apart at first cultivation, and use 24-inch sweeps. They use covered tent shields set close to the ground to keep weed seeds from being thrown back into the row. At last cultivation, they use 14-inch sweeps with ridging wings, and set disk hillers 9 inches apart to avoid root pruning.

Their five-year, corn-soybeans-corn-oats-hay rotation also helps control weeds. In '88, soybean ground in that rotation contained an average of just one velvetleaf plant for every 2 acres. In cash-grain demonstration plots where the Thompsons rotate ridge-tilled corn and beans, there were 807

velvetleaf plants per acre.

Covers Check Weeds

The Thompsons began experimenting with cover crops in the early '80s, by overseeding alfalfa and clovers into corn and beans at last cultivation. They soon discovered that perennial legumes were too tough to kill with the planter and competed with crops the next season.

Hairy vetch, a winter annual, showed more promise. "The planter does a good job taking it out," says Dick. "It worked for us a couple of years, but then shaded out when seeded at last cultivation. We realized that if we were working to shade out weeds, we were also going to shade out the overseeded cover crops."

So in '84, the Thompsons began aerial-seeding cover crops into corn and beans in early September. They tried hairy vetch, oats and grain rye alone and in combinations, and finally settled on a mix containing 30 pounds of vetch, 20 pounds of oats and 15 pounds of rye. "The vetch needs a companion," says Dick. Oats and rye grow quickly in fall for ground cover, then oats winterkill. The dead mulch protects both soil and vetch. It also provides some allelopathic (natural growth-suppressing) weed control in spring.

Total seed and planting cost for the mix is about $21 per acre. "These costs could be reduced by growing your own seed," says Dick.

In '88, the Thompsons switched from aerial seeding (which cost about $5 per acre) to using a highboy broadcast seeder built for $2,500 from a used corn detasseler. It seeds 16 rows per pass.

In spring, vetch and rye regrowth competes with early weeds. Vetch also provides nitrogen, while rye residues suppress weeds allelopathically. Together, the two crops improve soil structure and increase earthworm numbers, say the

Photos courtesy of Dick and Sharon Thompson

"We don't have all the answers," says Dick Thompson to the hundreds of farmers that attend his annual field day to learn about herbicide-free weed control. "We're always looking for something better."

By using a variety of cultural and mechanical tools, Thompson keeps most weeds between the rows, where they're easy to cultivate.

Thompsons. But don't be tempted to seed rye more heavily. The rank regrowth will be difficult to kill, use too much water and tie up too much soil N, warns Dick.

In fact, the Thompsons now seed no rye after soybeans. Instead, they drill a homegrown mix of 1 bushel of oats and 10 pounds of hairy vetch after harvesting beans. "Mid-Group II soybeans can be harvested by Sept. 21, and the cover drilled only on the ridge the same day as harvest," says Dick. Because cover seed is pressed firmly into moist soil, it normally germinates by October 1, the same as it would if broadcast into late-Group II soybeans at leaf yellowing around September 15.

On corn ground headed into soybeans, the Thompsons shred stalks down to the ridge, then drill 15 pounds of rye per acre in two rows 6 inches apart on the ridge. "The rye needs to be planted in the row area to be beneficial for in-row weed suppression," says Dick. "Rain will take its weed-killing chemicals down through the weed-seed zone."

150-Bushel Oats

The Thompsons' basic rotation hasn't changed much over the years. "We just picked up Dad's old five-year rotation in '67 and that was it," recalls Dick. They're still refining the details, though. For example, in hayfields to be planted to corn, they usually disk twice in fall, then build ridges and seed a vetch-oat-rye cover crop. In '88, they left some hay ground undisturbed until spring, when they incorporated manure and planted corn into a flat seedbed. That method yielded about 3.5 bushels more per acre compared with corn on fall-built ridges. But Dick considers spring plowing too risky.

After learning from some "mistakes" in '88, the Thompsons are getting as excited about oats as they are about corn and beans without herbicides.

First, the elevator broadcast 120 pounds of potash per acre — double what the Thompsons ordered. Then Dick accidentally drilled 4¼ bushels of oats per acre instead of the usual 3 bushels. The short-strawed DON oats averaged 142.5 bushels per acre, and tested at 38 pounds per bushel. "Some areas of the field were well over 150 bushels," says Dick. "I didn't think it was possible to grow that many oats and still have the hay seeding take, too."

Although they weren't hit by drought as badly as other areas were, the Thompsons say their soil-building rotation and cover crops helped them weather the '88 drought better than most. From '85 to '87, their soybeans averaged 5.4 bushels per acre more than the county average, and their corn averaged 8.7 bushels less. In '88, beans were 17 bushels above county averages, and corn was 27 bushels more. The farm received ⁸⁄₁₀ inch of rainfall during a 15-minute period on May 9. "It went in the ground here, while all around us it ran off and ponded," notes Sharon.

Better infiltration of moisture may have been enough to offset the water-robbing effect of the Thompsons' cover crops that year in most fields. But in one cornfield, yields were down 20 bushels per acre where the planter left some rye close to the corn row. "I blame most of that on the rye that didn't get taken out with the planter, not on the cover itself," says Dick. He believes drilling only two rows of rye on soybean ridges will eliminate this problem.

The Thompsons aren't satisfied with just perfecting their own farming system. They're also testing low-input rotations for cash-grain farmers who don't have livestock to eat forages and produce manure. They're most excited about a new, seven-year system they started testing in '89 with researchers from Iowa State University and the Soil Conservation Service. The rotation starts with a year each of corn and soybeans, then oats planted with an annual legume, then another year each of corn and beans. Oats are planted with a biennial legume the sixth year. And the biennial legume will be left as a cover during the seventh year — providing, in effect, a 14-percent set aside.

The rotation is established in eight-row strips on permanent ridges in a field with an 8-percent slope. To avoid point rows, ridges will run both up and down and across the slope.

Oats are drilled with ridges left intact, and the annual legume seeded with oats supplies N for the following corn crop. A vetch-oats-rye cover crop seeded into corn also adds N to the system. Any needed P and K is row-applied at planting. "There's no doubt in my mind this rotation will sustain the hillsides, the groundwater and the farmer's income, as well as reduce the taxpayer's subsidy to farming," observes Dick.

From The Heart

The Thompsons wonder if they'd still be farming today had they not quit relying on chemicals in '67. "We had a lot of borrowed money, then. The bank wasn't worried. But we knew what had to be paid back," says Dick. "It wasn't a crisis, but it would have been if we'd kept farming the way we did."

Today, the Thompsons are debt-free. But the changes they made affected more than their balance sheet. "There's a spiritual side to farming, too," says Sharon. "We just weren't satisfied with the way we felt inside about how we were farming, then."

They hope farmers catch that part of their message, too. "When the economics work with regenerative farming, people will go along with it," says Sharon. "But what happens when the economics are different? How long-lasting will changes be if they're only motivated by money? There also has to be a commitment from the heart."

What If It's Too Wet To Hoe?

Dick Thompson has developed what may be the closest thing, yet, to a rainproof mechanical weed-control program. The key is a cover crop sown in a double row atop his ridges.

If spring rains prevent timely rotary hoeing, Thompson simply lets the cover grow, and it virtually eliminates weeds within rows on the ridge. If it's dry in spring, he kills the cover a few weeks before planting, then follows his normal schedule of rotary hoeing and cultivating.

Now the best news of all: The idea may even work if the "cover crop" is *weeds*.

Thompson learned all of this with an experiment that began in late October 1990. After corn harvest, he shredded the stalks in one field. Then, using a Great Plains drill, he seeded grain rye at 15 pounds per acre in two rows 6 inches apart atop his ridges. "The space between the ridges is full of corn stalks, anyway. You couldn't grow anything there if you tried," he notes.

Rye grew slowly in fall, but Thompson says there was enough growth to let the plants survive the winter and regrow the next spring.

Thompson normally plants soybeans around May 15, but spring rains delayed planting until June 8. By then, he says, the rye was 2 to 3 feet tall and starting to head out.

Thompson shredded the rye and planted soybeans with his Buffalo ridge-till planter. The unit's ridge-cleaning sweep easily cleared the rye — including the crowns and most of the roots — from the ridges. "You have to make sure the crown is removed," warns Thompson.

Since the experiment was designed to measure rye's effect on weed populations, Thompson also planted corn with no cover crops in

Thompson's rotary hoe plays a big role in cutting herbicide costs. But his rye cover crop can replace the hoe in wet years.

some plots. "But because of all the rain we had in spring, the 'no cover' plots turned out to be 'weed cover.' Normally that wouldn't have happened, with bean planting on May 15."

The same thing occurred in a separate set of plots where Thompson had seeded rye into shredded corn stalks in April '91 instead of in fall. The so-called "control" plots — those without rye — were covered with foxtail and other grasses, plus some broadleaf weeds.

So, he wound up with some kind of cover crop on all plots.

Cover Replaces Hoe

In half of the plots, Thompson made three passes with his rotary hoe. The first took place three days after soybean planting. It was actually two passes — "up and back the same day," explains Thompson. The third hoeing took place a week later, after soybean emergence.

Other plots were not rotary hoed. But

Thompson cultivated twice in *all* plots — once on June 20 and a second time at ridge-building on July 8.

Thompson followed the same regime in corn plots where rye had been drilled into shredded stalks on ridges in spring.

By mid-August '91, after tallying weed counts, Thompson had made two observations: First, weed populations were extremely low in all of the plots, even in those with the "weed" cover crops. On average, there were fewer weeds in plots with spring-seeded rye (two to five weeds per acre) than where rye was fall-seeded (14 to 19 weeds per acre). But even the highest of those weed counts is nothing to worry about, notes Thompson.

Equally important, the three passes with the rotary hoe were not necessary. There was no significant difference in weed populations whether the plots were hoed or not. "If we got some kind of expression of a cover crop, we just didn't have any weeds in the first place," observes Thompson. "It's what we've suspected all along: Let early weeds control late weeds.

"All of this took place in a field that hasn't received herbicides in 24 years, and that normally has heavy weed pressure," adds Thompson.

The beauty of the program is the low-cost flexibility it gives a farmer. For less than $16 per acre ($1.80 for rye seed, $5.50 for drilling and $8.25 for three rotary hoeings), Thompson got excellent weed control without herbicides, plus all the soil-building benefits of a cover crop. And he could have managed with even less expense, because the hoeing wasn't needed.

Perhaps the rye cover wasn't necessary, either, given the excellent way his "weed" cover suppressed weeds.

But that's another experiment.

Whether the cover was rye or weeds, Thompson's subsequent soybean crop required no rotary hoeings.

Treatment	Broadleaf Weeds/A
Fall rye cover	15
"Weed" cover	19
Rotary hoe 3X	14
No rotary hoe	17
Spring rye cover	2
"Weed" cover	5
Rotary hoe 3X	2
No rotary hoe	4

Rotation And Tillage KO Weeds
While crop diversity reduces risks.

WINDSOR. N.D. — "All the studies show that 'conventional' systems do better under ideal growing conditions," says Fred Kirschenmann. "Well, my father has been farming in North Dakota for 58 years and he says he has yet to see an ideal season."

For many, the '88 drought was about as far from ideal as you can get. But for Kirschenmann, it was a year when the benefits of soil-building rotations, a diverse crop mix and careful management really paid off on his 3,000-acre farm. Despite receiving just 1.3 inches of rain between September '87 and August '88, he still harvested 13-bushel wheat. While that was a little less than half of his normal yield, "Some of my monocropping neighbors never pulled their combine out of the shed," Kirschenmann notes.

True, his oats and rye were a total loss. He just barely got back his buckwheat seed. But barley still yielded 9 bushels per acre and sunflower and millet yields were down just 15 to 20 percent. "Rotation reduces the risk of too much or too little moisture," Kirschenmann says. "If you have four crops and one fails, then you've cut your losses by 75 percent.

No Cookbook Recipes

"Diversity and flexibility are the keys to the economic advantage of sustainable systems." he continues. "Finding the right crop mix and rotation that works on your farm, that's half the battle."

Don't count on cookbook-recipe solutions, though. "That's what we've been taught to do, but it doesn't work. You need to find individual solu-

New Farm Photos by Craig Cramer

If his crop rotation doesn't get weeds, Kirschenmann's rotary hoe, rod weeder or Noble blade surely will.

tions because the biological systems are unique on every farm — indeed, in every field," he observes.

And don't be too hasty in abandoning chemicals. That's a lesson Kirschenmann learned the hard way. He simply stopped using chemicals on a third of his 2,000 crop acres in 1977. "We had terrific results the first year. There was less than one-half bushel difference in yields, and the weeds weren't any worse compared to our conventional fields," he recalls.

Kirschenmann quit chemicals on the whole farm the next year. "If you want a disaster on your hands, just stop using your inputs," he warns. "That's what we had for the next two years. We went too fast. Your soil responds to inputs, and it takes time for it to adjust when you stop using them."

Those first few years, Kirschenmann simply continued his father's wheat-oats-fallow rotation. He replaced standard NPK rates and 2,4-D with fish emulsion and humates. "But we didn't have a serious rotation plan," he remembers. "We thought we could rely on the other inputs. We quickly learned that rotation is absolutely critical."

During the disastrous second year, everything went wrong. Residual fertility had been drained from the fields that received no NPK the year before. Cool weather made the fish emulsion less effective. Weeds, especially pigeongrass (green foxtail), were rampant. Wheat yields were half of normal, and there was 20-percent dockage.

But Kirschenmann rose to the challenge. Instead of spreading raw cattle manure on the field closest to the cattle lot, he started composting manure and applying it to his poorest fields. "It took two or three years before we saw improvement," he says. He remembers one field where he spread compost only two-thirds of the way across a ¾-mile field, because that's how far it took to empty the spreader. "The oats were 10 inches taller where there was compost, and they yielded at least 20 to 30 percent better," he recalls.

Kirschenmann makes 1,200 tons of compost a year, enough to cover 400 acres at his usual rate of 3 tons per acre. "We just stack (manure) in windrows and leave it for about 10 days. We aerate it with a front-end loader before it reaches 140 F, because that's when you start losing nitrogen. Then it's ready to go to the field in eight weeks." He feels the time spent is worth the effort, considering compost's advantages over raw manure: reduced volume, easier handling, more stable nitrogen and fewer viable weed seeds.

Crops KO Weeds

While improving manure management, Kirschenmann also started to devise rotational schemes to build soil fertility and help control weeds. He added more row crops and warm-season crops, like sunflowers and buckwheat, and he started planting grain crops earlier in spring. "Spring wheat germinates at 40 F. Pigeongrass germinates at 50 F," he observes. "If you get the wheat in on time, it gets a jump on the pigeongrass.

"Buckwheat and millet like warm soil and hot weather. If you wait and plant them in the middle or end of June, it gives you a chance to kill a lot of weeds with tillage. It's like boxing. If you don't get them with the right, you can get them with the left. By alternating warm- and cool-season crops, you change the environment for weeds and get them off-balance."

All of Kirschenmann's grain is sold through the Mercantile Food Co., an organic grain exporter in Georgetown, Conn. He receives about a 15-percent premium for his certified organic grains over and above the extra handling and marketing costs.

The Right Rotations

Kirschenmann grows spring wheat because it

has the high protein and quality demanded by the organic grain market. "Winter wheat is an all-or-nothing gamble here," he says. "Plus, there's no organic market for it." His standard, five-year rotation is wheat-rye-sunflowers-buckwheat or millet (seeded with sweet clover)-fallow.

He drills wheat in 6-inch rows with a Morris disk drill. The drill is mounted behind a seeder-weeder — three staggered rows of narrow-shank Danish tines spaced 12 inches apart, followed by a single row of spring teeth. The unit disturbs the soil minimally, but still kills small weeds that have germinated.

After wheat harvest, Kirschenmann works the stubble with a Noble blade (V-plow), then drills 1.5 bushels of rye in late August or early September. "That's all we do until harvest. With all that competition and allelopathy (natural weed suppression from the small grains), weeds are never a problem in rye. Whenever my father had a problem with wild oats or mustard, he'd plant rye to clean it up." Yields average 40 to 50 bushels per acre. The rye sells for about $3 per bushel on the organic market.

Rye stubble is worked in fall with the Noble blade or chisel plow. "There's usually enough residue that we like to get some of it incorporated so that it can start breaking down," says Kirschenmann. In spring, a field cultivator or harrow is used to stimulate weed-seed germination and seal the soil with a dust mulch to prevent moisture loss.

"We plant sunflowers a little early (mid-May) to minimize seed weevil damage," notes Kirschenmann. "They (weevils) only eat about 10 percent of the meat, which is not a problem if the sunflowers are going to be pressed for oil. But it's a real problem for organic growers selling confectionery sunflowers. Consumers really don't like the damage." Planting sunflowers only once every five years helps reduce insect infestation, he says.

In '89, Kirschenmann planted sunflowers and soybeans in alternating 12-row strips. He got the idea from studies at North Dakota State University suggesting there might be less weevil damage to seeds in strip-planted sunflowers.

Kirschenmann rotary hoes sunflowers once before emergence, then twice after they're up. The final pass comes when plants are 2 to 3 inches tall. Usually, one pass with a vibra-shank cultivator finishes up weed control chores for the season. He disks sunflower stalks once in fall. "It's a tradeoff," he admits. "I'd like to leave them standing to catch more snow. But that makes insect problems worse. I still want enough trash to protect the soil."

Building Soil

The next spring, Kirschenmann kills the first flush of weeds with a shallow chisel plowing. A rod weeder destroys the next flush of weeds and volunteer sunflowers. Then Kirschenmann usually makes a second pass with the rod weeder just before drilling 50 to 60 pounds of buckwheat per acre (or drought-tolerant millet, if it's extremely dry) along with 7 pounds of yellow-blossom sweet clover. Buckwheat normally yields 900 pounds per acre, and sells for 16 cents per pound on the organic market, 40 percent more than conventional. "Still, it's the riskiest crop we raise." he observes. "Sunflowers take so much moisture, that we have to get rain to get a good crop."

Buckwheat smothers weeds and brings phosphorus up from the subsoil, says Kirschenmann. "The organic phosphorus is released from buckwheat residue back into the soil. I don't know if that's sustainable in the long run, but we haven't had any phosphorus deficiencies since we added buckwheat to the rotation," he adds. Deep-rooted alfalfa and sweet clover also pump subsoil nutrients into the root zone, he notes.

After buckwheat harvest, Kirschenmann lets the clover grow in fall and again in spring until it starts to blossom. "If you let it grow too much longer, it takes too much moisture," he warns. "If it's a good stand, I'll disk it, let it dry and then hit it with the Noble blade. If it's a light stand, one pass with the blade is usually enough.

Kirschenmann rotary hoes sunflowers once before emergence, then twice after they're up. Final pass comes when plants are 2 to 3 inches tall.

"Regular black fallow without the sweet clover burns up organic matter to release nitrogen. Kochia will thrive in a humus-depleted soil. But thanks to the sweet clover, we don't have that problem," he says. If there's inadequate cover in fall, Kirschenmann broadcasts a bushel of oats or barley per acre. The grains winterkill and provide ground cover until wheat is sown the following spring.

On lighter soils, Kirschenmann grows only two crops for every fallow year. "Organic matter is the limiting factor on these soils, so we're trying to build it," he explains. He applies about 3 tons of compost per acre and plants wheat. He follows

"Seeder-weeder" causes minimal soil disturbance, but still kills small weeds.

wheat with oats, millet or buckwheat seeded with sweet clover. On highly erodible land, he grows alfalfa for seven or eight years, then rotates to flax, oats or millet for a year or two before going back to alfalfa. He also works alfalfa into his five-year rotation to smother weeds in problem fields.

Waste Not, Want Not

Even when weeds manage to duck all of Kirschenmann's punches, he makes the best of it. In cooperation with North Dakota State University researchers, he's developed a winter cow ration consisting of alfalfa hay, oat and millet straw and ground weed-seed screenings. "There were no nutritional deficiencies and the calves gained just fine," he reports.

With both cattle and crops, Kirschenmann is somewhat reluctant to spell out the specific cost-savings of his farming practices. "When you look at the economics, your first reaction is that sustainable farming is cheaper. But it may not be," he observes. "You've got other input costs, like manure spreading and labor for weed control, to take into account.

"With sustainable farming systems, you need an early detection system," he explains. "When problems are easy to solve, they're hard to detect. And when they're easy to detect, they're hard to solve. For example, if your wheat or barley is 3 or 4 inches tall and mustard is starting to germinate, you can go out with a rotary hoe and take care of the problem. If you wait until the mustard is 3 or 4 inches tall, it's too late. You just can't check the fields from the pickup, anymore.

"The economic advantage is in the diversity," he adds. "You can spread the costs through the year. You don't have to go to the bank and borrow all the money at the beginning of the year and pay all the interest. With conventional farming, there are a lot of up-front costs.

"Once we add in the social and environmental costs, we'll find out just how expensive our current agricultural system is," he says. "But we can change it, if we want to."

245-Bushel Corn — Without Chemicals

Manure, rotations and cultivation help this farmer grow record corn yields for 80 cents a bushel.

BOONE, Colo. — Doug Wiley was disappointed with his 1986 corn crop. Low soil moisture before planting slowed germination, reducing his farm average to just 195 bushels per acre. His best field yielded only 207 bushels per acre. He'd hoped to better his 1985 record, when he was Pueblo County corn yield champ with a whopping 209.04 bushels per acre.

Wiley didn't take the news too hard, though. His '87 yields bounced back — and then some — with one early-harvested field producing 222 bushels per acre. And in '88, he set the county record with a whopping 245-bushel yield in a plot where he was testing a surge irrigation system.

What's more, he grew corn all four years without purchased fertilizer or pesticides. Intensive rotations, generous manure applications and an arsenal of mechanical weed control tools have kept his variable costs to just 75 to 80 cents per bushel.

"That was four years in a row, in different fields that I harvested 200-bushel corn. So it's no fluke," says the 1983 Colorado State University graduate. "Most farmers are inclined to believe yields will go to pot if you stop using chemicals. I personally don't like handling them. So we just quit in '83 and watched our yields steadily rise." Hail and late planting in '89 and '90 pushed yields down to around 190 bushels. But Wiley is confident he'll be back over the 200-bushel mark in '91.

Predators Replace Sprays

Wiley manages 250 acres of forage and grain crops fed to his family's 120-cow Holstein herd, which has a rolling average of about 20,000 pounds at 3.7 percent butterfat. Much of the credit for his low costs and rising yields has to go to the innovative farming system he developed to replace all purchased inputs except irrigation water.

New Farm Photos by Craig Cramer

To help break up plowpans and compaction, Wiley subsoils 18 to 20 inches deep before each corn crop that follows his triticale-sudax double-crop.

Take, for example, how he controls Banks grass mite (*Oligonychus pralensis* Banks; also called Date Mite). Left untreated, populations of this tiny pest can explode and ravage irrigated corn crops in the High Plains. In fact, the first year Wiley quit using chemicals, a mite infestation cut his yields in half.

Most local farmers used to spray Parathion or Furadan routinely, says Wiley. "You could get a kill that way, but chances were it wouldn't last. The populations would bounce back in six weeks and the mites developed resistance to the second spray."

The only pesticide that's still effective is Comite. "But it has to be sprayed pre-tassel, before you even know if you're going to need it. And it costs $18 an acre," says Wiley.

A hopeless situation? Not for Wiley. Since longer-season corn favors mite population buildups, he uses shorter-season hybrids than most of his neighbors do, and delays planting a week or two. He figures early planting pays off just one year in five, so it's not worth the extra risk.

But his main line of defense against the mite has been a six-year rotation: three years of alfalfa, corn, then triticale and sudax double-cropped, corn, then back to alfalfa. "By not growing corn on corn, I don't give the mite population a chance to build up," says Wiley.

Wiley established the rotation in six, adjacent 30- to 40-acre fields. That way, the two fields in corn each year are bordered on at least one side (usually two) by forages. When he harvests forage, a host of beneficial insects migrate into the corn and devour the mites. He provides additional habitat for mite-eating insects by only mowing his irrigation ditches when he absolutely has to.

By adding the triticale-sudax double-crop between corn crops, Wiley had no need to apply $10 worth of rootworm insecticide per acre. Total haylage yields from the two crops have topped 11 tons of dry matter per acre. And they make a perfect feed for dry cows and replacement heifers, because they have a lower TDN — but twice the protein — of corn silage.

"One of the biggest reasons I added the triticale is the effect of all those fine roots on soil aggregation," he explains. "It really improves tilth."

Wiley's rotation continues to evolve. To reduce labor, he plans to replace the triticale-sudax double crop with three years of perennial grass that he'll rotationally graze. He's also dividing his fields in half or quarters to take advantage of the border effects and increase his management flexibility.

Same Water, More Corn

Working to solve the mite problem also helped Wiley use his water resources more efficiently.

Wiley plows even productive alfalfa stands after three years, to maximize N production and weed smothering. "We may spend a little more for alfalfa seed," he says, "but I don't spend a dime for nitrogen or herbicides."

"Since mites attack stressed plants, I had a theory that I could get away from spraying by taking care of compaction and doing a better job of irrigation scheduling," he explains. To help break up plow-pans and compaction from heavy combines and manure spreaders, Wiley increased his acreage of deep-rooted alfalfa and other forages. He also subsoiled 18 to 20 inches deep before each corn crop that followed triticale and sudax.

Wiley used to irrigate corn every three weeks. "But it usually needs water every two weeks, so I was stressing it one week out of three," he says. Monitoring with a soil moisture probe revealed Wiley was losing much of his water to deep percolation. So he's now watering almost twice as often as before (based on results of soil probe), but he has shortened the length of his irrigation sets from 24 hours to 12 to 16, saturating the top 5 or 6 feet of soil.

All of this hasn't eliminated mite damage. "They're still out there," observes Wiley, noting that mites killed 30 percent of his record 209-bushel corn before it matured in '85. "It's just a race to keep them from getting off to a good start and then hold them off until the end of the season."

Forage Smothers Weeds

Wiley's crop rotation also plays a major role in his weed-control program. Corn always follows dense forage stands that reduce weed competition. Wiley takes some criticism for plowing productive alfalfa stands after just three years. (His alfalfa hay yields average about 8 to 9 tons per acre from four to five cuttings.) But he feels he plows down more N for corn and has less weed competition than he would if he waited longer and let the stand thin out. "We may spend a little more for alfalfa seed, but I don't spend a dime for nitrogen or herbicides," he quips. But with his new rotation, he plans to compromise and leave the alfalfa in a fourth year.

Weed control starts even before corn planting. To prepare the field, Wiley disks, spreads 20 to 30 tons of manure per acre, and disks again. Then he plows the field and forms beds with a power harrow followed by platypus shovels. The power harrow isn't as aggressive as rotary tillers are, says Wiley. It breaks up clods with a stirring action, and brings larger clods to the surface to form a moisture-holding mulch.

Once beds are formed, Wiley pre-irrigates to sprout early weeds before killing them with cultivator tools mounted on the front of his planter. Letting early weeds green up gives them a chance to release weed-suppressing (allelopathic) chemicals for late-season weed control, he explains. "It's almost like I banded on some herbicide," says Wiley. "When I pre-irrigate, I can get perfect weed control. That way, I don't have to rotary hoe after the corn is up. I'll hoe if the soil crusts, but I can just hear the corn screaming in pain when I do."

One reason the corn screams so loud is there's so much of it. Wiley plants 35,000 seeds per acre, shooting for a final population of around 32,000. He uses a French-built Monosem vacuum planter for more precise seed placement. Sweeps mounted in front of the planter slice off the top of the beds, and double-disk openers are set to plant corn deep enough to reach moisture — usually 2 to 3 inches.

Wiley looks for hybrids that germinate quickly, form a dense canopy, and stand well at such high populations. He tries to spread out planting time to avoid breaking his cardinal rule of non-chemical weed control: "Never plant so many acres of row crops that you can't keep up with the cultivation."

Customized Cultivators

"The most reliable and effective herbicide is cold, hard steel," he continues. Wiley is partial to

A pre-plant pass with his power harrow helps Wiley bring large soil clods to the surface to form a moisture-holding mulch.

the spyders and spring-hoe weeders made by Bezzerides Brothers Inc. of Orosi, Calif. (See Chapter 5, "Tools Of The Trade.") But he doesn't limit himself to one favorite tool. "The most important thing is to have a cultivator with different tools that can be adjusted to do any job under every condition," he says.

Wiley has hybridized his Alloway cultivator to handle just about any situation. For example, a typical cultivation schedule might start with spring-hoe weeders and spyders. The latter are offset-spiked wheels that break up and mulch soil close to the row, like a small weeding disk. Wiley sets these to throw soil away from corn when it's at the four- to five-leaf stage.

Bringing up the rear on this and all of Wiley's cultivation set-ups are S-tine furrow sweeps that run 1 to 2 inches deep between rows.

Second cultivation comes seven to 10 days after the first. On this operation, Wiley replaces the spring-hoe weeders with beet knives. These L-shaped half-sweeps cut weeds off the sides of the beds to within 2 to 3 inches of the corn without pruning roots. Spyders this time are set to throw soil back around the plants.

On the final cultivation, Wiley adds platypus shovels to smooth the irrigation furrows.

As effective as his pest and weed controls are, Wiley says he could never grow 200-bushel corn if it hadn't been for the thousands of tons of manure spread on Larga Vista Farm since his great-grandfather bought it in 1917. "The nutrients in manure are just the tip of the iceberg," he says. "It's the organic matter, soil-building and residual fertility from regular manuring that make our fields so productive."

While most local cropland contains just 1.5 to 2 percent organic matter and is vulnerable to wind erosion, Wiley's fields are protected from the wind by organic matter levels in the 2.5- to 3-percent range. "And it's hard to increase organic matter in this climate," he points out.

That kind of success makes Wiley bristle when he hears an occasional soil scientist claim that building organic matter isn't a valid goal. "It's backward thinking that you should build organic matter by growing high-yielding corn crops with a lot of fertilizer," says Wiley. "You should build the soil first. Then high yields will naturally follow.

"That's what my grandfather did," he adds. "He was such a good farmer that people said the soil talked to him. I want to carry on that tradition and pass the land on in even better shape than I got it."

Bin-Busting Yields On A Low-Herbicide Budget

Harrowing keeps chemical costs low and yields high

DELAVAN, Ill. — In the late '80s, Mark Graber typically spent just $47 to $56 per acre for seed and chemicals to grow 160- to 180-bushel corn. He only applied 70 to 140 pounds of N, and often skipped P and K completely. Plus, he controlled weeds with spot sprays and just one-sixth to one-third of the full broadcast preplant herbicide rate.

Likewise, Graber's 55- to 70-bushel drilled soybeans — which received no fertilizer and just 60 to 70 percent of labeled preplant herbicide rates — cost just $34 to $36 per acre to grow.

"I'll use chemicals when there's a good reason. But not automatically," says Graber, who calls these low-chemical practices CIRA — his tongue-in-cheek acronym for Controlled-Input Responsible Agriculture. "I'm not out on a limb at either extreme. I'm in a sensible middle."

And he has good reasons for being there, too — not the least of which is squeezing more profit out of his 830 rented acres. For example, Graber stopped applying P and K in one high-testing field in '86 because of planned highway construction. Since then, there's been no drop in yields or soil test levels.

"The standard practice around here is to keep putting on maintenance rates," he says. "But if I don't put on $40 worth of P and K that I don't need for seven years, at compound interest I'd save enough to put on $40 worth for the rest of my life," he reasons. "Putting money in the bank sure beats putting it into the soil."

With nitrogen — which Graber applies as 28-percent at planting and at first cultivation — his reasons for careful management are twofold: "With a split-shot, it saves at least 10 to 15 percent on material, and it helps keep the nitrogen out of our groundwater." He has cut his rate from 180 to 200 pounds per acre down to 140 pounds, and in some fields to as little as 70 pounds per acre.

But his decision to use as little herbicide as possible goes beyond short-term profits: "I cut herbicides for environmental and health concerns, not cost," he says matter-of-factly. "It wouldn't take more than a couple of extra bushels to pay for full rates."

A Little Dab'll Do Ya

Graber's bin-busting soybeans did just fine with less-than-label rates, even though drilling them on 8-inch rows eliminates row-cultivation as a weed-control option. "Because of their consistently higher yields, I can justify drilling beans in rotation with corn on my 630 acres of better, level ground," he says.

Those yields were as high as 70 bushels per acre before the '88 drought. But even that year, Group II beans still averaged 25 to 32 bushels, and Group III beans took advantage of late rains to top 40 bushels. "With my low costs, I still made money in '88," says Graber. In '89, beans rebounded to just shy of normal — 56 to 69 bushels per acre. "But your best bean crops always follow good corn crops," he explains.

Seedbed preparation those years started the previous fall when he moldboard plowed or chiseled and disked corn stalks. When plowing, Graber reduced the angle on the moldboard to leave more surface residue and prevent erosion. "It also pulls easier and uses less fuel, too," he observes.

Just because Graber drilled beans doesn't mean he relied solely on herbicides to control weeds. To prepare a seedbed and to flush and kill early weeds, Graber field cultivated twice in spring, a week to 10 days apart. On the second pass, he applied $4 to $6 worth of Sonalan at about two-thirds of the full rate. "I could probably get by with half of that three or four years out of five," he says. "But I'd have big trouble those other years."

He drilled beans with a JD 8300 as soon as possible after the second field cultivation, usually about the second week of May. His seeding rate was 80 pounds per acre — about 15 percent more than normal, to form a denser canopy and to compensate for plants that might be killed during later field operations.

Within four days of planting (before emergence), Graber harrowed once to kill weeds and to more evenly distribute what little herbicide he used. "I'm more of a believer in the harrow than the rotary hoe. And a field cultivator goes too deep and brings up untreated soil and weed seeds," he says. Occasionally, Graber has rotary hoed drilled beans when they're at the first or second trifoliate stage. "But I think that second pass with the hoe does more harm than good," he notes.

New Farm Photos by Craig Cramer

Corn without herbicides following alfalfa yielded 155 bushels per acre, just 2 bushels less than Graber's corn with herbicides, which was planted on better ground.

Graber built his own 25-foot-wide harrow by stripping the shovels off an old Glencoe field cultivator frame, building folding wings for easier transport, and mounting a section of Delta chain-link harrow to the frame. He can adjust the aggressiveness of the harrow by tightening or loosening the chain link.

Graber controlled broadleaf escapes by spot-spraying Basagran or a Basagran-Blazer mix. He usually used no more than half the normal rate, at a cost of $8 or less per acre.

"I keep diluting my herbicides until I have too little," he says. "If I don't see a scattering of weeds, then I've spent too much on herbicides, and I've probably hurt the crop, too. One of the reasons I have such good bean yields is that I don't damage them with herbicides. I apply just enough to keep the weeds from hurting yields, but not so much that the herbicide hurts the crop."

Banding Beats Broadcasting

Graber diluted herbicides even more in corn by banding, as well as harrowing. He field cultivated intact soybean stubble once or twice in spring before planting corn to germinate and kill weeds. Then at planting, he applied as little as half the regular rate of Dual ($3 to $5 worth) with 23 gallons of 28-percent N and 11 ounces of humic acid in a band 12 to 15 inches wide over 38-inch rows.

"The humic acid acts as an activator and extender," he explains. "When I apply a half-rate on a third of the ground, it means I'm only applying a sixth of the active ingredient in a normal broadcast rate.

"I've found that I can get good grass control with about a one-third rate of Dual, but not every year," he continues. "But a 50- to 60-percent rate should be OK most years. That's what works on my heavy silty-clay loam soils. You might get by with even less on lighter soils."

As with drilled beans, Graber harrowed corn within four days of planting, parallel to the rows to avoid herbicide streaking. "That distributes the Dual, erases tire tracks and helps emergence," he says. Harrowing also levels the small trenches left in the row by his JD MaxEmerge planter, and it increases yields. In '88, unharrowed corn yielded 65 to 80 bushels per acre, compared with 80 to 110 for harrowed corn. Graber sometimes rotary hoes or harrows again when corn is 2 to 3 inches tall.

At first cultivation, when corn is 6 to 10 inches tall, Graber applied another 23 gallons of 28-percent N. He cultivated at about 6 mph with a John Deere row-crop cultivator equipped with half sweeps next to the row, two staggered 7-inch sweeps and a 9-inch rear sweep. For the second layby cultivation, when corn is knee-high, he set the rear sweep to run deeper and increased his speed to 8 to 10 mph to throw more soil into the row. Graber spent up to $7 per acre to spot spray Banvel or 2,4-D to control buttonweed and other broadleaves.

No Herbicides Needed

On 200 acres of hillier ground, Graber worked small grains and alfalfa into his corn-soybean rotation, and eliminated herbicides in his row crops. Field operations for corn were almost identical to those he used on his better ground, except he skipped herbicides entirely.

Also, instead of drilling beans, Graber planted on 30-inch rows and harrowed, rotary hoed once or twice, and cultivated twice to control weeds. "Rotary hoeing packs the soil more than I'd like," he says. "I'd rather make an early, slow cultivation.

"Weed control in the no-herbicide beans wasn't as good as my drilled beans," he continues. "But it's tough to compare yields with my other ground because the no-herbicide crops were on poorer soil."

In '89, the no-herbicide beans yielded 52 bushels per acre, 11 bushels less than his drilled-bean average. No-herbicide corn following alfalfa yielded 155 bushels, just 2 bushels shy of this 157-bushel average for corn *with* herbicides. No-herbicide corn following beans yielded about 140 bushels.

Graber also double-cropped winter grains and beans on hillier ground. "In '89, I harvested 48 bushels of rye in the middle of July, and came back and no-tilled the beans in before the combine cooled off," he jokes. Graber applied Poast to the double-cropped beans to control grasses.

"I really haven't noticed much allelopathic effect on grasses from the rye," he says. "But the shredded straw conserves moisture and provides cover for erosion control. We didn't lose a drop of soil."

The double-cropped beans yielded 16.8 bushels per acre. "That was great, because I figured 11 bushels was breakeven for all my costs," says Graber. "Even if the beans fail completely, I still like to double-crop, because they fix N and make a good plowdown. I only wish we had a better market for rye."

Good To The Earth

To cut chemicals and diversify even more, Graber would like to add more wheat to his corn-soybean rotation. "But I'd have to drop out of the program and overplant wheat," he says.

Graber's three-year, low-chemical rotation is vastly different from his former cropping 'system.' Until '82, he grew continuous seed corn. "We were locked into a system that forced us to do our field operations at certain times, even if the soil conditions weren't right," he recalls. "We raised seed corn, buttonweeds, foxtail and compaction."

But with better timing, more care and fewer chemicals, Graber has turned all that around. "Our chisel plow used to bump along 6 inches deep. Now it goes down 12 to 14 inches," he says.

Graber gives part of the credit for reduced compaction to switching from anhydrous to 28-percent N. "You couldn't pay me to start using it again," he says. "Anhydrous over about 180 pounds per acre is going to hurt your other crops, too. I don't think I could be growing 60- to 70-bushel beans if I was using it on corn. The 60- to 70-bushel beans, in turn, help me grow better corn."

But just like his commitment to cutting herbi-

Mark Graber checks an average 1989 soybean field: $22 for seed, $4 to $6 for preplant grass herbicide, $8 or less for post-emerge broadleaf spot sprays — and 63-bushel beans.

cides, Graber's decision not to use anhydrous isn't motivated entirely by better crops and bigger profits. "For another thing, it's too dangerous to handle. And I'm not going to destroy myself or the earth just to get cheaper nitrogen."

$10 Weed Control In No-Till Beans
This farmer's cover crop saves soil and kills weeds.

WEST UNION, Ill. — In '86, Mike Strohm found a new product that controlled his weeds for as little as $10 per acre in his 200 acres of no-till soybeans. But he didn't buy it from his chemical dealer. He grew it himself.

His secret: A BALBO grain rye cover crop that Strohm shredded and used as a weed-suppressing mulch just after planting soybeans. "We were spending $35-plus an acre to control weeds in no-till beans, which was way out of line," says Strohm, who also grows hairy vetch seed and no-till corn on his 500-acre farm. "In '86, we spent $13 an acre — $5 for the rye and $8 for the herbicide. And I was as low as $5 for the herbicide in some places.

"I think this could work anyplace you grow soybeans," he adds. "Rye is very widely adapted, so I see no reason it wouldn't work on most any type of soil."

Strohm first tried the idea in '86 with the rye

Photos courtesy of Mike Strohm

Some rye volunteered after being shredded, but not enough to cut soybean yields, says Strohm. Planting beans a bit later could minimize rye regrowth, he suggests.

cover crop he'd sown on 160 acres of corn ground the previous fall. Immediately after corn harvest in October, he tore up the stalks with an AerWay (Holland Equipment Ltd., P.O. Box 339, 20 Phoebe Street, Norwich, Ontario, Canada N0J 1P0). This ground-driven tillage tool is equipped with rolling spikes that aerate the soil up to 8 inches deep without disturbing surface residue. "It helps get the decomposition cycle started and controls air and water levels in the soil," explains Strohm.

Into the partially chopped corn stalks he planted 1 bushel of rye per acre with a Tye no-till drill. "We had a real wet November, but the rye seemed to weather it well," he recalls. "It grew 2 or 3 inches tall before we got our freeze." The rye also withstood a winter marked by an unusual amount of freezing and thawing, Strohm adds. "I came out in spring '86 with probably a 75-percent stand."

Money-Saving Mulch

Strohm chose rye because he felt it would begin regrowing by March and take up excess spring moisture from his poorly drained soils. "If you can get the water out of the soil, it will warm up faster," he says. But that trait wasn't necessary in spring '86. Warm temperatures arrived early, and moisture was below normal.

By May 10, when soybean planting began, "the rye was shoulder-high, headed-out and pollinated," says Strohm. With a John Deere no-till planter, he planted beans in 15-inch rows directly into the rye, while another tractor followed with a flail-type stalk shredder.

Strohm used Williams 82 soybeans, a public, Group III variety. He saved his own seed, and aimed for a final population of just 120,000 plants per acre. Such a low planting rate virtually eliminates lodging risk, he says, but it also leaves him

with very little soybean canopy to shade weeds. "That's the reason we went to the mulch," he explains.

Strohm also relied on the shredded rye to cover soybean seeds. He ran almost all the tension off of his press wheels, and planted just deeply enough to allow good seed-to-soil contact. Still, the main purpose of the mulch was to control weeds. "We wanted to leave the rye on top, because when you incorporate it, you lose the weed control," Strohm emphasizes.

That's more than just a hunch. USDA and land grant researchers say rye is one of many crops containing allelopathic compounds — chemicals that, under certain soil and climatic conditions, inhibit the germination and growth of other plants.

While scientists don't fully understand the phenomenon, they find it's often less noticeable when the "weed-killing" crop is plowed or disked into the soil. For example, in a study at Purdue University, Dr. Marv Schreiber found that, "In systems where the moldboard plow was used for total incorporation of straw residue, giant foxtail control was poor. No-tilling corn into wheat residue gave excellent control of giant foxtail, whereas minimum-till showed only moderate control."

Bye-Bye Broadleaves

Strohm finished planting soybeans around May 20, and soon was convinced that smartweed and pigweed would no longer be the problem they'd been in the past. "The rye just completely took over the chemical control," he says. "I didn't have to chemically treat either of those weeds in '86." In fact, the only "weed" he did have to spray was the rye, itself, some of which regrew after being shredded. While many volunteer rye plants were taller than his beans, Strohm says the population wasn't heavy enough to affect soybean yields. "We only got one-quarter of the rye stand we had before," he says.

One thing he did notice was that rye seemed harder to control in the earliest-planted beans. "The later I planted, the less I needed to spray," says Strohm. The most likely reason is that, in the early-planted beans, "the young rye plants had more energy left in their roots for regrowth," he says.

Toward the end of soybean planting, the rye was more mature and was putting most of its energy into seed production, Strohm adds. "So we're probably looking at a trade-off, because the earlier you plant soybeans, the better your yields." On the other hand, later-planted beans may yield less, but require little or no post-emerge herbicide to kill rye.

Overall, Strohm applied from $5 to $8 worth of herbicide per acre to kill the rye. That's less than one-fifth what he spent on herbicides in his 40 acres of no-till beans not planted into rye.

The real payoff came at harvest. "We had yields as high as 64.35 bushels in the 'rye' beans, and my average over the whole 200 acres was 58 bushels," says Strohm. Yields in straight no-till beans were about the same as his farm average, he adds. "But the difference was I spent about $40 an acre on chemical weed control."

To put it all into perspective, "Where before we were giving the chemical company eight bushels of soybeans, this year we only gave them one, because I grew the rye seed myself," says Strohm. "The only reason I even included the rye seed in the total weed control cost is because we have to put some value to it."

Not surprisingly, Strohm drilled rye on all 200 acres of 1986 corn ground to be rotated to no-till

Immediately after planting no-till soybeans, Strohm shreds the shoulder-high rye to provide a weed-suppressing mulch.

soybeans in '87. "I feel like I've developed a system I can stick with," he says. "I'm looking for ways to eliminate all herbicide use. And if our planting dates are a little later, I'm sure we can do that."

Organic Matter Up 40%

In '88, Strohm found out the hard way how much moisture rye covers can use. Soybeans planted into rye mulch that year were a total disaster. "You've got to carefully monitor soil moisture in the spring," he says.

If moisture is short in spring, Strohm now kills rye with Roundup when it's 6 to 18 inches tall, or with Gramoxone if it's headed out. If he lets it go to shoulder height, he disks it once instead of mowing. He also makes one pass before planting with the AerWay to fluff up the soil — immediately after disking or after the burndown herbicide has killed the rye. With the high-carbon mulch from corn stalks and rye, Strohm says it pays to inoculate soybean seeds to assure good N fixation.

Strohm also has reduced his N rate on corn from 150 pounds per acre to 75 by drilling a hairy vetch cover crop at 25 pounds per acre following wheat. He disks the vetch once in fall to kill it. That speeds N release from the vetch in spring, he says.

Strohm says the rye and vetch covers have helped increase his soil organic matter levels by 40 percent. Fields that were running 1.5 percent organic matter are now up in the 2.2- to 2.5-percent range. "Commercial nitrogen can offset soil degradation, but it can't build the soil," says Strohm. "I use the rye to recycle leftover nitrogen back into organic matter. Organic matter is a perfect place to store N."

Listing Leaves Herbicides Behind

An "old-fashioned" tillage method helped this farmer control weeds without chemicals in first-year corn.

O'NEILL, Neb. — "When I started farming in '76, I used everything — all the fertilizers and chemicals everyone else used. It seemed like the only option," recalls Curt Morrow, who farms 420 acres and tends a 26-cow, cow-calf herd in north-central Nebraska.

The turning point came in '79, when Morrow invested $20,000 in his corn crop only to watch it be destroyed by hail. "It made me think that I'm

really sticking my neck out by putting all that money out there when so many things can come along and take it away," he says.

So, ignoring conventional wisdom, Morrow began rotating his irrigated corn with oats and alfalfa — a radical departure in an area dominated by continuous corn under center-pivot rigs. And with help from a tillage system most of his neighbors would call old-fashioned, he spent as little as $900 *a year* on pesticides and fertilizer.

First, Morrow stopped shooting for maximum yields and started substituting rotations and mechanical weed control for out-of-pocket chemical expenses. The result: In '86, he spent just $60 per acre to grow his irrigated crops, "including everything but payments on the land and the irrigation system," he notes.

While Morrow's 135-bushel average corn yields fell off a bit, his profits increased more than enough to offset that. "I was paying off the bills I built up farming the other way," he says.

No Herbicides Needed

One key to Morrow's comeback was "listing" — a specialized tillage system that allowed him to eliminate herbicides in first-year corn, and to get by with just a 7-inch band in second-year corn. "Listing used to be a high art in this area," says Morrow, noting that some nearby dryland farmers still use this traditional tillage system. "There's all the listing equipment you could want out here, and it can be had for a song."

After experimenting with two-row listing equipment his father had used since the '30s, Morrow purchased a late-'60s vintage, four-row lister planter in good condition for just $450. The machine resembles a standard corn planter, except each planter unit is mounted behind a small, double-sided moldboard that builds 8-inch-high ridges between 4-inch-deep furrows.

Seeds are planted 1½ inches deep in the bottom of the furrow. Morrow disked once before planting, but the lister's moldboards made additional tillage unnecessary. "We ran the rows north-south one year and east-west the next, so the whole field got plowed up over two years," he says. To incorporate the granular Sutan-atrazine mix he banded on second-year corn, Morrow dragged old car tire chains behind each planter unit.

Morrow's lister cultivator helped him eliminate herbicides in first-year corn, and get by with a 7-inch band in corn after corn. Here, the disks are set to throw soil into the row.

New Farm *Photos by Craig Cramer*

The moldboard on Morrow's lister planter digs a 4-inch-deep furrow between 8-inch-high ridges. Seeds are planted in the bottom of the furrow.

For $125, Morrow also purchased a four-row lister cultivator (known locally as a "go-dig" or "eli"). Each row of the cultivator has two adjustable disks, followed by two 6-inch sweeps that aerate the soil and clean weeds and crop residue off the ridgetops between rows. Morrow set the front disks to throw soil away from the row on the first two cultivations, enlarging the ridge. "We got in to cultivate just as soon as we could, often when the corn was only 2 or 3 inches tall," says Morrow, who added shields to protect young plants.

For the third (and sometimes fourth) cultivation, he set the disks to throw soil back against the knee-high corn to control weeds in the row. Guide wheels keep the cultivator on track so well that Morrow could turn completely around on the tractor to watch for plugging. "Cultivating and mowing hay were the first jobs my father let me do, it's that easy. If you can't kill weeds between the rows with an eli, you'd better find another job." he says.

Legume N Boosts Yield

Morrow also swears by another weapon in his weed control arsenal: "I just can't say enough about rotations. The longer you stay with them, the better it goes," he says. When listing, Morrow plowed 6- or 7-year-old alfalfa (often still a 75-percent stand) in spring. Then he disked and planted oats.

Instead of harvesting the oat straw, Morrow disked lightly to incorporate oats that slipped through the combine. Then he either turned cattle in to graze the volunteer oats, or he harvested oat hay in September. The following spring he planted the first of two years of corn.

What Morrow liked most about this rotation was its contribution to soil fertility and weed control. Even though his sandy soil isn't supposed to carry over much N from season to season, the alfalfa plowdown supplied all the N he needed for oats and for first-year corn the following year.

Morrow says he had fewer weeds in '86 in cultivated corn with no herbicides following oats than he did in second-year corn receiving a 7-inch herbicide band. He credits part of the difference to the oats' weed-suppressing allelopathy.

Morrow stopped listing in '90, when he added a second center-pivot to his farm and soybeans to his rotation. "But I didn't stop because listing didn't work," he quickly adds. "I was afraid the beans couldn't take having that much soil moved around. And with twice the crop acreage now, I have less time for field operations."

But he doesn't plan to give up on rotations. Morrow is starting a new eight-year sequence alternating corn and beans for four years, then establishing alfalfa with an oats nurse crop. After alfalfa, he'll plant wheat interseeded with clover. He'll plow the clover to provide N for corn, restarting the rotation. "I'm still amazed how much easier it is to control weeds when you get the rotation going," he says.

Courage To Quit Chemicals

A small test plot gave this farmer the confidence to quit herbicides and cut N rates by half or more.

DEWEESE, Neb. — What started as an experiment in a 12-acre field has steadily taken over Rich Mazour's entire 1,000-acre farm.

No, it's not an exotic new crop turned noxious weed, or a biotech trial run amok. "We just decided in '83 not to apply any chemicals around the farmstead," recalls Mazour. "We've been proving to ourselves that we can replace chemicals with rotations."

If Mazour had any doubts that was possible, 1988 erased most of them. "It was the first year we completely eliminated herbicides on all of our row crops. And we did just fine," he recalls. "Cutting back on chemicals is a little scary at first. But I'm getting more and more confident each year."

With just 11 inches of rainfall that year (less than half of normal), herbicide failure was common in south-central Nebraska. But Mazour kept his 220 acres of grain sorghum and soybeans squeaky clean with just two rotary hoeings and two passes with his six-row Buffalo ridge-till cultivator.

Weeds were no problem in grain sorghum following a sweet clover plowdown. With no additional N and just 2 to 4 inches of irrigation water, the crop yielded 97.5 bushels per acre. Irrigated soybeans ridge-planted into sorghum stubble yielded up to 40 bushels per acre. Wheat also averaged about 40 bushels per acre, but Mazour had to have some custom-sprayed with 2,4-D to control field pennycress. In '90, an armyworm infestation made spraying unnecessary. "Armyworms prefer pennycress to wheat, and they suppressed it," he observes.

Mazour figures he even made money on unirrigated fields in '88, where beans yielded just 15 bushels per acre and sorghum yielded 35 to 60 bushels. "With that kind of year, we fare a lot better than most, because we only have about $17.50 per acre invested in fuel and seed," says Mazour. Most local sorghum growers spend an additional $40 per acre on nitrogen, herbicides and insecticides, he notes.

Proving Ground

The experiment that got Mazour on the chemical-cutting track started in '83, when he drilled oats along with 5 pounds of sweet clover into the 12-acre field surrounding his farmstead. He didn't harvest oats, because of the PIK program. But the next year he harvested 6 bushels of clover seed per acre. He kept some for his own use and sold the rest for 50 cents per pound. Clover plowdown provided all the N Mazour needed for 40-bushel wheat in 1985.

New Farm Photo by Craig Cramer

Two rotary hoeings and two passes with his Buffalo ridge-till cultivator helped Mazour grow 97-bushel sorghum without herbicides.

In '86, the field gave Mazour his first experience with non-chemical weed control in row crops. Having only recently bought his first rotary hoe, he called another farmer for some hoeing advice shortly after planting soybeans. "He told me I had planted the beans too early and was already too late on my first hoeing," recalls Mazour. Mazour managed to get in one rotary hoeing and two cultivations that year, but the beans had to be walked. "They still made 40 bushels. But instead of giving my money to the chemical company, I gave it to the teenagers who rogued the field. I kept it in the local economy."

Even with average moisture that year, Mazour only had 80 percent weed control in his other beans that were solid-sprayed by the local elevator. Plus, the crop showed signs of stunting from herbicides, and it yielded just 25 to 30 bushels per acre.

In '87, Mazour followed beans with oats. To his surprise, a fine crop of sweet clover volunteered with the grain. "The clover was just 4 inches below the oats when we harvested," says Mazour. "If we'd had another rain, I'd have lost the oats to the clover." Instead, he harvested 70-bushel oats and cut the sweet clover for hay a few weeks later.

In '88, the sweet clover regrew to 12 to 18 inches by early June. Mazour undercut it with a V-blade, disked twice and planted grain sorghum. Two rotary hoeings and one cultivation provided excellent weed control. "But I should have cut the clover sooner. The sorghum just ran out of water and never filled," says Mazour, disappointed by the 20-bushel yield.

"These experiences have given me the confidence to try some of the same practices in other fields," Mazour continues. "If I'd gone cold-turkey, I'd have been in trouble and probably turned back. This is a whole different way of farming. It definitely takes more management, but I like breaking new ground."

'Millions' In The Bank

Like herbicides, nitrogen fertilizer may soon be a thing of the past for Mazour. Before working more sweet clover into his rotation, he often applied 100 pounds of N per acre to wheat or sorghum grown in the same field two or three years in a row. By '89, about half of his wheat and 80 percent of his sorghum received no purchased N, because they follow clover, alfalfa or soybeans. Where grains still follow grains, Mazour bases N rates on soil nitrate tests and on University of Nebraska recommendations, often applying just 40 pounds of N to wheat and 60 pounds of N to sorghum.

While he's now strongly against monocropping, Mazour follows no hard-and-fast rotation. He chooses crops based on weed pressure, the condition of the land, and farm programs.

Mazour likes to seed about 10 pounds of sweet clover per acre into wheat or oats headed for set-aside, then rotate back to grain sorghum or wheat after harvesting sweet clover seed. He has tested hairy vetch and red clover to see how they perform, and decided sweet clover is the best legume for his farm.

Adding sweet clover to the rotation has provided some unexpected surprises. In '89 for example, the clover volunteered in grain sorghum stubble headed for set-aside. "I'm building an account in the soil seedbank," observes Mazour. "There are going to be millions of seeds in the soil, so why not have good seeds in the bank? That way, when nature says it's time to cover the soil, I've got millions of sweet clover seeds out there ready to do the job, instead of weeds."

Often, volunteer clover is thicker than seeded stands, notes Mazour. "Once you've got the seed in the bank, you've got it made."

Before planting grain, Mazour undercuts sweet clover with a Noble blade, a wide V-plow resembling a field cultivator with oversize sweeps. Then he disks once or twice. He notes dramatic changes in the soil where he plants clover. "The rain soaks in better and the V-blade pulls easier in the clover than it does in fallow. You'd think it would be hard as a rock," he observes.

Mazour's son Mike caught his father's cost-cutting spirit, too. In '88, he grew 36-bushel dryland soybeans and 79-bushel dryland grain sorghum with no herbicides in a 120-acre field rented from his aunt. "They were the best-looking beans in the county," says Mazour, beaming with pride. "With the drought, there was a lot of herbicide stress on beans. But not on Mike's. Some farmers swathed their beans for hay, and most were real happy to get 20 or 25 bushels."

Mike died suddenly in June '90 from complications caused by a bout with mononucleosis. Rich was hospitalized later that year with the same condition, but he pulled through. "Mike was so involved and excited about farming without chemicals," he recalls fondly. "He was part of the next generation of sustainable farmers." Now, some of the Mazours' other children are catching Mike's spirit and getting involved in the operation.

7 Crops In 4 Years

Intensive rotations give this farmer continuous ground cover,
plus good weed control with next-to-no herbicide.

EASTON, Kan. — "My goal is to raise a crop for my cows and a crop to sell on every acre every year," says Eugene Kramer. And more often than not, the eastern Kansas farmer does just that on each of the 400 acres he farms — while at the same time building soil and growing corn for as little as $1.16 per bushel.

Two general principles guide Kramer's rotation: Follow legumes with grains; and alternate coarse-rooted crops like corn, milo and soybeans with fine-rooted small grains and red clover. Typically, Kramer follows corn with wheat, and overseeds wheat in spring with 8 pounds of red clover per acre. After wheat harvest, he cuts red clover haylage in fall and again the next spring — usually 4 to 5 tons per acre, total.

Milo follows clover. After milo harvest, Kramer broadcasts 1 bushel of grain rye per acre, which he pastures or chops for haylage before planting soybeans the next spring. Finally, he broadcasts or drills rye after beans before going back to corn.

Kramer deviates from this basic scheme as needed, sometimes substituting spring oats when he can't get a fall cover planted in time. "Sometimes we plant things we wouldn't normally plant, to keep our crop bases. But usually, I harvest seven crops in four years," observes Kramer, who started experimenting with double-crop rotations in the early '80s.

"What's more important, alternating coarse- and fine-rooted crops has improved my soil structure," he continues. "Because my soil can take up water, it not only helps the crops, but there's less runoff to erode the soil. You have to start with good, healthy soil."

Reduce Weather Risks

One key to Kramer's success with this system is the harvest-time flexibility provided by two, 20- by 70-foot Harvestore silos. "Because I can chop all my feeds and blow them into the silo, I can harvest earlier and the weather is less of a factor," he notes. "They give me 10 days to two weeks more time. And sometimes that's just what you need to make these double-crops work." Clover, alfalfa, oats, rye and other forages from the silos serve as the primary feed for Kramer's 60 brood cows and calves.

Kramer's intensive rotation not only provides continuous ground cover and high-quality feed,

but also helps him control weeds and cut fertilizer costs in cash crops. Because corn usually follows soybeans, Kramer finds he can get by with just 70 to 90 pounds of N fertilizer. The effectiveness of those rates was confirmed in replicated on-farm trials that Kramer conducted in cooperation with the Kansas Rural Center.

At planting, Kramer applies 10 pounds of 9-18-9-1S starter per acre, and bands about $2.50 worth of atrazine and a wetting agent 8 to 10 inches over the row. The combination of healthy soil and starter fertilizer allows Kramer to plant his 120-day hybrids a week to 10 days later than his neighbors do, and the corn still tassels at the same time.

Kramer rotary hoes row crops only about half the time. "It's a tool that's ready to go when we need it. If we get rain after planting and the weeds start coming up, we jump right on it. If it's dry and the crop gets a jump, we'll wait and cultivate," he explains.

Row crops are usually cultivated twice with four-row Buffalo or IH cultivators. Kramer sidedresses 10 gallons of 28-percent N per acre on corn during second cultivation.

In '86 — an excellent year for corn in his area — Kramer calculated production costs for one of his better fields by tallying input costs, using custom rates for field operations, adding hauling and land fees and charging 12 percent interest.

Two cultivations in soybeans killed weeds that weren't suppressed by Kramer's rye cover crop.

New Farm Photo by Craig Cramer

Result: His 155-bushel yield cost just $1.16 per bushel. Hillier fields that only yielded 125 bushels cost just 25 cents more per bushel. "Even in an average year with 100-bushel corn, I'm well under $2 a bushel," he observes.

'Crazy About Rye'

Kramer's soybeans yield about 40 bushels per acre without herbicides. "With these rotations, I can't use much chemical. If I did, my next crop wouldn't grow," he explains. Instead, Kramer relies on the same two cultivations and occasional rotary hoeing that his other row crops receive, and on the powerful weed-suppressing effects of his rye cover crops.

"I'm crazy about rye," says Kramer, who seeds more than 100 acres of rye cover crop each fall. "Not only does it hold back the weeds, but I just like what it does to the soil." But Kramer warns that rye's allelopathic effects can sometimes be too strong and can keep row crops — particularly milo — from germinating. So he usually disks rye about two weeks before planting.

Inspired by writers such as Louis Bromfield, Kramer started experimenting with conservation tillage 35 years ago. "The university experts said that it wouldn't work in my part of the state, because there was too much residue to handle," he recalls. "But compaction, erosion and dead furrows just weren't my way."

So Kramer started designing and building his own conservation tillage equipment before it was available on the market. Two examples: a chisel plow with coil shanks, and a planter with sweep openers so he could avoid one more trip over the field. In the late '60s and early '70s, he pioneered conservation tillage in the area, working with Extension to organize one of the first conservation tillage field days and serving as a consultant for several equipment manufacturers.

Today, Kramer selects his tillage based on the amount of residue he has to contend with. "I do just what it takes to get the soil the way I want it," he says. Sometimes he no-tills milo into red clover, knocking back the clover with 1 pound of atrazine and 40 pounds of 28-percent N per acre. He field cultivates soybean stubble before planting corn, because he feels he gets better N release from the residue that way. He disks rye before planting beans, while heavier crop residues might require a pass with a chisel plow.

Kramer also uses a penetrometer to assess soil compaction and to help him make tillage decisions. "If it takes more than 90 pounds to penetrate 12 inches, you need some kind of deep tillage. But if the soil is mellow, I'll just run a disk or a field cultivator," he says. By intensifying his rotations and not working his fields when they're wet, Kramer seldom has to use his subsoiler. To further avoid compacting wet soils in spring, Kramer spreads most of his manure (never more than 10 tons per acre) on wheat ground.

"I've always been conscientious about the soil," he adds. "By using all the manures from the livestock and intensive rotations, I've reached the point where my soil works like I'd like it. I use less fertilizer, have fewer weed and insect problems, my crops are healthier, and I have better livestock. Had I known all this 35 years ago when I started farming, oh what a better farm I could have had."

'Pretty Doesn't Pay The Bills'

But with broadcast soybeans and ridge-tillage,
this farmer has no herbicide bills to pay.

McLEAN, Neb. — It may not look good, but it works. That's the best way to describe the many soil-and money-saving practices that Gary and Delores Young have used over the years on their 320-acre farm.

Whether it's the time-worn solar collector that dries their grain and heats their home, or the crazy-quilt pattern of small paddocks on their 45-acre pasture. Their goal is always the same: to grow all of the feed they need for their livestock with as few purchased inputs as possible.

For example, before he switched from dairying to raising beef cattle, sheep and feeder pigs, Young used to broadcast about one-fourth of the soybeans he ground and fed to his cows. He harvested up to 38 bushels per acre that way, and says broadcast beans generally outyielded his ridge-tilled beans by as much as 5 bushels.

Broadcast beans cost next-to-nothing to grow, says Young. In spring, he disked corn or milo stubble, and broadcast 3 to 4 bushels of bin-run beans with 1 bushel of winter rye per acre using an endgate seeder. Then he disked again, and sometimes harrowed, to incorporate the seeds.

Seeded in spring, winter rye germinates along with beans to help smother early-season weeds, then dies within a few weeks. Its 3 or 4 inches of growth forms an allelopathic mulch to control later weeds.

Young planted broadcast beans a few days later than his ridge-tilled beans, to let more early weeds germinate before he wiped them out with the disk and/or harrow. He harvested beans with a reel head on his combine. "There aren't a lot of pods on each bean plant compared with ridge-tilled beans. But there are enough extra plants to compensate for the difference," observes Young.

That wasn't the case in '88, though. For the first time, Young's broadcast beans fell about 2 bushels short of his ridged beans, yielding just a little less than 16 bushels per acre. One likely reason is that Young only broadcast about 2 bushels of soybeans per acre, instead of his normal 3 or 4 bushels. Plus, with dry soil early that season, the beans were slow to germinate and had to compete with weeds and rye for scarce moisture.

Compared with ridge-tilled beans, he reports, "The economics were just about a toss-up."

Young thinks broadcast beans are an ideal way for farmers to meet conservation-compliance requirements in federal crop programs without spending a fortune on new equipment. "The real future for this is for farmers who need cover on sidehills for conservation compliance, and can't afford a drill to plant solid-seeded beans," he says.

Techniques That Fit

Young came upon the idea for broadcast beans through his work with the Small Farm Resources Project, a five-year program operated in the mid-'80s by the nonprofit Center for Rural Affairs (CRA) in Hartington, Neb. The project focused on helping farmers test and refine technologies that make them less dependent on purchased inputs and experts. A CRA staffer stumbled onto the broadcast-soybean idea buried in some pre-World War II research by the University of Missouri, and brought it to Young's attention.

But Young had started looking for ways to farm with fewer chemicals more than two decades ago, well before his involvement with CRA. Corn insecticides were making him sick, he recalls. His dairy herd's health was poor, and laboratory tests showed the family's well was contaminated by more than a dozen farm chemicals.

Two new ideas that really paid off for Young's dairy herd were rotational grazing and probiotics. But it was ridge-till that helped him cut crop pro-

duction costs and save soil. "Ridge-till really helps reduce wind erosion," he observes. "Our fields don't blow nearly as bad as others around here."

Young ridge-tills all of the row crops in his seven-year rotation. The rotation starts with corn, followed by either soybeans or milo. The latter is much more popular in drier regions to the south and west of Young's farm. But Young likes the security of having at least a few acres of milo each year. "It's my drought-insurance crop to make up for low corn yields in dry years," he explains. Homegrown milo is an important part of the ration for Young's lambs and feeder pigs.

Beans or milo are followed by another year of corn, then oats and three years of alfalfa. Those four years of weed-smothering sod crops are one reason Young needs virtually no herbicides. He usually controls weeds with just two cultivations, although he will resort to a little 2,4-D in rare instances when weeds get a head start. "Sometimes it hardly sets the weeds back at all. I'm finding that the cultivator usually cleans things up just as well," observes Young.

Young says he composts his cattle manure "by neglect." Even though he doesn't expend effort turning the windrows, they still heat enough to kill weed seeds, he says. To avoid compaction, he spreads compost in fall and winter — usually on fields between milo and the second year of corn in his rotation. His dryland corn yields are well within the county average of 65 to 70 bushels per acre, but the crop costs just 90 cents to $1.45 per bushel to grow — including seed, taxes, interest, and machinery and labor (based on University of Nebraska custom rates).

In addition to cutting chemical and fuel costs, ridge-till makes it easy for Young to plant corn and beans or milo in alternating four-row strips, by taking the guesswork out of row placement. This practice has worked so well for him that he has abandoned broadcast beans so he can strip crop more acres.

Depending on seasonal factors like temperature, moisture and wind, strip-cropping can boost yields of one or both crops by about 10 percent compared with either crop planted alone, he says. Border rows of the taller corn or milo can benefit from more exposure to the sun, while soybeans can benefit when the taller crop blocks moisture-robbing winds.

Young's biggest strip-cropping success was in '85. Strip-cropped beans and milo outyielded their monocropped counterparts by more than 9 bushels and 5.5 bushels, respectively. It would have taken 40 percent more monocropped land to equal the yields in the strip-cropped land, Young estimates.

Because Young's strips follow the contour, they also help reduce erosion by alternating soybean stubble with heavier corn and milo residue. The heavier residue also helps catch more snow in winter.

Forage Sorghum Whips Thistles

In '90, Young tested forage sorghum planted the first week of June as a way of controlling patches of Canada thistle on his crop ground. On part of the infested patches, he planted sorghum in rows at 5 to 8 pounds per acre, and cultivated twice. On the rest, he disked, broadcast 20 pounds of sorghum per acre, then disked again lightly.

Where sorghum was row-planted, there was an average of 2.5 thistles per square foot, compared with 3 thistles per square foot on bare-ground control plots. But where sorghum was *broadcast,* Young counted less than *one* thistle per square foot. He attributes the control to the concentrat-

ed shading, smothering and allelopathic effects of the broadcast sorghum.

Young's innovative cost-cutting practices aren't limited to crops. He was one of several farmers who spent $1,300 of their own money to build solar collectors in the late '70s as part of another CRA program, the Small Farm Energy Project. He mounted the device on a running gear so it could do double duty, drying grain in fall and heating the family's house in winter. As a result, it paid for itself in just four years, instead of seven if it had been used for grain drying, alone. In a way, Young's solar collector is a lot like his other ideas: The paint may have long since chipped away, he says. "But it's still going strong."

"It's not how things look, it's that bottom line that counts," Young adds. "Pretty doesn't pay the bills. And if you don't pay the bills, you won't be out there too long."

Early To Bed, Early To Harvest
This minimum-till furrow irrigation system uses
two-thirds less herbicide and saves cash, soil, water and fuel.

REPUBLIC, Kan. — During the planting-time crunch, Mike Charles has far fewer headaches than most folks. Instead of disking repeatedly to work up fine seedbeds, Mike and his father, Don, make just one tillage pass before planting.

Their time-saving secret: an Orthman "Tri-Level-Bed" farming system that not only saves soil, water and fuel, but helps the Charleses grow 150-bushel corn and 50-bushel beans with just a single cultivation and a 10-inch herbicide band. "We don't end up back at square one and have to rework the fields every time it rains," says Mike. "Even after a heavy rain, we can get back in the field in just two or three days and continue planting.

"And with this system, we use only about one-third of the herbicide we would use with a broadcast rate," he adds.

By not overworking their well-drained, sandy loam river-bottom soils, the Charleses conserve precious moisture that's easily lost with each tillage pass. "Conventional planters require a clean, fine seedbed," explains Mike. "All that tillage is not only expensive, but it would turn our sandy soil to powder and leave it exposed to

spring winds."

If the Charleses used conventional tillage, they might have to disk four or five times before planting, some years. Instead, they make just four or five trips across the field in an entire season. They shred corn stalks in late winter, apply dry fertilizer and split the old beds in March, plant in April, cultivate and sidedress N in June, and harvest in October. "We try to plant corn a little early — starting around April 15-20. In a wet season, farmers who use conventional tillage may still be reworking their fields when our corn is up," observes Mike.

Early Hybrids Pay Off

The Charleses use hybrids that mature five to 10 days earlier than the 120-day hybrids commonly grown in the area. So, their corn usually is below 14-percent moisture by mid-October, and is out of the field by November 1. "A lot of people feel you won't get the yields with shorter-season hybrids," says Mike. "But for us, it's not worth harvesting into late November or December for a few extra bushels."

In fact, early harvesting lets the Charleses save

money on drying costs, by reducing the risk of damage from fall rains or early frost. They have only had to run the grain dryer about two years out of 10.

The Charleses' first trip across the field is to shred corn stalks, which are left undisturbed through winter to catch snow and protect the double-row beds from erosion. Next, last year's beds are 'split' down the center with wide, heavy-duty V-blades that bury residue and raise new, trash-free seedbeds centered over the old furrows.

"The splitter really doesn't throw that much dirt, or pull as hard as it looks," says Mike. A 125-hp tractor easily pulls his three-bed, six-row split-ter. "A 100-horsepower tractor would probably be enough," he says.

To conserve moisture, the Charleses work one field at a time, immediately following the splitter with the bed shaper-planter. This implement con-sists of lighter V-blades that run in the new furrow formed by the splitter. The blades form a double-shouldered bed with a slight ridge rising in the center.

John Deere planter units are attached directly to the shaper. These plant corn or soybeans in 30-inch rows on the flat areas between the outside shoulders of the bed and the ridge in the center of the bed. In this well-drained area out of the furrow, seedlings aren't likely to be drowned by heavy rains, or hampered by crusted soil during emergence. Though they haven't had to yet, the

Charleses can irrigate immediately after planting with this system, if the soil is dry.

In sandy soil, it's important not to build the center ridge too high, warns Mike. Heavy spring rains can wash soil off the ridge and cover fragile seedlings. He also likes to throw a smaller ridge with soybeans. The flatter bed makes it easier to run the combine header close to the ground.

Mike finds it possible — but difficult — to plant corn into bean stubble without first splitting the beds. Because he has to drive on the beds rather than in the furrows, it's harder to keep the planter units on track, he explains.

Weed-N-Feed

The bed system makes it possible for the Charleses to get by with two-thirds less herbicide than they'd use in broadcast treatments. They use minimum rates of pre-emergence herbicides applied in 10-inch, over-the-row bands at plant-ing. "That gives us manageable weed control," says Mike. "It keeps weed populations down in the rows, and I can control those that grow on the ridges and in the furrows with timely cultivation."

The last pass before irrigation is a lay-by cultiva-tion to control weeds in the center of the beds and to deepen the furrows. Barring-off disks on the Charleses' Orthman cultivator cut soil away from the row, while 14-inch sweeps throw soil off the center ridge, burying small weeds in the rows. Half-sweeps cultivate the sides of the beds, and do

A variety of tools on their Orthman cultivator let the Charleses kill weeds within and between rows, apply nitrogen and smooth and reshape irrigation furrows in a single pass.

New Farm Photos by Craig Cramer

a better job than the L-shaped beet knives that were standard on older Orthman cultivators, says Mike. Furrowing shovels and half-sweeps kill weeds between the beds and reshape and smooth the furrow. In '91, Mike switched from Richardson platypus shovels to Hawkins hillers.

Mike doesn't rotary hoe, because he's too busy planting. "By the time I'm ready, the weeds are too big to hoe," he says. "But there's no doubt a second cultivation is advantageous. It doubles our weed kill and loosens the soil."

But until '89, limited time and manpower made a second cultivation nearly impossible. That year, Mike bought a Lilliston rolling cultivator, and he now does all he can to make the time to squeeze in an early cultivation in addition to the layby pass. He removes the sweeps from the rolling cultivator that would normally run on the ridges, and he sets the spider gangs to throw soil away from the newly emerged crop. The remaining sweeps loosen the furrows, and coil shanks running behind the tractor wheels help break up compaction.

While cultivating, the Charleses also sidedress corn with 75 pounds of N per acre as 28-percent. They also apply needed P and K and preplant nitrogen (about 75 pounds after beans, and 85 to 90 pounds after corn) just before bed splitting. They inject the liquid behind the sweeps that run on the ridge-top in the center of the beds, weeding and feeding at the same time. "You know how 'hot' 28-percent is. Where it hits exposed weed roots, it helps ensure a kill," says Mike.

In addition to splitting N applications, the Charleses feel they get the most out of their nitro-

Mike Charles shows off his 1987 corn crop, planted in well-drained areas above irrigation furrow, where seedlings aren't likely to be drowned by heavy rains or hampered by crusted soil.

gen by incorporating it immediately.

Rotations Break Weed Cycles

The Charleses rotary hoe row crops when crusting is a problem. But because they can run the rolling cultivator on small crops, they don't need to hoe for weed control. Mike sometimes hoes their 50 or so acres of wheat in early spring to reduce annual weed populations. "It fluffs up the soil, kills a lot of the newly germinated annuals, and — if the soil stays dry and loose — discourages more weeds from germinating," he says.

Wheat plus set-aside acres make it possible for the Charleses to rotate at least some of their ground out of row crops from time to time. But all too often, rotations in their dozen 10- to 50-acre fields are determined by ever-changing ASCS allotments. "We generally try to follow soybeans with corn, then to wheat or set-aside — just so long as we capture the N fixed by the soybeans and rotate enough to break up the pest cycles," says Mike.

Mike has experimented with hairy vetch as a green manure crop, but he feels it has only limited potential with his farming system. Because he plants corn so early, the vetch has little time for regrowth in spring. But he has found that it makes good winter grazing — even during January thaws.

Mike has established good stands broadcasting vetch on unworked soybean stubble in early October. In '87, he shredded 2-foot vetch regrowth just before bloom in early May, then split the beds and planted soybeans. "The vetch went right under, and covered and killed well. Planting was no problem," he says.

Cattle play a small but important role in the operation. The Charleses run about 25 cow-calf pairs on crop residues during the winter, and on set-aside land plus about 20 acres of pasture and sudangrass during the summer.

Mike also drills wheat around field borders, paths and irrigation ditches to suppress weeds and provide more forage for his cattle. He harvests some hay and silage for additional winter feed. "The small fields we've planted to pasture and hay weren't very productive ground, anyway. It's a good way to use areas with highly erodible soil or lots of point rows and are difficult to irrigate. All I buy is mineral salt and veterinary services. The cattle are always in excellent condition just from grazing around the farm. So it's a pretty low-input herd," says Mike.

Chapter 3

GREENER PASTURES

*Try these spray-free solutions to weed problems
in hayfields and pastures.*

Three words sum up the best way to manage weeds in your pastures: Intensive ... Rotational ... Grazing.

That's right. Making sure animals graze *all* pasture species *at the best point on the plants' growth curve* will keep pasture weeds at bay more cost-effectively than anything on sale at your local chemical or machinery dealer. Researchers have proved it in their experiments. And farmers have proved it in their fields.

Because of its growing popularity, Intensive Rotational Grazing is the subject of many excellent books. You've seen them advertised in *The New Farm* and in other magazines. Maybe you even own a few of them.

We won't rehash the subject, here. Our goal in this chapter is to summarize many of the other innovative ways you can manage weeds to boost pasture productivity.

Weed Feed Rivals Alfalfa

*Farmers can save up to $25 an acre by knowing what weeds
not to spray in forage crops, research shows.*

If you're spending $15 or more per acre to control dandelion, quackgrass and other weeds in pasture and hay crops, recent forage research may 'recalibrate' your bottom line. Depending on the species and growth stage, certain weeds that invade forage fields may actually be as nutritious and/or palatable as alfalfa and smooth bromegrass. In fact, a few weed species may occasionally exceed the quality of these popular forages.

"Some of those weeds farmers have been indiscriminately spraying over the years may be doing more good than harm," says Dr. Craig Sheaffer, an agronomist at the University of Minnesota (UM). "And even in cases where the weed quality is less than that of alfalfa, you still have to justify the expense of the herbicide application."

Sheaffer and two other scientists compared the taste and nutritive value of alfalfa and smooth bromegrass with those of 10 perennial weeds most often found in forage crops. The list includes quackgrass, dandelion, white campion (white cockle), swamp smartweed, perennial sowthistle,

Jerusalem artichoke, curly dock, hoary alyssum and Canada thistle. Among the nutritional factors studied were crude protein, minerals, digestibility and fiber content.

Packed With Protein

The scientists found that, when alfalfa was in the vegetative to bud stages, its crude protein level was no higher than—and sometimes lower than—that of N-fertilized Jerusalem artichoke, Canada thistle, curly dock, common quackgrass, swamp smartweed and perennial sowthistle.

As with alfalfa, crude protein levels in the weeds declined with maturity. But even when alfalfa was at mid- to full-bloom, its crude protein concentrations were matched (or nearly so) by Canada thistle, quackgrass and curly dock during the first year of the study.

In the second year, Jerusalem artichoke, dandelion, Canada thistle, quackgrass and curly dock had protein levels similar to mid-bloom alfalfa. But in the third year, the researchers found that

Weed Feed

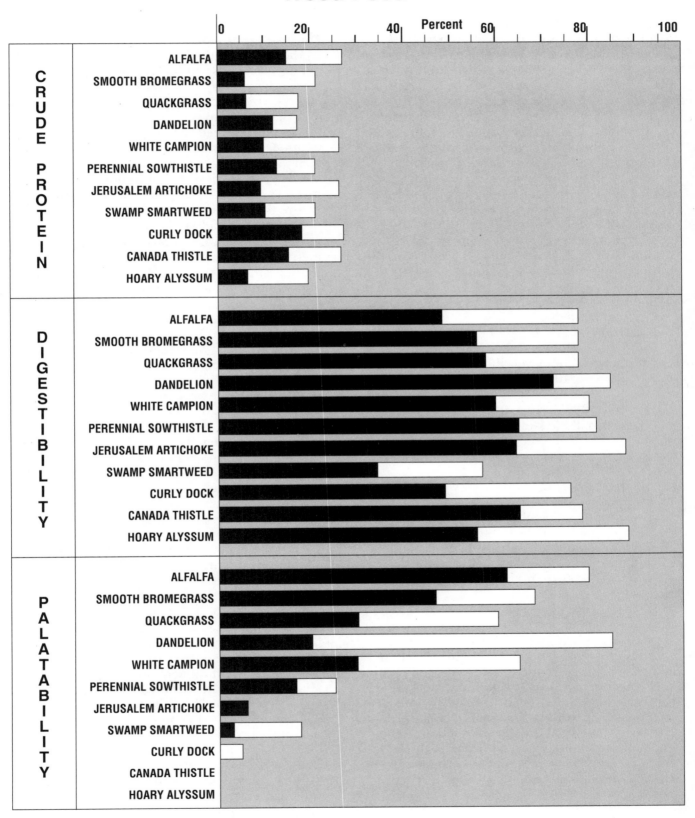

Some weeds are not only as nutritious as alfalfa and bromegrass, but as palatable, too. This graph summarizes University of Wisconsin research on the subject. In general, crude protein and digestibility were highest in late May and early June (white bars), and lowest later in the season (dark bars). Palatability, shown here as a percentage of plants consumed by sheep, was highest in early June. The one exception is dandelions, which were most palatable in midsummer.

all broadleaf and grass weeds had less protein than alfalfa at the full-bloom stage.

Both types of quackgrass also had greater protein concentrations than smooth bromegrass. And while high populations of quackgrass in bud-stage alfalfa can reduce forage digestibility, Sheaffer says smooth bromegrass can reduce it even more.

Besides protein, the researchers studied a number of micro- and macrominerals, including calcium, phosphorus, potassium and magnesium. As with protein, mineral concentrations in the weeds were highest at the least mature growth stages.

Overall averages showed higher concentrations of calcium in swamp smartweed, hoary alyssum and Canada thistle than in alfalfa. Phosphorus content for Canada thistle and the grass weeds was lower than that of alfalfa in the first year. But in the second year, it was greater than alfalfa in all species.

Potassium levels were consistently higher in the weeds than in alfalfa, but magnesium levels in both alfalfa and weeds were inconsistent from year to year. Grass weeds had much lower calcium and magnesium levels than alfalfa and broadleaf weeds did.

But Do They Taste Good?

Using a small flock of sheep, Sheaffer and his colleagues also conducted taste tests of the various species. Few surprises, here: Alfalfa almost always came out on top.

Still, quackgrass was consistently close behind, as was smooth bromegrass. White campion achieved high palatability in late spring, but became less tasty as the summer progressed. Dandelion also scored well in taste tests during its midsummer vegetative stage, and was the only plant occasionally found to be more palatable than alfalfa.

The scientists based palatability estimates on the amount of each crop or weed that remained after sheep were allowed to graze each plot for periods ranging from four to 16 days. Separate stands of each weed and forage had been established before the experiment began, and the scientists created "lanes" leading to each species, so that the sheep would have a clear choice.

Palatability for all species was compared to alfalfa in early bud, as well as in the mid- and full-bloom stages. Consumption was estimated by trained observers several times a day during each grazing cycle.

Canada thistle, hoary alyssum, curly dock, Jerusalem artichoke, swamp smartweed and perennial sowthistle showed the lowest palatability, with 80- to 100-percent rejection by the lambs.

Sheaffer says these results probably would hold true for other grazing animals, too.

Haying Beats Spraying

Making hay with weeds is another good way to cut herbicide costs in forages, according to scientists at the University of Wisconsin (UW).

Take white campion, for instance. "This weed is very palatable and nutritious," says Dr. Gordon Harvey, a UW weed specialist. "I'd be very hesitant to advise controlling it." When Harvey fed goats alfalfa hay containing 35 percent white campion — the heaviest concentration of this weed he'd ever seen — the animals ate the campion before they would eat the alfalfa.

Spraying dandelions is also unnecessary, in most cases. Apparently, this weed's greatest detriment to forage and livestock production is a matter of aesthetics, suggests Harvey. "Farmers hate dandelions," he says matter-of-factly. "They especially don't like those bright yellow flowers poking out of their green hay fields for their neighbors to see."

Still, he adds, "We've never been able to document an improvement in animal production by controlling dandelions. Though the weed has slightly less crude protein than alfalfa, it's palatable and doesn't affect consumption and overall quality."

Nor does it seem to affect forage yields. "Dandelions are more of an invader than a competitor," explains Harvey. "They don't tend to reduce alfalfa stands, except in rare cases where winterkill has set the alfalfa back. The weeds simply fill in the bare spaces, keeping out more competitive weed species.

"If dandelions outnumber alfalfa, the field should be replanted, anyway," he adds. "As long as the alfalfa is well-managed, dandelions won't cause any decline in forage yield or quality."

Notes Dr. Jerry Doll, another UW scientist: "Even if a field had 25 percent dandelions in the harvested forage, there would only be a 1-percent drop in protein content in the forage, on the average. We found that dandelion protein content is lowest at the first alfalfa cutting (4 percent less crude protein than alfalfa), while the weed has the same protein content as alfalfa in the second and third cuttings."

Save $20 To $25/A

What does all this mean to farmers? To begin with, says Harvey, "At a $20- to $25-per-acre herbicide cost for spraying dandelions, I think the money could be better spent on forage management, such as good alfalfa seed, fertilization and crop rotations."

UW researchers say there's no sound way to determine an economic threshold for weed populations in forage crops. But they do advise farmers that, to justify the cost of herbicides, an alfalfa stand should contain at least four to five crop plants per square foot, and the field ought to be kept in production for at least two seasons after treatment.

If the alfalfa stand is older and thinner, spraying could well be a waste of money. For example, in 1985, UW scientists applied a herbicide to an alfalfa field with five dandelions per square foot. A year later, there was only one dandelion plant per square foot.

The herbicide seemed to pay off, but that wasn't the case, reports Doll. Though the number of dandelions was smaller, the total forage tonnage—and dandelion concentration per ton—were identical both years. "You couldn't justify applying the herbicide in this case," says Doll.

The main potential drawback the researchers can find with dandelions is the weed's high moisture content, which can make hay drying more difficult. "All this means is waiting an extra day to dry your hay, for the most part," says Doll.

Another invader of hayfields is yellow rocket. Once again, unless the weed is seriously competing with alfalfa, spraying the typical $15 to $20 worth of herbicides per acre may not be justified, says Harvey.

Hoary alyssum is about the only broadleaf weed that poses a serious threat to alfalfa, according to UW research. That's because, unlike yellow rocket, hoary alyssum is in bloom throughout the growing season and has caused substantial declines in forage yields and quality. "There is no real good product for controlling it, so rotations and other management practices that make alfalfa healthy are important," says Harvey.

Periodic forage testing may be the best way to determine if weed populations are heavy enough to damage crop quality. "Without testing, your decision will be subjective," says UM's Sheaffer. "The advantage of testing is that it removes guesswork and quantifies what you have. This is true whether you're looking at protein, minerals or what have you. Farmers need to compare the cost of using a herbicide versus the economic gain achieved from weeds."

It's also a good idea to survey the predominant weed species in your forage fields before hooking up the sprayer. Often after harvesting alfalfa, many annual weeds cut along with the forage — including lambsquarter and pigweed — will not regrow, notes Sheaffer.

"We're not telling farmers to never use herbicides," Sheaffer points out. "But where farmers can avoid using them, they should do so. Just because they have weeds doesn't mean they should spray."

Harvey agrees. "I think if farmers could look at forage management rather than herbicides to solve their weed problems, they'd be better off," he says.

Pastures That Weed And Feed Themselves

ANGLETON, Texas — Southern cattlemen face a real dilemma when they depend on warm-season grass pastures like bahiagrass and bermudagrass. While these forages can often support more than one cow per acre, their nutritional quality is low during the summer. What's more, they require up to 200 or more pounds of nitrogen fertilizer per acre to support high stocking rates, and they produce their best quality forage during spring and fall.

Dr. Gerald Evers, a forage specialist at the Texas Agricultural Experiment Station in Overton, Texas, has a simple, low-cost solution: Overseed subtropical grasses with cool-season annual legumes, like arrowleaf, crimson, rose, bull and subterranean clovers. In his research, a bahiagrass-subterranean clover mix produced as much forage as bahiagrass alone receiving 225 pounds of N per acre. "The clovers add 30 to 45 days to the spring grazing season," says Evers. "That means the farmer can reduce his winter-feeding period and lower the amount of hay, silage and supplements needed.

"By incorporating nitrogen in the pasture system through the legume, there is a slower release of the nitrogen from the organic matter, so less gets in the groundwater," he adds. "Plus, the legume improves the friability of the soil."

Free Herbicide

Finally, overseeded annual clovers can reduce

or eliminate the need for herbicides and boost forage quality. "If a solid clover stand develops during the winter, you can eliminate spring herbicide spraying," says Evers.

The cool-season clovers shade out tough spring weeds that germinate and thrive in March and April when the grasses are still dormant, he explains. In his studies, bermudagrass treated with 1.25 pounds of Princep per acre (about $4 worth) had just as many weeds in May as plots overseeded with clovers receiving no herbicides.

In late spring, the clovers also compete with the forage grasses, but not enough to reduce overall production. That's because subterranean clover bows out in early May and arrowleaf in June — a month or two after warm-season grasses start producing. The more even forage production through the longer growing season makes it easier to determine stocking rates, too, says Evers.

The bottom line for beef producers is better animal performance because of the higher-quality forage. "When you add clovers, you increase milk production, weaning weights and conception rates," notes Evers. "It's possible to increase stocking rates 50 to 100 percent compared with unfertilized grass, but what's more important is you reduce your per-unit production costs."

Texas farmers have no problem understanding that message. Extension efforts helped increase clover acreage in the state more than 40 percent from 1980 to 1985. "Farmers are starting to realize it's just more economical to have clovers in their pastures," says Evers.

In his study, Evers broadcast 6 pounds of YUCHI arrowleaf clover or 16 pounds of MT. BARKER subterranean clover per acre into established bermudagrass and bahiagrass sods in Octo-

ber. The clovers produced little additional forage that fall, but came on strong the next spring before the grasses broke dormancy, producing as much as 2,200 pounds of forage per acre by the end of March.

Farmers may be tempted to boost summer grass production by topdressing full nitrogen rates, but Evers recommends using low N rates and relying on residual N from the clovers. "High nitrogen fertilizer rates will stimulate grass growth, but then you'll have problems getting the clover to volunteer in the fall. If you do get a (clover) stand, it will be poor and late," he says.

To help get volunteer clover stands off to a good start, Evers suggests keeping pastures grazed short until late October or early November, when cool weather slows down grass growth. This reduces grass competition when the clovers germinate. Annual clovers will continue reseeding themselves if managed properly and fall rain is adequate.

Clovers are more soil-specific than grasses, says Evers. Care needs to be taken to match the best-adapted annual clover with your soil type. He recommends checking with your local Extension agent for help.

Cattle enjoy the benefits of extended grazing on high-quality clovers almost as much as cattlemen. "On pure stands of subtropical grasses, conception rates might be 80 to 85 percent. Adding clover might increase that to 90 to 95 percent, if breeding coincides with peak clover growth," says Evers. "A lot depends on pasture management. Clovers might increase production 30 to 40 percent for one producer, but only 20 percent for another."

Beef Up Northern Pastures Without Herbicides

In northern pastures and hayfields, locally adapted legumes can reduce herbicides, boost forage quantity and quality, and produce almost as much free N as the annual clovers in Evers' Gulf Coast study. (See above, "Pastures That Weed And Feed Themselves.") For example, pure grass stands required 200 pounds of nitrogen fertilizer per acre to match forage yields of alfalfa- and red clover-grass mixtures, according to a University of Minnesota study. With no N, pure grasses pro-

duced 60 to 70 percent less forage than grass-legume mixes.

Since many northern farmers already have well-established legume-grass pastures, they can benefit most by planting switchgrass, big bluestem, indiangrass and other warm-season grasses to supplement cool-season forage production. And to extend the grazing season into January, northern farmers can rely on forage turnips, rape and other high-protein forage brassicas.

Intensive rotational grazing is a good way to control weeds and make the most of pastures just about anywhere. "But not everyone wants to move their animals every day," says Ken McNamara, program manager of the Farmland Stewardship Center, Marine, Minn. "There's a middle ground between neglected pasture and intensive rotational grazing."

'Cows Replace Roundup'

The first step toward that middle ground is reducing competition from unwanted grass and weeds before seeding legumes. Many farmers do this by applying herbicides in fall and/or spring, then seeding new pastures with a sod drill rented from their local Soil Conservation Service.

But frost-seeding would accomplish the same thing without herbicides or tillage, says Dr. Mike Tesar, a pasture management specialist at Michigan State University. The technique is simple: Just broadcast legume seed in late March or early April, when alternate soil-freezes and -thaws plant the seed naturally.

Graze the pasture until late May to suppress grasses until the legumes germinate. "Let the cow be your herbicide," says Tesar. "She does the same thing as Roundup." Legumes also can be established with an oats nurse crop, but Tesar recommends chopping the oats as silage. If harvested for grain, oats can out-compete the legumes and reduce the stand, he explains.

Seeding straight alfalfa for pasture is not a good idea, says Dr. Vaughn Holyoke, an Extension crops specialist at the University of Maine. In addition to the possibility of bloat, alfalfa is difficult to manage in pastures, especially under short-term rotational grazing. "Alfalfa needs to rest at least 35 days to build up root reserves," says Holyoke. "Few farmers will wait that long."

Avoid 'Shotgun' Mixes

Holyoke recommends carefully selecting legume-grass mixes that match your pasture conditions.

The mulch effect of the grasses protects legumes from winter injury, increasing legume stand longevity, he says. "You're also not forced to reseed the pasture when the legume does fade out." To keep legumes from fading, maintain pH above 6 and potash levels medium or higher, and frost-seed legumes at reduced rates every two or three years.

For new seedings, Holyoke cautions that "shotgun" mixtures of three or four grasses and a like number of legumes can be expensive and counter-productive. "Normally, one grass plus one legume make up a desirable forage mix," he says.

The long-term, best-adapted species aren't always the most aggressive in the seeding year, he explains. For example, on poorly drained pastures, Holyoke recommends 2 pounds of Ladino clover per acre, plus 6 pounds of timothy or 8 pounds of reed canarygrass. An alternative is 8 pounds of EMPIRE trefoil with 6 pounds of timothy. Adding ryegrass to the mix would choke out the preferred grasses in the seeding year and reduce long-term pasture productivity.

"But there may be some situations where a second legume can be used to advantage," says Holyoke. On well-drained sites, for example, he recommends 2 pounds of Ladino clover per acre, plus 4 pounds of IROQUOIS alfalfa and 6 pounds of orchardgrass. "The Ladino is slow to take off," he explains. "The alfalfa will add 1 ton of dry matter to the first-year grazing — enough to justify the seed cost even though it may be gone by the second year." Orchardgrass thrives under rotational grazing, he notes, while timothy will quickly give way to lower-quality bluegrass.

Brome Beats Alfalfa Weeds

In addition to reducing weevil damage by more than 95 percent and improving soil structure, adding brome and trefoil to alfalfa fields can also help fend off invading weeds. In a Wisconsin study conducted by the Michael Fields Agricultural Institute (MFAI), brome and trefoil mixed with alfalfa kept weed content to 1 percent, reports MFAI agronomist Dr. Walter Goldstein.

Quackgrass is a tenacious invader of aging alfalfa fields in southeastern Wisconsin. But mixing brome and orchardgrass with alfalfa kept the plots quack-free. Adding trefoil to the mix also slows grass invasion by gradually taking over as alfalfa disappears, Goldstein reports. Because brome is less competitive than orchardgrass, it works better with alfalfa, filling in where needed rather than crowding out the legume.

Weed-Eating Weevils Whip Musk Thistles

And eliminate pasture herbicides for thousands of farmers.

ARCADIA, Neb. — Cattleman Jim Holmes has an interesting arrangement with his neighbors: They let him pick all the musk thistles he wants from their pastures, and he saves them tens of thousands of dollars a year on herbicides.

Holmes isn't the world's fastest hand-weeder. In fact, he doesn't even pull the entire musk thistle plant. All he wants is the seedhead, because inside it are about two dozen larvae of the musk thistle weevil (*Rhinocyllus conicus*). This tiny, voracious bug not only devours the insides of musk thistle seedheads, but lays its eggs in them as an adult. When Holmes accumulates enough of the heads — say, 1,300 or so — he dumps them into a 50-pound seed sack and sells them. The result is about $10,000 profit each year, which according to Holmes makes him the largest seller of biological thistle controls in the country.

So what's in it for his neighbors? Plenty. The weed-eating weevils are so effective that, by Holmes' estimate, only about one in 50 local farmers now use herbicides to control musk thistles in their pastures.

Other Controls Fail

Musk thistle (*Carduus nutans L.*), a tall-growing biennial native to Europe, infests thousands of pasture acres in Nebraska and elsewhere. Controlling the weed with chemicals can be risky, because it must be treated at times of year when farmers are typically busy with other chores: during spring planting, or fall harvest, when the plant is storing root reserves.

Mechanical controls can be equally ineffective. Continuous, well-timed mowing eventually depletes the weed's root reserves, but can be cumbersome and expensive when large acreages are infested.

While there are several herbicides now registered for use on musk thistle, 2,4-D is the cheapest and most widely used in Holmes' part of the country. In fact, he says, "Up until the late '60s, 2,4-D was the only thing we had to control it." But entomologists from the USDA-ARS Rangeland Insect Laboratory in Bozeman, Mont., changed all that in 1969, when they made the first release of musk thistle weevils in the United States.

The insects, imported from their native France and Italy, spread over 500 square miles within four or five years. And by 1977, thistle populations had declined enough to virtually eliminate the need for chemical controls in that area, says

USDA Entomologist Norman Rees.

Fortunately for Holmes, a similar study by the University of Nebraska failed miserably. U of N scientists released weevils at seven sites throughout the state in the early '70s, but could find little trace of them a few years later. So the university temporarily abandoned the project.

But Holmes managed to clip about 30 or 40 musk thistle seedheads harboring weevils at one site, and took them back to his farm. He released them in a secluded part of a pasture. "After three years, I had thousands of them," he says.

During the next few summers, U of N scientists visited his farm periodically to document that weevil populations were, indeed, increasing. "It took five to eight years, but my thistle control is great," he says. "If I were to try harvesting seedheads from my own farm, I'd be out of business, because there aren't many thistles left."

By 1976, Holmes was selling the weevil-infested seedheads commercially to farmers in his and several surrounding counties. Each summer, Holmes hires students from town to clip the heads from nearby farm fields. The weevil eggs, which are laid in early spring, have hatched by then. The white larvae literally eat their way out of the plant, leaving undeveloped seeds and ending the weed's reproductive cycle.

After about a month in the larval stage, the weevils pupate for up to two weeks, then emerge as adults and overwinter. Holmes sells the heads in 50-pound seed sacks while the weevils are pupating. Each sack contains from 1,200 to 1,400 seedheads — or at least 20,000 weevils — and will cover about 160 acres.

Holmes recommends farmers release the weevils in one of two ways: in equal amounts at four sites within a pasture (preferably where the seedheads will be protected by brush or buildings) or over a 15-acre area located in the middle of the pasture. No need to locate the weevils near musk thistles. "As long as you get them in the general area, they'll seek out the thistles," says Holmes.

'Recreating Nature'

Musk thistle weevils have been used successfully in at least 20 states from Montana to New York, and in virtually every Canadian province, says Rees.

Still, both he and Holmes are quick to point out that thistle control doesn't happen overnight. "It's going to take awhile to get the weevil popula-

"Burp!" By eating itself out of house and home, this musk thistle weevil (and two dozen siblings in the same seedhead) can eliminate chemical musk thistle controls.

New Farm Photo by George DeVault

tion sufficient so that every seedhead is hit," says Rees, who's been studying musk thistle weevil since 1974. "Our first release was in '69, and our first real 'crash' in thistle populations was in '77. So that was an eight-year period."

One reason for the delay is that only about 75 to 80 percent of the larvae survive and reproduce, explains Rees. Another is that some thistle seeds do survive (although germination potential can be reduced to as little as 2 percent in a well-infested seedhead, compared with nearly 70 percent in a healthy one). "What we're trying to do is recreate that normal, healthy balance of nature that occurs in the native country," says Rees, noting that weevil feeding naturally prevents thistles from becoming pests in Europe.

Farmers can give that natural process some help by following three simple guidelines, Rees adds:

◆ **Don't allow cattle to graze near the release site when weevils are laying eggs** — generally around May or June.

◆ **If rainfall is low, water the thistles.** When the plants suffer moisture stress, the weevils do, too, Rees explains.

◆ **If pasture fertility is low, or if the field has been grazed heavily, remove livestock so grasses can recover.** Otherwise, "the farmer will unknowingly be selecting for thistles," says Rees, noting that the weed sends up new shoots to repopulate sparsely covered ground.

No More Herbicides — Ever

During the first year or so, farmers may want to avoid spraying certain insecticides near the release site. "If you spray before they are in the seedhead, you may lose the weevils in the spray zone," warns Rees.

Same goes for herbicides, although it's unlikely farmers will even want to spray after a few years. "If you can get the biological control regime established, you can just sit back and let Nature take its course," says Rees.

Compared with the $5-per-acre cost of aerially applying 2,4-D, the $200 sack of thistle seedheads (enough for 160 acres) can save a farmer at least $600 a year. The technique requires careful management, Rees warns. "But at least you won't have the year-by-year herbicide expense."

Rees suggests that collecting adult weevils in spring is even more effective than gathering seedheads. Between late May and mid-June, clip rosettes and shake the plants inside a garbage bag. Then dump the bag onto a tarp and sort out the adult weevils.

One drawback is that, as the weevils multiply — and as musk thistle populations drop — the bugs will eventually head out in search of a larger food supply. "They're very mobile. They can migrate 5 to 10 miles in a year," Rees points out.

That's not necessarily bad news for the farmer who buys the weevils, but it presents a challenge for Holmes. Since the migrating weevils have decimated thistle populations within a 20-mile radius of his farm, his seedhead supply is growing more scarce each year. He's not too worried, though. "The only place I can get them now is that one in 50 farmers who kept on spraying," he says. "But they have plenty."

Editor's Note: *Musk thistle weevils are available from Jim Holmes, R.R. 1, Box 179, Arcadia, NE 68815; and Norman Rees, USDA-ARS Rangeland Insect Laboratory, Bozeman, MT 59717-0001.*

Weed-Eating Bugs

They take time, but give cleaner pastures.

Rick Nelson has been battling weeds on his 1,200 acres near Olympia, Wash., with some of nature's own allies — weed-eating bugs.

Released on untilled range or pastureland, the USDA-approved beneficials seek their favorite plant, tansy ragwort, in this case. Flea beetles (*Longitarsus jacobaeae*) feed on the weed's basal growth, crown and roots. Cinnabar moth larvae (*Tyria jacobaeae*) defoliate the plants.

"I wanted to establish biocontrol because repetitive spraying was only marginally successful," says Nelson. "I used cinnabar moths as early as 1966, and saw good control for a few years. But the weeds kept returning and the moth population seemed cyclical. So I also started releasing flea beetles in 1988, and they're spreading well now."

In northwestern Missouri's Daviess County, agronomy specialist Rodney Hexem says: "We've had good success with seedhead weevils in controlling musk thistle on pastures. About 50 growers here have used some of the weevils the past three years. I check every release and have found weevils feeding every place we've released them."

Phil Morris, an Iowa rancher and farmer, agrees. He released 5,000 of the weevils, *Rhinocyllus conicus*, in June 1990 on three half-acre sites on his 317 acres of pasture in Lenox, Iowa. He paid $200 for the insects, plus a $25 shipping charge.

"We found some activity within two weeks," says Morris. "Of course, it's hard to tell how many musk thistle weed seeds were destroyed in 1990 — the proof will be over time."

With musk thistle weevils already well-established in southeastern Idaho, wildlife refuge manager Dick Sjostrom started a biocontrol program against Canadian thistle last spring. "We released a few hundred stem-mining weevils, *Ceutorhynchus litura*, on four small sites in Bear Lake National Wildlife Refuge," says Sjostrom. "First-year biocontrol is usually iffy — and Canadian thistle is tough to knock out because it propagates by seed and by rhizomes — but we saw quite a few stems bored by the weevils by the end of summer." He describes the insects as "good weapons to use against the weeds, especially near wetlands and other protected areas."

The local weed-control board provided Nelson's insects, at no charge. Most of the insects were locally reared, many from releases purchased from BioCollect, an Oakland, Calif., company specializing in weed-eating insects.

Three former USDA weed researchers started the firm in 1987, to help public agencies and private growers meet an increased demand for weed-chewing insects.

"On rangeland, you really need something to control weeds without spending a lot of money," says Aubrey Mayfield of BioCollect. "We offer practical expertise in collecting and shipping weed bioagents."

Another former USDA weed researcher, Noah Poritz, in 1986 started a similar company, Biological Control of Weeds (BCW) in Bozeman, Mont. "If you have rangeland weeds and cultural means have failed, you should be starting biocontrol now," says Poritz.

Different beneficials are available for troublesome weeds such as leafy spurge, thistles, St. Johnswort, knapweeds, puncturevine, Mediterranean sage, Scotch broom and gorse. The insects weaken the weeds, providing a competitive edge to forages without use of herbicides.

Once established, the insect populations persist as long as specific host plants are available, according to Everett Dietrick, a beneficial-insects pioneer and the president of Rincon-Vitova Insectaries Inc., Oakview, Calif. Given time and the right conditions, the insects branch out to protect adjacent fields, too.

Research in weed biocontrol since the 1940s has shown that dozens of insect and mite species prefer weeds to crop plants. More than 40 species have been introduced for this purpose in the United States.

At prices ranging from $4 to $100 per 100 insects, BCW provides more than 300,000 weed-chewing beneficials per year. BioCollect ships more than 65,000 insects annually at prices from $10 to $75 per 100.

Biocontrol Works

Dietrick, who has more than 40 years of experience with insects, says you can count on building a population from as few as 10 insects in most cases. "It's an inoculation rather than a control at first. So expand it as you can afford it," he says. "I'd suggest going with half of what you might have been tempted to spend on herbicides. Or use multiple releases if you can afford to build the population faster."

The companies recommend purchasing more than one insect species for some weeds. "We sell two different puncturevine weevils," says Johnson, of BioCollect. "One type feeds on seeds, and the other on stems, so they complement each other."

Against musk thistle, Poritz also suggests a second weevil, *Trichosirocalus horridus*, which targets top growth of the thistle. A branching growth habit then makes it easier for *Rhinocyllus conicus* to attack the thistle seedhead. To keep costs down, Morris purchased only the *Rhinocyllus*. He plans a second release of the same species near the original release sites, "just to be sure they're established."

Getting Started

It's easy to get insects working for you once you have a positive identification of your rangeland weeds.

◆ **Contact a supplier.** Have at hand details on location, number of acres, type of land, and a description of your weed problem including weed emergence times and previous control efforts. The supplier will advise you on insect choices and release times, which can vary by location.

◆ **Plan ahead.** Availability and price vary depending on the time of year. Decide where you'll release the insects before you order any. Choose small sites, preferably less than a half-acre, and certainly no more than an acre each. Pick spots near water, woods or protected field corners you won't be cultivating or spraying for a few years. "Sprays, tillage and poorly timed mowing make it harder to succeed in establishing the desired insect populations," says Jerry Johnson of BioCollect.

◆ **After checking with you to confirm the presence of host weeds, the supplier collects and ships the insects within a 24-hour period.** They are sent by overnight express (UPS or USPS) in styrofoam packages with blue ice packs. Insects are guaranteed to arrive alive, with replacements or refunds made on request. Suppliers send a few more than ordered, though, and have had almost no problems with deliveries, even to remote areas.

"Adult beetles are pretty hardy," says Johnson. "Moths, flies and flea beetles are more fragile and

shorter-lived, so we ship them as pupae or larvae."

◆ **Disperse insects by sprinkling them around the base of weeds in early morning or late in the day to avoid the heat.** "I tell growers to put at least one weevil on each weed until they get tired of that, and then just spread them around," says agronomist Hexem. BioCollect suggests a higher concentration. "Be sure to put a couple dozen on a good-sized plant," says Johnson.

"The less delay and handling of a live organism, the better," says Poritz's partner and wife, Leona. "Adult insects are shipped on some of the host weeds for a ready food supply, but it's best to release them as soon as possible unless you have massive numbers to release. If you must store them, one night in a refrigerator is fine — but don't freeze them!"

◆ **After distribution, check some weeds a week later, and again at mid-season.** You'll probably see little evidence of real weed control. It takes time for populations to build. If you haven't found any chewed weeds by season's end, call your supplier.

"Unless you release an awful lot of insects, it'll probably take at least one to three years to start seeing the kind of results you'll want. But in most cases, that'll be fine for small operations. You can't expect overnight control with biocontrols," says Johnson.

Poritz takes an even longer view. "Don't be concerned if you see no damage the first two years," he says. "Damage depends on how the weed propagates and what population levels of insects you have. Just be patient — biocontrol benefits often will be seen as much as 10 to 25 years down the line."

Don't be tempted to hurry the eradication program with some spot spraying of Roundup or other herbicides that could reduce insect levels fast. "Make a commitment to the insect population," Johnson recommends. "Don't cultivate or spray the sites, and stick with it."

You might try a few other measures in tandem with biocontrol, such as hand scything or mowing small areas at appropriate times, or even grazing sheep on heavy spurge.

"Try to have good, competitive vegetation in there," suggests Lloyd Andres, another BioCollect founder. "Whether pastureland or orchard, try for vigorous, locally adapted grass cover or other vegetation to outcompete the weeds, and don't overgraze."

Following The Rules

Interstate shipment of insects requires permits, but suppliers already have current open permits for most Western and Midwestern states. Wherever necessary, suppliers should send you a permit application before shipping insects.

Find out if any state or local regulations prohibit specific predator insects, and if tax-supported supplies are available. Your Extension service and weed advisory board can help, as can your state department of agriculture. Wisconsin prohibits shipment of the musk thistle weevil out of concern that it might attack a native dune thistle. California prohibits importing virtually any insect, so use in-state suppliers there.

Some weeds are easier to control than others. "I'm more confident recommending insects for St. Johnswort and tansy ragwort than I am for insects against Scotch broom and gorse," says Johnson. "But those insects are the only approved ones for Scotch broom and gorse."

Questionable results also have been seen for Mediterranean sage, says Andres, but you can attain great results against many thistles and puncturevine.

"Musk thistle only reproduces by seed, so the beneficial weevils really work well against it. Those reproducing vegetatively can be a little tougher," says Poritz.

"Don't worry about the weed level needed to sustain the feeder-insect population," says Dietrick. "When the weeds diminish or disappear, so will the insects. If the weeds return, the feeders probably will too. And overwintering usually won't be a problem as long as some weeds remain."

Suppliers of weed-eating insects forecast a rising demand for their fledgling industry, which so far has only a few thousand customers and annual revenues under $1 million.

"Eventually, we can expect bioagent distribution centers to be found all over the country," says Norman Rees, entomologist at the USDA Rangeland Weed Laboratory in Bozeman, Mont. "But there's a need for more research and funding first. They may not realize it, but when ranchers obtain weed-eating insects, they're contributing to screening and educational efforts as well as to the future success of biocontrol."

Where To Get Weed-Eating Bugs

◆ Biological Control of Weeds
Noah and Leona Poritz
1140 Cherry Drive
Bozeman, MT 59715
(406) 586-5111

◆ BioCollect
5841 Crittenden St.
Oakland, CA 94601
(415) 524-9492 (Jerry Johnson)
(415) 436-8052 (Aubrey Mayfield)

County weed-control boards or Extension services can supply insects in some locations.

Tougher Than Weeds
Native prairie plants, better management trim roadside spraying 90%.

Al Ehley is working to reduce or eliminate herbicides on more than 600,000 acres. No, he's not a big-time IPM consultant scouting weeds in corn and soybean fields. Ehley is Iowa's SCS roadside specialist. And his "crop" is the 6 acres or so of vegetation that borders every mile of road in the state.

As part of Iowa's Integrated Roadside Vegetation Management (IRVM) program, Ehley helps counties and individual landowners spray less by taking better care of their roadsides. "Our focus is on preventing weeds and soil erosion by promoting the best management practices and species mix along our rural roadsides," he says. "In many cases, re-establishing mixes of native prairie vegetation is what's best for that land."

Photo courtesy of USDA-SCS

Burning at the right time every several years benefits roadside prairie plantings.

Re-establishing native prairie plants cuts mowing and spraying costs.

That's because native prairie is tougher than weeds. Its dense cover and extensive root systems make it difficult — if not impossible — for weeds to get a foothold. Once it is established, occasional spot sprays and periodic burning are all that's needed to keep weeds out. Where IRVM programs have been implemented, there is typically a 90-percent reduction in herbicide use, reports Ehley.

"Many counties have been spending $50,000 a year on herbicides and watching their roadside weed problems get worse, instead of better," he observes. "In the short run, a county won't save money by investing in these programs. But they'll get more for what they spend by getting on the road toward a long-term solution."

Weeds Indicate Problems

Like many Corn Belt states, Iowa can trace the roots of its roadside weed problems all the way back to the state's original settlers. They plowed up the prairie — a diverse plant community often made up of 300 or more species — and replaced it with grasses they brought from Europe. These cool-season grasses — like brome, fescue, timothy, bluegrass and red top — grow rapidly in spring and fall, but go dormant during hot, dry Iowa summers.

Because they were easy to establish and readily available, these same grasses were used when roadsides were first seeded in the '20s and '30s. The only trouble is, monocultures of cool-season grasses become sod-bound, lose vigor and die back, usually less than 10 years after planting, says Ehley.

In this weakened condition, roadside plantings are easy prey for invasion by annual and perenni-

al weeds, like thistles, teasle, mullein, hemp, horsetail, wild parsnip, pigweed, field bindweed lambsquarters and others. Bare spots in the sod also leave soil vulnerable to erosion. "The weeds are indicators of problems that need to be solved," observes Ehley, "especially where you see ragweed or foxtail. It's usually because there's been some erosion or spray drift from cropland."

Since the '60s, the usual response has been to spray invading weeds. But in the mid-'80s roadside workers in Iowa's Mitchell and Black Hawk counties began to take a different approach. They started replanting roadsides with native prairie vegetation and taking other steps to reduce the need to spray. When Ehley's Integrated Roadside Vegetation Management office was created in '88 to serve as an information clearinghouse, six counties had active IRVM programs. Since then, interest has exploded and programs are now in place in more than 27 counties.

That interest has been fueled, in part, by strong support from local garden clubs and conservation and wildlife organizations, says Ehley. "When you re-establish prairie, the roadsides become avenues for wildlife to move between the remnants of prairie scattered around the state," he explains. "They're especially important for small mammals, birds and butterflies."

IRVM efforts were also aided in '89 when the Iowa legislature created the Living Roadway Trust Fund. The fund provides $600,000 to $1 million per year to counties with roadside management plans to help inventory roadsides, conduct research and demonstration projects, and buy the special seed and equipment necessary to establish roadside prairies.

Avoid Monoculture, Develop Community

The prairie sod that was so quickly turned under a century ago is difficult and expensive to re-establish. Most restoration efforts are concentrated on sites that are already disturbed by new construction, ditch clearing or herbicide spills, says Ehley. Prairie plants are usually slow-growing at first, so they are often seeded with an oats or rye nurse crop to help suppress weeds.

The species are carefully matched to site conditions and other constraints. "You wouldn't want to plant a tall grass prairie in front of someone's seed corn plot," Ehley points out. "And even with natives, it's important to avoid monocultures. You want to develop a stable community of plants resilient enough to resist insects and disease."

Seed mixes are typically made up of five to seven prairie grasses — like big bluestem, switchgrass, indiangrass and sideoats grama — and three to six flowers — black-eyed Susan, grayheaded coneflower, blazing star, bush clover and prairieclover, for example. In addition to being an essential part of the stable plant community, the prairie flowers' showy blooms make for a more visually pleasing roadside, notes Ehley.

Most of the plants used are warm-season species. But on some sites, cool-season prairie grasses like Canada wildrye or less-aggressive introductions such as timothy are added to the mix to compete with cool-season weeds. To encourage warm-season prairie plants and suppress cool-season weeds, established prairie stands should be burned in late spring every three to five years. If they're properly managed, even spot spraying may be unnecessary, and the stands will also resist encroachment by woody shrubs.

While they are stiff competition along roadsides, there's no need to fear prairie plants will invade neighboring cropland. "Because they take a long time to get established and depend on their extensive root systems, they can't tolerate periodic tillage," Ehley points out.

Frequent mowing reduces the vigor of native vegetation. So natives are not a good choice where roadsides need to be kept closely mowed to maintain safe visibility, like field and farmstead entrances and hazardous intersections. Likewise, tall prairie plants should not be grown close to the shoulder in places where they are likely to cause snow drifts. But Ehley is testing a solution for such troublespots: buffalograss, a prairie species that only grows about 6 inches tall.

Roadsides already disturbed by development or ditch cleaning are the focus of Iowa's plant restoration efforts.

Encouraging The Natives

Counties with active IRVM programs are restoring roadside prairies at an average of about 5 miles per year, reports Ehley. But reseeding is only one part of IRVM. Perhaps even more important is helping counties and private landowners do a better job managing existing roadside vegetation. Counties that have conducted roadside inventories typically find that one-third to two-thirds of their roadsides already have some native prairie species present, reports Ehley. He would like to see those roadsides managed to encourage natives, rather than go to the effort and expense of re-establishing them from scratch.

"Much of our work is educational," he continues. "People think that they are controlling weeds by mowing their ditches like they mow their lawns. But often, they're just weakening the sod and encouraging the weeds. Many farmers burn ditches at the wrong time; that encourages weeds instead of natives. Or they spray their ditches more than they need to. Some think that if it's good for corn and soybeans, it's good for the roadsides, too. But that's not usually true."

To help remedy that situation, Ehley's office offers farmers' guides to basic roadside management, burning and controlling disturbances. For copies, write: Alan Ehley, USDA-SCS IRVM Program, Biology Dept., University of Northern Iowa, Cedar Falls, IA 50614-0421. Phone: (319) 273-2813. For information about similar roadside programs in your area, he suggests contacting your state's natural resources or transportation department.

Cattle And Woodlots Can Mix

Careful management benefits livestock, native vegetation and wildlife while reducing weeds.

It's no secret that cattle can make a mess of woodlands in a hurry. Improperly managed, livestock can destroy understory plants that provide cover and food for wildlife. They also can encourage weeds, increase soil erosion and even kill mature trees.

But those damaging effects aren't inevitable. Research in southern Illinois shows that allowing cattle in the woods in late summer can actually increase plant diversity, compared with ungrazed woodlands.

"In the past, foresters have taken a uniformly negative view of pasturing cattle in woodlands," says Ann Dennis, the Illinois Department of Energy and Natural Resources ecologist who conducted the study. "But it's possible to manage the shade, vegetation and soil resources of woodlands for cattle production without damaging them."

Illinois woodland used heavily by cattle year-round (top photo). Site grazed only in summer and fall (bottom photo) had increased plant diversity.

Photos courtesy of Ann Dennis/Illinois Natural History Survey

It's not surprising foresters take a dim view of running cattle in the woods. Some farmers use woodlots like feedlots, sheltering cattle at very high stocking rates through winter. "That eliminates understory cover and wildlife habitat," says Dennis. Such practices can also cause erosion on steep ground and around streams, and injure mature overstory trees, reducing their value, she adds.

Dennis found in her study that even at modest stocking rates, cattle pastured over winter in woodlands drastically reduced plant diversity. The study compared upland oak-hickory forest sites with four different management histories at the Dixon Springs Agricultural Center in southern Illinois. Shrubs and saplings were virtually eliminated on sites where cattle were pastured and fed in the woods from December through March and had access to the woods through the growing season. In addition, weeds replaced many native woodland herbs, and trampling exposed bare ground on up to 10 percent of the area.

No Excuse For Abuse

Where cattle had access to the woods only from March through November, Dennis noted less damage. But her most striking findings came where access was deferred until late June or early July. "I was surprised at how diverse the vegetation was there," she says. "We found more woodland species than on sites that had been protected from grazing for 15 years." Deferred sites also had relatively few introduced and weedy species, she reports.

Dennis says the increase in diversity may be due to cattle disturbing the litter layer, perhaps releasing some species suppressed by that cover in the unpastured forest. She also surmises that keeping cattle out of the woods in spring increases diversity by protecting understory plants at a critical time in their life cycle. Deferred use also helps reduce tree-root injury.

"On the sites in this study, dividing pastures to exclude livestock from woodlands until June or July appears to enhance the diversity of plant communities," concludes Dennis. "That improves habitat quality for wildlife that requires well-developed understories for food and cover." She's eager to see if studies on other sites with different forest types confirm her findings.

Dennis is also concerned that with the emphasis on livestock diversification in sustainable farming, more and more farmers will view woodlands as low-cost facilities to feed and shelter animals. "Farm woodlands account for about 70 percent of all remaining native vegetation in Illinois," she observes. "There's no good excuse for allowing complete destruction of vegetation and habitat when this can be avoided with better management."

Her suggestions:

◆ **Fence pastures and woodlots so that you can control when and how many cattle are in the woods.** Cost-share money is often available.

◆ **Locate fences, gates, feeders, water, salt, etc. to keep cattle out of streams and to encourage cattle to travel across slopes.** That way they won't make trails up and down hillsides.

◆ **Pay as much attention to forest soils as you do cropland soils.** When it's wet, don't hold cattle in areas with heavy clay soils or poor drainage.

◆ **Know what you value in your woodlands, and manage accordingly.** If you value shade, make sure cattle don't damage the trees that provide it.

"The conservation community has identified and preserved some of our best forest lands," says Dennis. "But that doesn't mean we should abuse the rest. We can manage cattle and woods together for the benefit of both."

Chapter 4

HIGH-VALUE WEED CONTROL

These tips and tools will help reduce weeds and chemical costs in your fruits and vegetables.

The intensive nature of fruit and vegetable production offers plenty of opportunities for low-cost weed control.

Many farmers grow two vegetable crops — sometimes three — on the same ground in a single year. If properly managed, that kind of frequent tillage and seedbed preparation, alone, can help awaken and kill weed flushes. Crop rotation, a key to controlling the soilborne diseases that plague many high-value crops, serves much the same purpose.

Double-cropping and crop rotation become even more effective when you include weed-smothering covers such as grain rye or buckwheat in the system.

Mulches and row covers, which are popular among farmers looking to meet early markets and to conserve soil moisture, can also double as excellent weed control tools. Likewise, well-timed transplanting gives crops a head start on the competition — especially when it follows a pre-plant tillage regime designed to kill early weeds.

To give these and other cultural methods a helping hand, farmers use a variety of innovative *implements* to manage weeds in high-value crops, including:
◆ Customized cultivators for in-row weed control
◆ Modified mowers that clip weeds and lay mulch at the same time
◆ Propane-fired flame weeders that ... well, you can pretty much guess what these do!

You'll read about all of this, plus a few surprises, in the pages that follow.

Getting The Jump On Vegetable Weeds
Timing, mulches and tillage keep fields clean.

RALPH MOORE

Organic vegetable growers are finding new ways to beat weeds. Like a forward-thinking physician, they focus on prevention, natural processes and early intervention to give their crops the advantage.

Good weed control begins with tillage long before planting. The competition begins as soon as the soil has been prepared for planting. I like to give our crops at least an even start with the weeds. We begin by incorporating cover crops four to six weeks ahead of planting. This allows time for the vegetation to decay and the first round of weeds to begin sprouting. If a rye cover grows beyond the 12-inch lush green stage, it gets stemmy and should be mowed before being tilled.

A flail mower does the best job of cutting stems into short lengths that incorporate easily. We use a 6-foot International Harvester flail chopper.

To incorporate the cover crop, we use a combination of tools. A five-shank Ferguson chisel plow (list price: $1,487) set a foot deep is followed by a 70-inch Howard Rotavator (list price: $3,605) set 7 inches deep. The tiller produces a loose soil texture full of oxygen to help decompose the green matter. I leave the field undisturbed for two to four weeks to allow weeds to germinate.

Next, I make a second pass with the Rotavator set only an inch or 2 deep. This scarfs out young weeds which have sprouted, without bringing up new weed seeds. Few weed seeds deeper than 2

A three-row Lilliston rolling cultivator with sidedresser attachment makes quick work of weeds in green beans.

inches will sprout early in the season. I repeat this scalping method the day of planting.

In the days when we used to plow and harrow, the weeds were up ahead of the crop by the time we got the whole field planted. That can turn into a real disaster. With the Rotavator, you can scarf-till only the beds that are ready to be planted. Using the chisel plow ahead of the Rotavator provides a subsoiling action and an overall loosening effect, while lessening the wear and tear on the tiller. The Rotavator does the best job of mixing the soil and preparing a level seedbed. This flatness is especially important for laying plastic mulch tight to the soil surface.

After harvest, crop residue can be tilled under immediately, and a cover crop can be planted rather than letting fall weeds take over and go to seed. Since the Rotavator is able to work in small areas, an early planting of peas can be incorporated while a bed of peppers and tomatoes grows alongside.

Timing Critical

We have a weed flush in spring and in fall, times when soil moisture and temperature are ideal for Nature's own cover crops to develop. Well-timed crop planting can greatly reduce weed pressure in some crops.

Some growers use fluid-gel seeding for slow-germinating vegetables like carrots. In this technique, pre-germinated seed is planted in a gel medium. Quicker emergence decreases the time weeds have to catch up after a pre-plant scarfing. In-row hilling techniques won't work if the weeds are as tall as the plants. Some crops can be transplanted, which gives them a head start on the weeds and for harvest. For many crops, however, direct seeding is just more practical.

We grow a few acres of snap beans which are succession-planted nine times for continuous harvest. The first three plantings in May and early June always are the weediest, and may need three cultivations. Later plantings have much less weed pressure and are usually cultivated only once. We use a Lilliston rolling cultivator, which is one of our favorites (list price: two row, $1,534). Timely attack is extremely important in controlling the early weed flush. Weed emergence and development must be carefully scouted. Weeds should be removed when they are young sprouts, because most cultivators lose some of their effectiveness as weeds get taller.

Our worst weed competitor is ragweed. It is a fast grower and gets a good foothold early, developing a strong root system. It doesn't take too many plants to make the field look really bad. We feel good when a patch of green beans doesn't

Piling greenchop between beds covered with plastic mulch is hard work. But it's worth the effort, as these lush green peppers and staked tomatoes show.

have any weeds towering above the bean plants. A few can be tolerated or hand-pulled easily.

Keep Weeds In The Dark

A mulch of grass, straw or black plastic is a way to prevent weeds from developing. Grass and straw shade and cool the soil to inhibit weed growth. Black plastic heats the ground, forcing weed seeds to germinate quickly in the warm, damp environment. The plastic then kills the struggling plants by keeping out sunlight.

Seeds or plants are hand- or machine-planted through the mulch. The plastic is most efficiently laid by a mulch-layer implement that furrows-in the edges and covers them with soil. Many kinds of mulch layers are available. Our dealership alone handles 10 models. Prices start at $465 for a basic machine capable of laying 3- or 4-foot rolls flat on the ground. More expensive layers are able to lay wider plastic, apply fabric covers or clear plastic tunnels, and work on raised beds. There even are mulch layers that form a raised bed and wrap it in plastic in a single operation. Cost of the plastic is about $100 per acre.

Many vegetable crops grow and yield better on black plastic mulch. In the Northeast, crops such as melons and peppers don't mature without the increased soil temperature from a heat-retaining boost.

Weed control between the beds and their plastic covers is a concern. Some growers cultivate the wheel paths, careful not to snag the plastic and pull it loose. We like to mulch the paths with green-chop grass applied mechanically with our 12-foot John Deere forage wagon, which we bought used for $400. It side-unloads the grass onto the adjacent wheel path where it is hand-tended. One wagonload takes about an hour to unload and covers 400 linear feet of wheel paths. The wagon also can be used to apply organic mulches right on the bed for crops that can tolerate a cooler soil. An automatic spreading system could be devised for doing larger acreages.

Growers who don't have grass crops can use baled straw to mulch the paths. This can be applied by hand or with a Berri King straw mulcher designed for mulching strawberries (list price: three-point hitch model, $2,475). The mulch should be applied before weed growth so established weeds don't grow through the straw. In addition to the weed-control benefit, the grass mulch retains soil moisture, eliminates mud splashing on the crop, adds organic matter to the soil and allows better harvest conditions. Rye can be harvested to provide a natural mulch for earlier crops.

Another method I have observed, with similar

A 70-inch Howard Rotavator gobbles up young weeds. Crumble roller on the rear is optional.

results, is to let weeds and grasses grow between the plastic beds and mow the wheel paths with a rotary mower to keep them under control. This can make hand-removal of the plastic mulch difficult, however, since quackgrass roots can grow through the buried edge of mulching plastic, anchoring it to the soil.

Weed growth in the mulch's plant holes also can be a problem, more so with bare-rooted plants than with plugs or pots. There is nothing worse than having to hand-weed around each plant. Keep the hole as small as possible. One trick is to place rotted sawdust around each set to keep weed sprouts from reaching sunlight.

Smothering Benefit Lingers

Smaller-scale growers can use wide sheets of black plastic to solarize their soil and smother weeds. Norman Hunter, an organic grower from Berkley Springs, W.Va., gave it a try for the first time in 1990. He rototilled first, then laid a wide sheet of black plastic down and secured it with soil three weeks ahead of planting. When he removed the plastic, the soil was bare. Seeds of lettuce, kale and spinach were planted with a Planet Jr. walk-behind planter. The seeds sprouted quickly ahead of the weeds. As later weeds emerged, they were cultivated with a walk-behind tiller.

Other growers use the solarization technique to double-crop a fall planting. After early crops grown on black plastic have been harvested, the plastic is removed and a new crop is planted. Often, very little additional weed control is needed.

Burning, By Flame And By Spray

Flame weeders use a propane burner directed at the soil to kill sprouted weeds. These devices are used mainly on direct-seeded crops that are slow to germinate, such as carrots. Weeds are flamed once before planting and once after, just before crop emergence. Once the rows are up, mechanical cultivation can commence.

Safer has an organic herbicide for vegetable use called SharpShooter which is accepted for restricted use by the Organic Crop Improvement Association (OCIA). SharpShooter is non-selective, and will burn any plant it comes in contact with. Though not yet labeled for crop use, it will work like a flame weeder to kill weeds before and soon after planting. It will also be used for spot spraying and controlling weeds between beds of plastic mulch. Be sure to get the 18-percent formulation that comes in 2.5-gallon jugs and not the weaker solution meant for garden use.

Right Tools Make The Difference

We've tried quite an array of cultivators over the years. If there is one thing we've learned, it is that the right tool used at the right time can make all the difference. Knowing the variables in your fields *and* between implements can help you decide what combinations might keep your crops in the clear — and herbicides in the can.

Mechanical cultivation can begin as soon as the crop is planted. One or two cultivations should take care of a crop, at least to a level of weed control that will not reduce yield.

Cultivators differ widely in how they disturb the

Mechanical weed control for horticultural crops can involve something as simple as a pair of 16-inch hiller disks on a toolbar. These adjustable earthmovers can make furrows, cover planted rows, or hill up soil around maturing plants.

soil. There are two types of cultivating action — between the row and in the row. Some cultivators do both. Selection of the best piece of equipment depends on a number of variables: How quickly has weed pressure developed? How tall is the crop relative to the weeds? What is the soil type, texture and surface condition? What type of cultivating action is needed to ensure control?

Working Between The Rows

The least aggressive cultivator we've come across is the Buddingh Model K, known as the "basket weeder." It doesn't move soil into the row, but it's good for very early cultivation and can be used even before the crop has sprouted. It works best in loose soil before weeds get a good footing. The front wire cage wheel or "basket" drives the trailing rear basket twice as fast as ground speed, which makes it break up and loosen the soil. It can be fitted with optional sweeps in front of the drive basket to open up crusted soil. These cultivators are custom-made to each row spacing and are not adjustable.

The most aggressive cultivator is the rototiller-like Multivator. It has rotating, PTO-driven tiller blade heads mounted on a toolbar. The width of each head is adjustable and the heads can be positioned anywhere across the back of the tractor. The heavy-duty model can be used to strip till, leaving sod grassways between the rows. It does not move soil for in-row cultivation unless the optional ridgers are mounted behind the heads. Only heavy-duty models are recommended for rocky or hard soil conditions. This type of cultivator is widely used by strawberry growers to renovate their perennial beds.

Sweep cultivators are used most widely. Mounting sweeps on a toolbar using trip shanks or spring tines protects them against damage when they hit a hard object. They are generally between-row cultivators, though they do move some soil to the row. They may or may not do a complete job of hilling, depending on ground speed. The sweeps travel below the soil, severing weeds in hard and soft soil conditions. They are good at cleaning up tall weeds that have grown out of control between the rows. Sweeps come in many sizes. Shanks are adjustable to fit various row spacings.

The Lilliston and BHC rolling cultivators have ground-driven spider tines that work the soil. These cultivators are highly adjustable and can be set to lightly hill the row to perform in-row cultivation, or to pull soil away from the row. The aggressiveness can be changed by adjusting the angle of the gangs. They can also be swiveled to hill crops like potatoes. The spider tines leave weeds on top of the soil where they will dry out. Fist-sized rocks can sometimes jam a gang, but they usually can be removed by backing up. This type is one of our favorites.

Working In The Row

In the row is where the weeds are most difficult to remove mechanically. In-row cultivation is accomplished two ways: by hilling the row with a wave of soil from both sides, which buries young weeds; or by stirring the soil around the plants. To be successful, the crop must have a size advantage over the weeds. The objective is to get the seed up quickly and tall enough to cultivate before the weeds recover. When our snap beans are 3 inches tall, the weeds are just sprouting. At this stage, the crop can be hilled lightly and the weeds buried with good results.

The Buddingh Model C Finger Weeder is primarily an in-row cultivator. It has rubber fingers that go around the plants, gently scuffing the soil while bringing a wave of soil in under the planted row. The fingers wiggle the plants without damaging them. We use the finger weeder on cucumbers and other vine crops with good results. The rear steel fingers cultivate between the rows, as well. The Model C is usually set up as a one-row cultivator for wide rows.

The Bezzerides Spring Hoe, another in-row cultivator, brings in a wave of soil from both sides to hill the row while scuffing out weeds between the rows. Toolbar mountings enable the spring hoes to be mounted on other cultivators to create a custom unit, such as we did on our Lilliston Rolling Cultivator for the early weed flush.

Wheel hoes are an old standard on small organic farms. They are manually pushed but are much more efficient than hand hoeing. They can be used for between-row cultivation with sweeps and for in-row cultivation with a moldboard plow to hill the row lightly. Prices start at $85 for the Jupiter Wheel Hoe and range up to $400 for the deluxe Real (pronounced ray-AL) hoe we import from Switzerland. It's worth the money.

We have found many uses for a pair of 16-inch hilling discs mounted on a toolbar. They provide excellent weed control in potatoes and other specialty crops that can be aggressively hilled. They also can be used for building raised beds and for making furrows for small-scale growers to hand-plant potatoes, garlic and flower bulbs. The disks can then be reset to cover and cultivate the rows.

Keeping On The Straight And Narrow

Precision cultivation is easiest if you have straight rows. Always match the cultivator to the planter. If you use a two-row planter, use a two-row cultivator. This gives you perfectly spaced parallel rows to follow.

Belly-mounted cultivators are best, since you can see what you are doing. However, tractors of this type are becoming harder to find in some places. We handle custom-built tool-carrier tractors that have belly mounts, high clearance, three-point hitches and PTO access. Most cultivators can be belly-mounted with the right brackets.

For growers who need to use rear-mount three-point-hitch cultivators, adding mirrors allows the operator to check tracking of the unit while still looking forward. Offering more assistance is a cultivation guidance system, such as the arrangement Bezzerides and Lilliston offer. These low-priced units use a chisel foot mounted on the planter to make a groove in the soil. At cultivation, a guide wheel mounted on the cultivator tracks the groove. By removing sway blocks or loosening chains on stabilizing bars, the tractor can drive off the track a little bit without pulling the cultivator out of the groove. The chisel foot and guide wheel also could be adapted to mount on other cultivators.

The Friday Wiggle Hoe uses a low-technology approach to staying on the row. One person per row seated on the unit guides two shanks around plants in the row. More sophisticated guidance systems also have been developed using hydraulics and electronic-assist systems (see Chapter 5, "Tools of the Trade").

New in 1991, Friday's Robotic Hoe adds an electronic eye and robotic arms to the wiggle hoe, allowing it to work even in the dark. It is suitable for use on transplanted crops that are spaced apart, such as peppers. Plants must be sufficiently

Photos courtesy of Ralph Moore/Market Farm Implement

The aggressive Multivator (shown with metal shrouds removed to expose multiple-bladewheel heads) provides maximum incorporation between rows. Tillage width and position on toolbar are adjustable for each head.

larger than weeds for the system to distinguish between the two. Plant tops break a light beam, which triggers two hydraulic arms to open then close around the plant. All the tractor operator has to do is steer along the row.

Timing is everything in vegetable weed control, especially if you choose mechanical rather than chemical means. In-row hilling won't work if weeds are as tall as the plants. Some crops can be transplanted, which gives them the height advantage and provides an earlier harvest. Weed development must be carefully monitored. Most cultivators — especially in-row types — lose some of their effectiveness as weeds get taller.

Vegetable growers have an old saying: "If you can see the weeds, it's too late." That may be a little strong, but *just* a little.

Editor's Note: *Ralph Moore and his brother David grow 20 acres of certified-organic vegetables in southwestern Pennsylvania, and operate a speciality-crop machinery business (Market Farm Implement, R.D. 2, Box 206, Friedens, PA 15541; (814) 443-1931).*

Weapons For Winning The Weed War
They'll make your high-value crops more profitable and enjoyable.

TOM MORRIS

You can't use just any old herbicide with vegetable crops. Planting many different crops requires many different herbicides. Trying to match the proper herbicides with a number of relatively small patches of crops planted at various dates

Notched, rolling shields protect young crops during cultivation. They also destroy weeds close to the row.

can drive you crazy, and waste both your time and money. It can also greatly limit your ability to rotate crops to control disease, insects and weeds, since many vegetables are very sensitive to herbicide carryover. Many consumers are increasingly sensitive about chemical use on vegetables, too.

So what can you do? A whole lot more than the chemical companies would like you to think. Non-chemical weapons for winning the weed war include crop rotation, weed-suppressing cover crops, mulches (black plastic and organic materials like straw), mechanical cultivation and, as a last resort, hand hoeing. Cultivation is your best defense.

The keys to effective cultivation are:
◆ Optimum fertility for fast-growing crop plants
◆ Good, uniform crop stand at the proper stage of growth
◆ Straight rows with accurate spacing
◆ Optimum soil moisture
◆ Enough time to cultivate when conditions are right, which might be only for a couple of hours in one afternoon
◆ Using the proper cultivators for each crop at the correct speed, depth and spacing

Mid-Mounted Cultivators

Mounted under the belly of the tractor, mid-mounted cultivators are raised by hydraulics or mechanically with a large lever. The cultivating tractor should be purchased with a set of cultivators. When fitted with sweeps, these cultivators will be used to cultivate between beds of black plastic, which is used on warm-season crops such as tomatoes, peppers, eggplant and all of the cucurbits. Sweeps usually work better than shovels in throwing soil onto the buried edge of black plastic to kill weeds growing there.

The cultivating tractor, when fitted with a specialty mid-mounted cultivator, will also cultivate the narrow rows of direct-seeded and transplanted specialty crops. Many custom welding shops make specialty cultivators for narrow rows. These units are quickly and easily attached to tractors. Most of these shops are in the vegetable growing regions of California, Michigan and New Jersey. They are most commonly located by word of mouth, or sometimes by ads in local newspapers. Most of the cultivators made by these firms are smaller and can be arranged in many different ways to suit specific soil and crop needs.

Custom-built cultivators will vary widely in price, depending on their complexity and construction. They cost from $500 to $1,000. One unique type of cultivator which I have used with good success is the rolling cage cultivator made by the Buddingh Weeder Co. (6987 Hammond Ave., Dutton, MI 49316). This cultivator does an excellent job of removing weeds in the two- to four-leaf stage. It is easy to mount and dismount. Cost of a two-row unit is about $400. Another company that makes specialty cultivators is Bezzerides Bros. Inc. (P.O. Box 211, Orosi, CA 93647).

Rear-Mounted Cultivators

Rear-mounted cultivators are attached to the tractor by the three-point hitch. They are not as precise as the mid-mounted cultivators, because side sway cannot be completely eliminated from rear-mounted implements. Sway blocks or bars on the tractor and stabilizing disks on the cultivator keep rear-mounted cultivators steady enough to do a good job on wide-row, large-seeded crops such as corn and on transplanted crops on wide rows.

Used cultivators often are available at half the price of new cultivators. Just make sure the one you buy has shields. Shields alone are not usually available in the used market. Buying new shields would cost almost as much as a new cultivator. Cost of a used two-row cultivator with shields should be $200 to $250. Another useful attachment is a set of 14-inch disks-on-shanks that will fit your cultivator. These disks do a good job of hilling sweet corn on last cultivation.

Rotary Hoe

This implement is an absolute necessity for controlling weeds with fewer herbicides. It breaks up crusted soil on large-seeded crops such as corn, peas and beans, and controls weeds in the row between young crop plants.

The rotary hoe is used before the crop is large enough for regular cultivation. It works by kicking out small-seeded weeds as they germinate, leaving large-seeded crop plants unharmed. Rotary hoes work best when the soil is crusted and weeds are just emerging. After weeds have reached the two-leaf stage, the rotary hoe cannot remove them, so timeliness is important.

There are two types of rotary hoes. The newer, spring-loaded type is mounted on a toolbar with a three-point hitch attachment. The older, pull-type hoe is not spring-loaded. The spring-loaded hoe is much better, because the springs allow each hoe on the implement to float independently, providing better coverage on uneven ground. And, with three-point-hitch mounting, you can easily control the depth of soil penetration from the tractor seat. This optimizes the effectiveness

Hundreds of spoons on a rotary hoe quickly pulverize crusted soil and uproot small weeds. If you're looking to cut herbicide costs, a rotary hoe will be one of your best machinery investments.

of the implement by allowing the operator to quickly adjust the depth for varying soil conditions.

In contrast, controlling the depth of penetration on the old, pull-type hoe is much more difficult, since it involves adding weights to the implement's frame. The other weakness of the pull-type hoe is that it does not float on uneven ground. Despite that, the pull-type rotary hoe still does an adequate job. When adapted to a three-point hitch, it could become one of your best machinery buys.

Planting Tips

When growing direct-seeded vegetables with few, if any, herbicides, it is cheaper and better to solid seed the crop. There are three reasons for that:

1. Solid-seeded crops compete better against weeds than do plants spaced 12 inches apart.

2. Cultivation is faster and easier. Because of the higher plant populations in solid-seeded rows, knocking out some crop plants with the cultivator is not as big a concern as it is with precision-spaced plantings. Cultivators can be run much closer to crop plants and at higher speeds.

3. Thinning and hand-hoeing a solid-planted row is faster and easier than trying to clean up a weed-infested row with crop plants a foot apart. With solid-seeded rows, no time is wasted trying to distinguish crop plants from weeds.

For all those reasons, I recommend buying a Planet Jr. planter to plant small-seeded crops. A new three-row unit on a toolbar set up for a three-point hitch costs about $1,200. It will plant both wide and narrow rows. The middle unit is left empty when planting wide rows. This includes the brushes necessary for small seeds and a 2-inch scatter shoe for proper spacing of root crops such as carrots, beets and radishes.

Editor's Note: *Tom Morris is former farm manager of the Rodale Institute Research Center, Kutztown, Pa. He is currently a researcher in the agronomy department at Iowa State University.*

Your Mower—The Best Orchard (And Pasture) Herbicide Yet

Introducing a broad-spectrum weed killer that's cheap and effective.

Efficiency is the only way to make it in farming these days. For Virgil Bareham, who grows 150 acres of tart and sweet cherries near Sutton's Bay, Mich., that means getting two jobs done at once with his mower.

"I'm mowing anyway, why not get a little extra weed control and mulch in the bargain?" says Bareham, who has modified his mower to blow all of his orchard driveway cuttings into the tree rows. "Mulch has a lot of values. It holds moisture, smothers weeds and puts nutrients back into the soil."

Field-crop farmers can also turn their mowers into broad-spectrum herbicides, thanks to research into the life cycles of weeds, which has revealed when they're most vulnerable to cutting. Many weeds are best cut when they are in flower, but the timing of subsequent mowing can make the difference between eliminating the weed or allowing it to survive.

For Bareham, the mowing and mulching system has saved one or two $10-per-acre herbicide applications per season. It has also relieved water stress on his trees at critical blossom and fruit set times, and helped his trickle irrigation system provide moisture more evenly to his trees. Bareham grows the traditional, long-lived perennial ryegrass and Kentucky bluegrass for his driveway cover crops. He makes his first cutting in mid-spring when the grass is about 18 inches high.

"That machine lays down an inch of mulch just as fast as you can cut," says Bareham. His Woods 120 mower is a side-by-side tandem unit which he modified to give strong side-delivery of cuttings. First, Bareham changed the drive mechanism to reverse the direction of his left side cutter so that it feeds clippings to the right side blades. Then he cut away a portion of the mower body and installed a grass chute to direct the flow.

Don't reach for the cutting torch right away, though. Some mower manufacturers, including Woods, offer models with built-in or bolt-on chutes for safely directing cuttings where they're needed.

Boosts Tree Growth

Bob Gregory, who with his brother, Don, manages the family's 650-acre cherry and apple orchard near Traverse City, Mich., says mow/mulching not only helps control weeds, but is crucial to the survival of costly new plantings. "We know that mulch increases the survival and growth rate of young trees. Blowing that mulch in is fast and easy. Where we don't have enough mulch, we'll apply hay by hand. It's that important." Gregory also uses a modified mower to distribute cuttings in an 8-foot-wide strip in the tree rows. Unlike Bareham, the Gregorys first mow orchard middles when the cover is 8 to 12 inches tall. "You want to cut it before it sets seed, so you're not blowing seed into the rows."

The Gregorys are still trying to find the best cover crop for the system. They have experimented with sorghum, oats and annual rye. The rye is managed much as a traditional driveway cover, but oats and sorghum require some new and different approaches, says Bob. "With oats, you're seeding in late summer and letting the crop winterkill. It leaves a mat that provides fairly good control and a nice layer of mulch until you plant again next year."

With weed-fighting covers, Gregory has eliminated three of his usual four herbicide applications at a savings of about $20 per acre. He has increased his planting costs by only half that amount for a net savings of $10 per mow/mulched acre. But just as important to Gregory are those tough-to-put-a-price-on advantages: the survival and fast growth of young trees under mulch, recycling of nutrients to the dripline area, and the gradual improvement of soil tilth.

Natural Weed Killers

Researchers are finding that some types of mulches can pack more weed-controlling punch than others. Plants such as annual rye, sunflowers, sorghum and oats release substances that are toxic to other plants, says Alan Putnam, a Michigan State University plant scientist.

These toxins inhibit the germination and growth of weeds, benefiting the source plants and — if the grower plays his cards right — the cash crop. "Right now, annual or grain-type rye looks like the best crop to use," says Putnam. "We have the most experience with orchard situations, but annual rye is doing a nice job in vine crops and certain vegetable crops, too."

Finding cover crops that could be grown for weed control, water conservation *and* nitrogen could tip the balance even further in favor of mow/mulching, says Putnam. "White clover does nicely as a nitrogen-fixing cover crop, but we haven't worked with it enough yet," he says. One disadvantage of using a legume is that bees, which should be pollinating fruit trees, are distracted by tempting clover flowers.

Mow Pasture Weeds, Too

Mowing is one part of a total weed control program for pastures, field edges and other parts of the farm where row crops aren't grown, says M.K. McCarty, a weed scientist at the University of Nebraska, who has conducted a 20-year comparative weed control study. "One of the most effective ways to use the mower is to prevent seed production in annual weeds," he says. Annuals should be mowed when flowers first appear, because some weed seeds will manage to germinate even though the plant is cut soon after pollination.

McCarty says mowing is less effective on perennial weeds and low-growing weeds, which can set seed below the blades. He recommends wick application of systemic herbicides for persistent weed problems.

But perennials can also be controlled by well-timed mowings, which can prevent seed production and starve underground parts, research shows. To control tall perennial weeds, repeated and frequent cutting may be required for one to three years. Never let weeds replenish their stored food supplies. The best time to start mowing or cultivating is when root reserves are at a low ebb. For many species, this is between full leaf development and the time when flowers appear during late spring. New stems can only grow by using up stored food.

In pastures, adequate soil fertility, drainage and near-neutral soil pH can help desirable legume and grass species out-compete weeds. Controlled, rotational grazing, rather than prolonged set-stocking and continuous grazing, can also suppress weeds and favor good pasture regrowth.

Safety First

Providing bark-chewing rodents with cover is one possible disadvantage of mow/mulching. Most of the Gregorys' trees go through winter, the riskiest season for rodent damage, with a layer of mulch. But routine anti-rodent measures are enough to prevent tree damage, says Bob Gregory. "We protect our younger trees with the white plastic spiral tree guards. In mature orchards, we don't leave crates or junk around, because that's the main rodent habitat. If we have to, we'll use poisoned baits. The trees are too big of an investment to leave the rodent problem to chance under any conditions."

Can mulches tie up nutrients that should be

going into the trees? "I go by the theory that grass mulches tie up a little extra nitrogen at first, but then gradually release it back," says Bob. He applies about 2 pounds of actual nitrogen per tree in split spring-fall applications. As mulches decompose, they also return micronutrients to the tree root zone, he says.

Both Gregory and Bareham say they minimize the dangers of the mow/mulch system by not mowing in the vicinity of orchard workers. Reducing the risk of thrown objects is another reason to keep the orchard clean, they add.

It's also important to protect mower operators, who can fall under the cutters. "In a blade con-

tact situation, the tissue usually can't be restored. It often results in amputation," says Wesley Buchele, Iowa State University agricultural engineer and an authority on mower safety. How to avoid such an accident? He rates a full cab as the best protection. Next is the use of a tractor seat belt and roll cage.

Nearly every farm has a mower. Used wisely, it can do two jobs at once — like mowing/mulching. With good timing, a mower can be used to kill annual weeds before they can set seed, or starve out perennial weeds. "Herbicides work fine on certain weeds. But I can't find one to do the whole job like the mower," says Bareham.

Direct Seed And Flame Weed
That's his secret for effective weed control.

VIROQUA, Wis. — Richard de Wilde has a rough rule of thumb about which vegetables and ornamentals to plant: "Don't grow anything that doesn't have the potential to bring in at least 50 cents a pound or row-foot, wholesale," he suggests. "And I prefer to get a dollar."

Choosing the highest-value crops helps. And adding value to some after harvest boosts his bottom line. But de Wilde, who farms 20 acres of silt-loam bottomland, also pays special attention to every detail of production, harvest and transport to make sure his certified organic crops are the best money can buy. That includes using just about every technique available to control weeds without herbicides.

Precision Planting

Many growers transplant crops or rely on plastic mulch to control weeds. But de Wilde direct seeds whenever possible. In fact, only about 20 percent of his crops are transplanted. "Why transplant 1,000 plants an hour when you can direct seed 1,000 in five minutes?" he asks.

Still, de Wilde transplants crops when there are distinct advantages. To get a jump on the season, he transplants his first lettuce crop. And he transplants cucurbits to avoid cucumber beetle damage. De Wilde also starts cucumbers in the greenhouse to transplant in July to help fill the late-summer production slump. Onions, leeks, celery root and tomatoes are also transplanted.

De Wilde uses a pair of Stanhay belt seeders to direct seed on two-row beds. The units, which list for about $1,500 each, allow him to space plants

precisely. "They save me a lot of time and money because I don't have to come back and thin," he observes. "But you have to have excellent weed control first if you're going to direct seed." De Wilde bought the units used, but feels that even at the full price they would quickly pay for themselves. For his baby salad mix and large-seeded crops where thinning isn't needed, he uses Planet Jr. planters.

Tobacco growers in the area taught de Wilde the key to better weed control. "They say to never let any weeds go to seed. We've stuck to that rule since we came here in the mid-'80s. And we've noticed that our fields have gotten incredibly cleaner. There's a lot less hand weeding to do now."

De Wilde's second rule is to use a chisel plow whenever possible. "A moldboard plow just turns up your old sins, causing more weed problems. I only use it when I absolutely have to." De Wilde sometimes chisels a second time, then disks at least twice and cultipacks to prepare the seedbed.

One way de Wilde helps direct-seeded crops get a jump on weeds is to use a flame weeder to kill weeds between planting and germination. His flamer was set up by Thermal Weed Control Systems, 3403 Highway 93, Eau Claire, WI 54701. Phone: (715) 839-7242. (See Chapter 5, "Tools of the Trade.") Pregermination flaming works particularly well for slow-germinating crops like carrots, parsnips and larkspur, says de Wilde.

Timing is critical. To predict the best time to flame, de Wilde sets a pane of glass over the row after planting. The crop seeds under the glass

Cucumbers started in the greenhouse and transplanted in mid-July help fill the late-summer production slump. Transplanting can also give crops a head start on weeds, but de Wilde prefers the labor- and cost-savings of direct seeding and flame-weeding.

germinate several days before uncovered seeds. When they come up, de Wilde knows it's time to flame the early weeds that have sprouted before the rest of the crop germinates.

Timing is even trickier with fast-germinating crops, like spinach and lettuce. De Wilde admits he's had less success flaming these crops. His strategy is to prepare the ground, then delay planting for four or five days to give weeds a chance to start sprouting. He direct seeds the main crop, then flames three or four days later. Without the delayed planting, weeds and the crop would germinate simultaneously, making flaming impossible, he explains.

De Wilde also flames potatoes. "They're tough. They can take a flaming even after they're up," he observes. In 1990, he flame weeded potatoes as they emerged, and then he cultivated just once. The crop required no additional hand weeding.

To work close to the rows without throwing too much dirt, de Wilde equips his midmount cultivator with narrow, 1-inch-wide "snake points" set as close as 2 or 3 inches from the row. Narrow, 3-inch-wide shields make it possible for him to cultivate young crops without burying them. Wider, 4-inch shovels kill weeds between rows. De Wilde is also testing Bezzerides Brothers cultivator tools, and feels a combination of the company's spyders and torsion weeders will help him cultivate closer to the row and further reduce hand-weeding.

De Wilde limits mulching primarily to tomatoes and strawberries, mostly to keep the fruit off the ground. He greenchops overgrown rye cover crops and augers the mulch out of the chopper box along the tomato row. Garlic is mulched in fall with a manure-sawdust mix trucked in from a local livestock breeding operation and stockpiled for six months before being applied with a manure spreader. In addition to suppressing weeds, the mix helps hold moisture and supplies nutrients, says de Wilde.

Carpets Of Cover Crops

Cover crops play a big role in de Wilde's weed control strategy, as well as supplying other benefits. Normally, covers carpet about 17 of his 20 acres in winter. His most dependable cover has been a rye/vetch mix. He drills the mix wherever it's possible to get it in by mid-September. Where he knows that won't be possible — on peppers and fall cole crops, for example — he prefers to broadcast red clover and annual ryegrass at final cultivation.

De Wilde chops covers the following year before working them with his chisel plow. "The downside of covers is that if they get away from you, you have to plow them with the moldboard to get rid of them," he cautions. With a wet spring in '90, that happened more often than de Wilde would like. Rye, especially, got out of hand. So more and more, he is replacing rye with oats. Seeded alone, oats winterkill, making them an excellent cover where early spring crops will be seeded. Seeded with vetch, the winterkilled oats mulch protects the legume over winter. Then the vetch can be left to regrow in spring before de Wilde incorporates it for later crops.

De Wilde also broadcasts annual ryegrass into his asparagus. The asparagus is planted deep enough to let him disk any ryegrass that doesn't winterkill. He also flames asparagus residue in spring to kill asparagus beetles. To try to keep quackgrass from creeping into the asparagus from the field edge, he's planting a border of rhubarb. "An old gardener friend pointed out to me how you never find quackgrass in a rhubarb bed," he recalls. "So I'm going to try to take advantage of that to keep quack out of my asparagus."

Cover crops also help de Wilde reduce insect damage. He often lets narrow strips keep growing through the season so that their blossoms will attract beneficial insects into the field. Every few years, he'll also work up his semi-permanent picking roads and seed them to white clover, which also attracts pollinators and pest predators. The picking roads divide his fields into long strips about 70 feet wide. Crops that need daily picking are planted next to the roads to reduce the distance they need to be carried and to minimize field traffic and compaction.

De Wilde uses a Reemay cover to keep flea beetles away from late crops of the baby salad mix and other mustard-family crops direct seeded in the field. He's found that a double layer of Reemay can protect tomatoes, zucchini and other frost-sensitive crops down to temperatures as low as 23 F. After the threat of hard frost is past, he removes the top layer of Reemay and leaves the bottom layer in place until the weather settles.

De Wilde runs a 40-ewe sheep flock on an additional 20 acres of land that's too marginal to crop. "The sheep aren't a big moneymaker. But they make use of the steep hillsides and they supply some compost for the crops," he observes. "There's a good marketing overlap with the crops, too."

Compost from sheep manure is supplemented with purchased turkey manure compost, so that at least a little is broadcast on almost every field each year. De Wilde also has applied calphos, potassium sulfate, high-calcium lime, kiln dust and trace mineral products. He determines fertility needs based on annual soil tests.

Except for the tank containing liquefied propane, de Wilde's flame weeder looks like any other cultivator.

Composting helps kill weed seeds, and de Wilde also avoids spreading raw manure because of the potential for nitrate accumulation in his greens. "I feel just being organic isn't enough," he says. "You have to be responsible, too."

Keep Weeds On The Ropes

By using tillage and crop rotation to keep them constantly off balance.

BOB HOFSTETTER

"Weeds are only a problem if you let them become a problem."

That quote comes to mind whenever I get behind in field operations and end up pulling weeds out of one corner of a vegetable patch by hand. Whoever said that should be sentenced to hard labor — pulling weeds, of course — for the rest of his or her natural life. That's because this person was absolutely right — weeds don't have to become a problem, especially in a few acres of high-value crops. You can win the war against weeds — without herbicides. Just think like a prizefighter in a title bout.

Throw First Punch

"Moldboard plowing 6 inches deep buries a bunch of my weed problems," says Terry Holsapple, an Illinois grain farmer who plants 30 acres of organic vegetables on his 400-acre farm. "The moldboard action buries the weeds deep enough to keep them from germinating, and any seeds brought to the surface can be taken care of before planting."

Holsapple plows in early spring, then disks lightly. "In four or five days, or when a good flush of weeds has appeared, I'll either disk about 1½ inches deep or take them out with a Danish-tine field cultivator," he says. Those operations are repeated if another flush of weeds appears. One or two row cultivations control late-germinating weeds.

The whole idea is to never let weeds become established. For example, when you're converting an old hayfield or row-crop ground to vegetables, try to attack weeds the year before you plant, if at all possible. Plow, then disk several times. By late summer, plant a winter grain like wheat or rye at 2 bushels per acre, or plant barley at 3 bushels. These crops will overwinter and provide lush spring regrowth. "It's usually muddy in the spring. So I like to have something green growing out there to pump out the water," says Holsapple.

If excess soil moisture isn't a problem in spring, you can fall-plant spring oats, wheat or barley early enough to allow 40 to 60 days of growth before a killing frost. They will winterkill and form a weed-suppressing mat. Check Extension for the best varieties. The following spring, plow early if deep-rooted perennial weeds like dogbane and thistle are a problem. If they aren't, you can probably get by with lighter tillage if your soil is friable. Then control emerging weeds by harrowing or disking as often as necessary until planting time.

In either case, avoid direct-seeding crops, because of residual weed pressure. Use transplants and vegetable varieties that can be cultivated well into the season. Avoid growing sprawling or tall-growing plants like tomatoes, potatoes and sweet corn, since their growth habits soon limit cultivation. Instead, plant beans, broccoli, cauliflower, peppers or other easily cultivated crops.

Keep 'Em Guessing

Faced with fulfilling a contract, organic vegetable growers Dick Prochazka and Lynn Lyndes of Savona, N.Y., were unable to rotate fields. They planted onions two years in a row on the same ground. "We had decent weed control the first year. However, weeds were beginning to appear near harvest," explains Prochazka. "We moldboard plowed shallow, planted a rye cover crop and hoped for the best.

"The late seeding of rye didn't take well, so we didn't have much of anything for early weed suppression and plowdown," he continues. "The following year we did a shallow plowing again and planted the onions. We had a terrible weed problem. Purslane, pigweed and crabgrass had practically taken over these fields."

Following harvest, the field was moldboard plowed again, this time to a depth of 8 inches. A rye cover crop was planted. In spring, another 8-inch-deep plowing was used to incorporate the rye and bring up weed seeds. As they germinated, weeds were tilled with a tractor-powered rototiller. The field was then planted to squash and melons, and cultivated once with a one-row cultivator. "Few weeds were evident in that field," says Prochazka.

On another field, Prochazka and Lyndes had a serious nutsedge problem. They plowed about 8 inches deep, then disked. As a thick green carpet of nutsedge began to reappear, it was rototilled. That procedure was repeated three times. "You would have thought we used an herbicide!" exclaims Prochazka.

Crop rotations are essential to a good weed-control program. "I never rotate vegetables with vegetables," says Illinois farmer Holsapple. "I like to keep them on new ground. In this way, I can keep weed and disease problems from getting out of hand," he says.

Rotating tillage systems can be as important as rotating crops. Why? When using minimum and no-till systems, only the top few inches of soil are being worked. After two to four years, perennial weeds may become dominant. One of the best remedies is two or three years of deep moldboard plowing to tear up the roots of hard-to-control perennials. For control of annual weeds, the disk, harrow and field cultivator are excellent tools. Best control is achieved when weeds are just emerging.

Fall-sown cover of AROOSTOOK grain rye and hairy vetch towers over the tractor when it was mowed in June '89. Mowed rye was left on soil surface for two months before field was plowed, disked and planted to vetch-rye again in fall '89. Mowing and disking were repeated in spring '90 before the field was finally planted to vegetables.

Keep Your Guard Up

Be sure to include a cover crop in your rotation. It doesn't really matter what you use as a cover crop, as long as it provides good cover that will both suppress weeds and help build soil organic matter. Legume covers are also a major source of nitrogen.

Your main concern should be how efficient a specific cover crop is at physically suppressing unwanted plants. That's why Holsapple uses hairy vetch. "It smothers practically all the weeds in my rotation, adds tilth to the soil and, in some cases, can supply all my nitrogen needs," he says. "I use it wherever it will fit into the rotation." Vetch should be drilled at 20 pounds per acre or broadcast at 40 pounds per acre.

"We mostly use grain rye seeded in fall," says Prochazka. "However, in the 1989 growing season, we began to look at the weed-controlling benefits of hairy vetch." Some of his broccoli plantings were overseeded with hairy vetch after the first cultivation, four to six weeks after transplanting.

"We had excellent weed control in the overseeded broccoli with no need for additional cultivations," says Prochazka. "The broccoli that was not overseeded required two to three additional cultivations to get the weeds under control."

Cover crops can be overseeded into vegetable plantings after vegetables have become established. Cultivate prior to overseeding to remove any weeds, loosen the soil and allow the overseeded crop to germinate quickly.

You can also plant cover crops after crop harvest. Fall-planted cover crops must be planted early enough so that they put on sufficient growth prior to winter dormancy or a killing frost. I have found that in most cases at least 6 to 8 weeks of fall growth is needed to get covers through the winter and give good regrowth in spring.

If your overseeded cover crop has become well-established and weed pressure is light, let the overseeding be your winter cover and spring plowdown. But if you have a poor stand after harvest, plow deeply and seed a winter cover. In spring, plow deeply to incorporate the cover crop and bring up any viable weed seeds. When weeds germinate, cultivate as often as necessary until it is time to plant.

Hairy vetch and grain rye combinations are an excellent choice for late-season seedings. They produce large amounts of biomass that protect the soil, smother weeds, and increase soil tilth and organic matter. You can mow a vetch-rye cover then give it a heavy disking to make it easier to plow. Holsapple prefers to leave it attached so the furrow flips over without plugging. Don't let all that scare you. The extra effort is well worth it.

When I need a quick cover more than I need nitrogen, I overseed annual ryegrass in my tomatoes, peppers and bush beans. I can't say enough good things about it. At a seeding rate of 20 pounds per acre (about $6 worth), it establishes quickly, does a superb job of smothering weeds, aids water infiltration during rainy periods, and acts as a nutrient trap by using residual nitrogen. During the season, it reduces splashing and diseases. And after you harvest, animals can graze it.

In '89, I overseeded annual ryegrass in my peppers and tomatoes four weeks after they were transplanted and in beans when they were at the bud stage. There was no evidence of yield reduction in any of the crops. What was noticeable was the absence of weeds. The ryegrass growing between the rows makes picking easier and cleaner because the vegetables don't get splattered with mud.

Wear 'Em Out

Some plants produce chemicals that can inhibit the germination and growth of other plants. Scientists call this phenomenon allelopathy. Research has found that crop residues of wheat, grain rye, oats and the sorghum family suppress weeds with naturally occurring chemicals.

No matter what allelopathic crop you use, it must remain on the soil surface. The slightest bit of incorporation can greatly reduce the allelopathic effect. Otherwise, short-term weed control is all you should expect. Environmental conditions are a determining factor in how long allelochemicals will last. Current research puts it at anywhere from 30 to 75 days.

Researchers at North Carolina State University found that, when row crops were no-tilled into a killed-back rye mulch, it controlled ragweed, pigweed, lambsquarters, morning glory, cocklebur, sicklepod and prickly sida. Poor control was observed in conventionally tilled systems.

Michigan State University scientists found similar results. Fall-planted rye was used on established strawberry and asparagus plantings. Also, peas and beans were planted no-till into a killed-back rye mulch. Results showed good control of most annual broadleaves and moderate control of annual grasses. There was practically no effect on perennials.

Avoid direct seeding of small-seeded vegetables into rye mulch, warn Michigan State researchers. Severe injury to direct-seeded carrots and onions has been reported. Large-seeded crops like cucumbers, peas, beans and corn, and transplants of all types, have shown no ill effects when plant-

New Farm *Photo by T. L. Gettings*

Farmer and New Farm *editor Bob Hofstetter overseeds annual ryegrass in 1 acre of peppers with hand-cranked Cyclone seeder.*

ed into a killed-back mulch of rye or wheat.

Light — or the lack of it — can also be used to help control weeds. Large-leaved crop varieties, as well as those that produce a dense canopy, can suppress newly emerging weeds. Cultural techniques such as bed planting, narrow rows and increased plant populations can help shade out some weeds.

By using cover crops, rotations, timely cultivations and crop competition, you'll be doing all you can to promote a profitable harvest — and to prevent weeds from becoming a problem. When it comes to weed control, an ounce of prevention is worth about 100 gallons of herbicide.

Editor's Note: *When he's not writing for our magazines and books,* New Farm *Associate Editor Bob Hofstetter grows 4 acres of vegetables and raspberries on his farm in Limeport, Pa.*

Covers Cut Costs In High-Value Crops
Legumes and grasses can control weeds and insects while building soil.

BOB HOFSTETTER

Farmers have used cover crops to control erosion and improve soil fertility in cash grains for many years. But cover crops may be even more important for vegetable growers.

One reason is that vegetables are very hard on the soil. They not only take nutrients out of the ground, but they need more personal attention, which means lots of compaction from foot and mechanical traffic.

Vegetable ground is also managed more intensively. It's not unusual for a vegetable grower to plant three or more crops back-to-back on the same piece of ground. These intensive cropping regimes can quickly deplete organic matter, reducing soil fertility and water-holding capacity.

Cover crops can help. By adding a grass or legume to your vegetable rotation, you can maintain or increase productivity while often reducing or eliminating pesticides and purchased N at the same time.

Best of all, cover cropping can be less risky for a vegetable grower than for someone growing field crops. Think about it. A main worry with cover crops is that they'll rob moisture from your cash crop. The likely solution, irrigation, is rarely cost-effective with cash grains (except in areas with extremely low moisture, of course). But if you're producing vegetables in a region with unreliable rainfall, you should have irrigation available whether you use cover crops or not.

While there are still many questions to be answered about using cover crops with vegetables, farmers and scientists are learning more and more each season. Before you can use any of their ideas, you much decide what species and establishment techniques best suit your operation.

The Easiest Cover Crops

If you typically grow several high-value crops in succession on the same piece of land in a year, your best bet is probably a fall-planted cover that you can incorporate in spring.

In fact, fall-planted cover crops are generally the easiest to manage no matter what type of vegetable system you use. Sweet-corn growers in my area of southeastern Pennsylvania typically seed grain rye at roughly 2 bushels per acre after their last crop comes off in September or early October. Most of these farmers grow nothing but sweet corn and recognize how hard that is on their soil. Rye is a perfect solution. It can be planted as late as November and will still establish well before winter. And it regrows quickly in spring so it can be plowed down as a soil-builder before the next crop of sweet corn.

You can use most any winter-hardy grass, legume or legume-grass mix as a fall cover crop after harvesting vegetables. If it will overwinter in your area, it should perform just fine. Examples include annual ryegrass, crimson clover (in the Mid-Atlantic and Southeast) and winter grains. An advantage of winter grain covers like rye, wheat and barley is their ability to control weeds with natural, weed-suppressing (allelopathic) compounds in their roots, leaves and/or stems.

One of my favorite fall cover crops is a mix of 20 to 40 pounds of hairy vetch per acre with 2 bushels of rye. It not only provides substantial ground cover and plowdown material, but it adds nitrogen to the soil, too. Such a mix provided at least 75 pounds of N per acre in my cover-cropping experiments at the Rodale Institute Research Center.

Field preparation for fall covers does not need to be fancy. A light disking to loosen the soil is sufficient. If you have a grain drill, use it. It will provide even seed distribution and good seed-to-soil contact for better germination. Tractor-mounted broadcast seeders also work well, but I suggest you follow them with a cultipacker or light harrowing to incorporate cover crop seed and provide seed-soil contact. In either case, plant your fall cover early enough to allow it to put on a few inches of growth before winter.

If you can't plant a fall cover, you can get many of the same soil-building benefits by sowing a fast-growing, cool-season cover in spring. Species like annual sweet clover, crimson clover, oats, and annual ryegrass work really well as spring-planted cover crops in most areas for growing fall broccoli, cabbage and cauliflower.

I can't grow good broccoli in spring, because the weather gets too hot too fast. My broccoli turns bitter and quality is reduced. Instead, early in the season, I broadcast an annual legume like annual sweet clover (10 pounds per acre) or crimson clover (15 pounds per acre). I plow the legume a week or two before transplanting broccoli as a fall crop in July or August. Sometimes I use starter N, but normally all of my nitrogen comes from the legume and the 2 to 5 tons of horse manure per acre that I plow down with it.

If you try this idea, don't use a biennial clover as your cover crop. It will cost more and won't put on as much growth during the seeding year.

'No Need For Cultivating'

Not interested in fall- or spring-planted cover crops? Then consider overseeding a grass or legume directly into your vegetables. With the right management and moisture, it's an excellent way to help control weeds while improving soil.

Kit Casper uses this technique with great success on his organic farm in Rangeley, Maine. Casper transplants broccoli three times a season at two-week intervals. Immediately after transplanting, he broadcasts medium red clover at 10 pounds per acre into his broccoli. "The broccoli outgrows the clover and I get great yields," says Casper, who overseeds summer squash the same way.

Casper simply lets his clover grow after he finishes harvesting broccoli. He plows the clover, along with compost and animal manure, the following spring a few weeks before he starts transplanting again. Aside from a little hand-hoeing, his broccoli requires virtually no weed control. "There's no need for cultivating the broccoli when I have a solid stand of clover in there," he says.

Casper is lucky: He typically gets enough rainfall to provide both his cash and cover crops with sufficient moisture. "I've never had suppressed yields because of the clover overseeding," he says. If you can't count on adequate moisture, you should have irrigation for your vegetables whether you grow cover crops with them or not. You must avoid competition for moisture between your main and cover crop. Otherwise, the plant that is established best will take advantage of any water there is.

Moisture competition can be especially troublesome with direct-seeded crops like beans or peas. Make sure the plants are well-established before you sow a cover crop. There's no real guideline on this. You just have to observe the cash crop and be sure it is growing vigorously before you overseed.

Transplanted vegetables often are better-able to tolerate moisture competition. Give the plants a week or so to overcome transplant shock and you should be able to overseed a cover with little risk of it robbing moisture. "Transplants are weeks ahead of anything that is direct seeded, so I can't see how an overseeded cover crop could be competitive to a main crop that is maturing in 70 days or less," says Dr. Greg Hoyt, a soil scientist at North Carolina State University.

Hoyt has been testing a way to combine overseeding with minimum-till vegetables. His experimental method begins with an 18-inch band of herbicide applied to kill weeds. Hoyt then rototills the strip and plants broccoli. About a week after transplanting, he broadcasts Quail Haven soybeans, a prostrate, trailing variety, at 5 pounds per acre right into the broccoli. Quail Haven is an SCS release developed primarily as a wildlife food. (Seed is available from: Mississippi Foundation Seed Stocks, Box 5267, Mississippi State, MS 39762.)

"The soybeans worked exceptionally well in this system," reports Hoyt, who irrigated the plots as needed. "There was excellent weed control and they didn't affect the growth of the broccoli." Another benefit is the large amount of N the beans will provide: about 200 pounds per acre, according to Hoyt's calculations. That would be enough for even a heavy-feeding crop like corn or potatoes.

Hoyt had similar success with crimson clover broadcast at about 15 pounds per acre into broccoli, except the clover produced only half as much N as Quail Haven soybeans.

Herbicides may not be needed in Hoyt's system. "The mechanical action of strip tilling may be all that's needed for pre-plant weed control. I can't see why it won't work if it's done properly," he says.

Nor would you have to overseed a warm-season crop like soybeans. Cool-season legumes or grasses like hairy vetch, annual ryegrass and winter grains should work fine in an overseeding system with broccoli, cauliflower, Brussels sprouts and possibly cabbage. As the temperature rises, growth of these cool-season covers will slow and be less competitive to vegetables.

If your overseeded crop comes on too strong, you can minimize competition by cultivating along both sides of your vegetables to create a clean strip of soil between them and the cover. That's how I managed the crimson clover and annual ryegrass cover crops I've used with my tomatoes and peppers. Since I don't irrigate, I didn't want to take any chances with moisture. Plus, cultivating helped stimulate growth of my vegetables by aerating the soil.

High-Value Hillsides

On hilly ground, you may want to try growing vegetables with a permanent living mulch. Bob Cathey of Hendersonville, N.C., plants his drip-irrigated tomatoes on sloping ground into rototilled strips of sod consisting of 85 percent orchardgrass and 15 percent Ladino clover. Like Hoyt, Cathey applies an 18-inch band of burn-down herbicide two weeks before transplanting, then rototills his starter fertilizer into the strip. Tomato plants are set 2 feet apart within rows that are 5 feet apart, leaving a 3½-foot strip of sod between the rows.

Tomatoes receive additional fertilizer through drip irrigation. Cathey mows his sod strips with a small, tractor-mounted rotary mower. "I mow whenever I feel it's necessary and up to the time the tomatoes grow into the strips," he says.

He doesn't rely on nitrogen from the tilled mulch to cut his N bill, but he probably could. Ladino clover overseeded into corn at last cultivation added 100 pounds of N to the soil in my experiments. The amount would be less in Cathey's mix, but it's still worth considering.

Cathey does plan to try eliminating the burn-down herbicide, though. "I may need to till the planting strips a couple of times to get incorporation of the heavy sod, but I'm sure it can be done," he says.

While Cathey's sod cover reduces compaction from traffic at harvest and increases water infiltration, it doesn't affect tomato production, he says. "My yields are above average for my area. The yield from my '88 crop was 23 tons per acre," he notes.

Moisture competition could be a problem with these living mulch systems. It depends largely on the type of sod you plant into. For example, Dr. Ray William, an Extension weed specialist at Oregon State University, is studying the effect of well-established perennial ryegrass on interplanted vegetables.

"Established perennial ryegrass is very aggressive and forms a dense sod that is necessary to support heavy field traffic during harvest," he observes. "This rank growth habit will need to be controlled in some way to eliminate crop yield reduction by competition. Some recent research has shown that it may be necessary to remove one-half to one-third of the established sod from around the crop plant, so some type of cultivation is necessary."

In other research, perennial ryegrass solid seeded at roughly 20 pounds per acre in an uncropped field cut weed populations by 80 percent, says William.

Since water and N will stimulate grass growth, you may have to avoid using overhead irrigation and broadcasting fertilizer in living mulch systems. Drip irrigation and timely, row-applied fertilizer may help reduce the risk of competition, because any additional nutrients and moisture are applied directly to the cash crop and not to the cover.

Besides their ability to improve your soil and cut fertilizer and herbicide costs, cover crops may also help you reduce or eliminate insecticides. Research is just beginning on the subject, but results are promising.

University of California entomologists have found that various legumes and legume-grass mixtures can reduce mite problems in orchards. The nectar produced by the flowers attracts bugs that prey on mites. Entomologists at the University of Georgia, meanwhile, have discovered that cover crops in pecan trees will reduce aphid damage. Ladybugs are lured to the covers and then migrate to the trees to feed on aphids.

Since all cover crops appear to attract some type of insects, a good future practice might be to blend several different species into kind of a cover crop 'tank mix.'

If you are going to try using cover crops with your vegetables, I recommend you start slowly. Limit yourself to a small amount of land and try a couple of test strips in different areas of your farm. Not every system or species will work everywhere. If your first trials don't succeed, try a different cover crop, a different establishment method — or both.

Cover Crops Replace Plastic

Oats and peas help control weeds, pests and erosion.

LAKE CITY, Minn. — Instead of using plastic, organic-produce grower Steven Schwen uses an oat/pea cover-crop mix to mulch his winter squash and other vine crops. In addition to smothering weeds, the cover helps control erosion, build soil and even appears to reduce pest pressure. "I use it mostly for squash. But you could use it for just about any crop grown in wide rows," notes Schwen.

In early spring, Schwen drills a commercial forage mix of oats and Canadian field peas at a rate of about 120 pounds per acre. The seed costs about $26 per acre. But Schwen notes that the peas and oats mature at the same time, so growers could harvest their own cover crop seed to reduce out-of-pocket expenses.

The cover is usually about 6 inches tall when the soil is warm enough to plant squash. Schwen then field cultivates or rototills 2½- to 3½-foot-wide strips on 6-foot centers, and immediately direct seeds or transplants his main crop into the strips. His horse-drawn cultivator and occasional hand-hoeing help Schwen keep the strips free of weeds while the crop is small.

By late June or early July, when the oat/pea cover is about 3 feet tall, Schwen cuts it with a walk-behind sickle mower. Then he rakes the cuttings by hand into the squash row to form a weed-smothering mulch. "The raking goes real fast, especially if you catch the plants when they're large and bushy, just before they start to vine," he observes.

In '90, Schwen tried drilling about 12 pounds of a clover/alfalfa mix per acre along with the oat/pea mix. He also broadcast about 12 pounds of clover following a field cultivation after the cover had been raked into the rows. In both cases, the added legumes established well. The squash vines smothered them later, however, especially the broadcast clover. Schwen doesn't feel the broadcast clover paid off, and adding it or the clover/alfalfa mix eliminated the option of cultivating if weeds came on where the peas and oats had been planted.

Early Spinach

Another innovative way Schwen uses cover crops is to plant oats along with fall-seeded spinach. He drills oats at a rate of 2 bushels or more per acre, then seeds spinach in 12-inch rows with a Planet Jr. planter. While mid-September is ideal, Schwen has had success planting the combination as late as early October.

The oats winterkill, usually when they're about 10 inches tall, and form a protecting mat over the spinach. "The oats also catch snow. That helps insulate the spinach and keep it from drying out," observes Schwen. "Then I harvest spinach in mid-May, a good three to four weeks before anyone else's spring-planted spinach is ready."

At final cultivation, Schwen also overseeds clover, alfalfa and vetch into many of the dozens of other crops he grows on his 5-acre farm. "Covers are especially great for onions, because you can dry them in the field and the cover crop keeps them off the ground."

In three years of planting squash into an oat/pea cover, Schwen hasn't had to resort to botanical insecticides to control cucumber beetles. "I'm not sure why. But I think they have a harder time finding the squash," he speculates.

In '91, Schwen planted strips of squash into a field of oats/peas as before. But he also had an established field of alfalfa/clover, from the previous year's seeding. "I spread manure down the middle of the strips I made there, then planted broccoli and cauliflower." After harvesting those crops in mid- to late July, he can direct seed baby Chinese vegetables and also transplant late-storage Chinese cabbage. "Hopefully that combination will throw off any flea beetles, which seem to like open spaces, especially under droughty conditions.

"Our land is pretty steep, so cover crops are essential for erosion control," adds Schwen. "The oat/pea strips have saved our field from washing."

Cover Crops Replace Herbicides In Berries
And protect plants from frost for $100 less per acre.

MARNE, Mich. — "With cover crops, I don't need any herbicides at all," says Michigan strawberry grower Steve Carmody. "I've found that cover crops make a tremendous difference in controlling weeds."

Carmody's claim may frighten most commercial strawberry growers, who are used to spending up to $130 per acre for weed control. But farmers and scientists are finding that such expenses — which include $80 to $100 an acre for straw mulch and $25 to $30 for herbicides after harvest — simply aren't necessary. "Cover crops offer the same benefits at a lot lower cost," says Dr. Alan Putnam, a horticulturist at Michigan State University.

How much lower? An average of $100 per acre — while producing better-than average yields, he says.

But cover crops offer more than just savings, Putnam adds. During two years of research, he found that grain rye or hard, red winter wheat fall seeded between strawberry rows actually control weeds, prevent erosion and reduce frost damage as well as — or better than — mulch and chemicals, combined.

The only exception is in extremely cold winters, when a heavy mulch may offer more protection, he notes. But unlike mulches, well-managed cover crops don't harbor weed and grain seeds that can germinate and cut yields, says Putnam. In fact, strawberry production in his study averaged more than a ton higher than state averages.

Putnam conducted his research during the '83 and '84 growing seasons. In fall before each season, he broadcast either hard, red winter wheat or grain rye at the rate of 1½ bushels per acre into strawberries.

Because the cover crops grew within strawberry rows, Putnam had to suppress them the following May by broadcasting 1 quart of Fusilade per acre. Three weeks later, Putnam also mowed the still upright wheat and rye to minimize competition for light.

By early June, weed growth in cover-cropped plots was from 80 to 95 percent lower than in control plots which had no cover crops but received the same herbicide treatment. Some five weeks later, weed control had dropped somewhat in cover-cropped berries, to an average of 55 to 85 percent better than the control. Putnam attributes the decline to decreasing levels of allelopathic (weed-suppressing) chemicals in the cover crop residue.

Save Up To $115/A

But yields were fine. Putnam harvested an average of 2,900 pounds of berries per acre from the cover-cropped plots in late June. Had he picked two more times, as is typical in Michigan, yields would have been about 8,700 pounds per acre, he says. That's from 13 to 23 percent less than the control plots, says Putnam. But it's still more than a ton higher than the 6,000-pound state average. The difference is that Putnam's system cut weed control costs by from $88 to $115 per acre.

Most of those savings come from not having to apply mulch. Typically, strawberry growers in the Midwest and Northeast mulch plants with straw or chopped corn stalks in fall. The idea is not only to smother weeds, says Putnam. Mulch also helps reduce soil erosion and winter injury to plants, and stunts early-season crop growth, reducing frost damage to buds, he explains.

But whether mulch is applied manually or mechanically, labor and material costs can be from $80 to $100 per acre, he says. Add $25 to $30 for Devrinol, a broad-spectrum herbicide applied after harvest to control weeds, and the tab comes to more than $105 per acre.

In contrast, reports Putnam, "Cover crops are essentially living mulches that interfere with weeds, shading them out." And they do it for just $15 to $17 per acre, according to his research. That includes $6.50 for cover crop seed, $8 to $10 for Fusilade (to suppress sod growth in spring), and about 50 cents worth of fuel.

Putnam also has tested oats and winter barley as cover crops in strawberries. Barley provided some early season weed control. But its overall weed-suppressing ability was no better than in control plots with no cover crops, Putnam reports.

"Oats winterkills in Michigan, so it doesn't work well, here," he adds. "Oats would definitely work in areas where there isn't winterkill. But you'd have to be careful as to when to sow the cover crop. If it's planted too soon in fall or late summer, it could compete too strongly with the strawberry crops."

Could cover crops be suppressed without herbicides? Not if they're growing within rows, says Putnam. "While mowing can considerably reduce cover crop shading between rows, there is nothing you can use to reduce competition within rows other than using a herbicide to suppress the cover crops." In fact, even herbicide-treated covers should be mowed three weeks after application to reduce shading, Putnam adds.

No Chemicals Needed

Michigan grower Carmody doesn't have that problem. He sows his grain rye cover crop only *between* strawberry rows, not within them. Carmody's non-chemical weed-control program actually involves two different cover crops. It starts during the season before he transplants strawberries. Carmody selects a field where he has just harvested a cool-season vegetable, and broadcasts 80 pounds of buckwheat per acre ($10 worth) in late June. "It's a fast-growing, dense cover crop that smothers out weeds real well," Carmody observes.

"Cultivating a lot that summer would control quackgrass, too. But it would take more time, and you wouldn't have the added organic matter," he explains.

Buckwheat grows 3 feet tall and reaches full bloom in his area by late July or early August, he says. At that point — just before buckwheat produces seed — Carmody plows it. "If you don't till it under before it goes to seed, you'll have a lot of volunteer buckwheat on your hands," he points out.

The field is fallowed until fall, when Carmody drills 1½ bushels of grain rye per acre in 2-foot strips between the 4-foot rows where berries will be transplanted.

Care-Free Berries

Carmody transplants strawberries in late April. He uses fast-growing cultivars (SPARKLE and HONEOYE) that produce many runners for developing daughter plants. The result is greater ground cover and more weed-shading, he says. "After the first season, the berry plants take care of themselves."

In mid-May, he mows rye leaving just 2 inches of growth, then incorporates it with an 8-foot rotary tiller powered by the PTO on his John Deere 80 tractor. The tiller covers two rows of berries, so Carmody removes the tines above the plants.

To keep rye residue near the soil surface, Carmody only tills 2 inches deep — just enough to kill most of the rye. Though some grain regrows, it's seldom enough to compete with berries for water and nutrients, he says.

Hand weeding is all that's necessary during the first season. "There's no labor cost except for my own time, and that of my family," says Carmody. "And it's only necessary during the first season." Each year after that, the fall-seeded cover, thick berry canopy and narrow rows (4 feet wide instead of the 5-foot rows in Putnam's experiment) provide all the weed control Carmody needs.

As for protecting his berry plants from winter frost-injury, "We have enough of a snow cover that I really don't have to put any mulch on. Plus, our sandy soil prevents the heaving I'd get from freeze-thaw cycles on heavier soils."

The bottom-line cost for Carmody's weed control program: $18.50 per acre, including $10 and $6.50 for buckwheat and rye seed, respectively, and roughly $2 for fuel to plant and plow cover crops, he says.

You don't have to grow strawberries to benefit from cover crops. Putnam says his system also could be used with peas, beans, sweet corn and vine crops. "Cover crops are great in tree fruits too," he stresses. "Weed control is very good. And cover crops provide just as good protection from erosion as mulch does. But the most important factor is better moisture conservation. Rainfall penetrates into the soil better with less evaporation.

"I'd say cover crops are one-fourth to one-tenth less costly than mulching plus herbicides, depending on how much machinery, labor and mulching materials are used," Putnam adds. "I don't see cover crops eliminating herbicides, but they certainly substantially reduce the need for them. It's clear that, across the board, consumers and growers would prefer fewer herbicides to be used."

Plastic Mulch, A Blessing — And A Curse

It grows great crops, but disposal is a big, big problem.

BOB HOFSTETTER

You just can't beat plastic mulch when it comes to controlling weeds, retaining moisture, warming soil, conserving nutrients, boosting vegetable yields and hitting the lucrative early markets.

That's the good news. The bad news is that once it's been used, you just can't get rid of the darn stuff. Oh, sure. You can put it in the landfill. In fact, that's where virtually all of our 200,000 acres of agricultural plastic mulch winds up these days, says Carl Hoeffer, executive secretary of the American Society of Plasticulture (ASP).

And that's exactly where it will still be 100, 250 or maybe even 500 years from now. No one knows for sure how long plastic will last after it has helped fill up our limited landfill space.

So-called degradable mulches are being introduced. But they cost two to three times more than regular plastic, and may or may not be the "green" answer growers and manufacturers are hoping for. Questions remain about how, or if, the new plastics really decompose and about the environmental impact of any resulting products. If you want to try degradable mulches, experiment with them on a few beds to see how they perform. Keep accurate records on installation, plastic condition at various dates, general weather conditions and composition of the soil the following year.

"The ASP recently established a task force to come up with alternatives to landfilling," says Hoeffer. "Currently, about 99 percent of it is being landfilled. Some of the remainder is being recycled and some is incinerated. Incineration and recycling are the most logical alternatives. Plastic film generates a lot of heat when burned and it could be used as a heating source. However, before this occurs, the problem of emissions needs to be addressed. We're actively working on a solution."

Sooner or later, answers will be found. But what are environmentally conscientious growers supposed to do with their used plastic until then? Nothing. Just hang onto it, at least until recycling or other options become available, advise groups like the Natural Organic Farmers Association and the Organic Foods Production Association of North America. Compress used plastic as tightly as possible and store it in a little-used location around the farm. Whatever you do, don't send it to the dump. Some growers are making an effort to reduce their use of plastic mulch by switching to natural mulches like straw on selected crops.

Plastic Replaces Herbicides

Steve and Gail Ganser grow about 16 acres of mixed vegetables in southeastern Pennsylvania. "We wouldn't think of growing our peppers, cucumbers and melons without plastic mulch," says Steve. "We don't need to use herbicides with the black plastic, plus I like being able to have produce earlier than my competition."

New Farm Photo by T. L. Gettings

Vegetable grower Ward Sinclair still uses plastic mulch on tomatoes and other crops. But he's replacing plastic with natural, straw mulches in many fields.

Ganser begins harvesting his mulched crops up to two weeks sooner than his bare-ground plantings. "Yields have practically doubled and the quality is high," he says.

Not all plastics are created equal, and you need ones made for the field. "You can't get *bona fide* agricultural plastic film just anywhere. You have to deal with a distributor who specializes in them," says Mary Winter, president of PolyWest in Encinitas, Calif. She imports high-tech agricultural polyethylene films and non-woven row covers. "The black and clear poly films one generally finds in a hardware store are commercial- or construction-grade. They cannot withstand the handling and environmental stresses they would be subject to in the field."

Plastics vary in thickness, pigmentation, texture and longevity. The "best" plastic for you is the one with the right combination of variables to match your needs. "So much depends on one's specific growing conditions and the crop being grown, so results can vary from one section of the country to the other," says Winter. "I'm a real strong advocate of telling growers to use different plastics to see which works best for them. It's like vegetable varieties. What does well for one grow-

er may not do well for the next person."

The industry reports the plastic mulches used most often are black and clear. This is mostly due to familiarity and cost, not necessarily because they are the most appropriate. Let's take a look at these two, then at others that are available.

Black For Heat

◆ *Black polyethylene film* absorbs solar radiation (which weeds need for photosynthesis) and transfers heat to the soil. With few exceptions, it gives excellent weed control. Only hard-to-kill weeds like thistle, mallow and nutsedge can survive under black plastic. "Black or any dark-colored mulches which absorb heat must be in direct contact with the soil in order to maximize heat transfer," says Winter. "They could actually *lower* soil temperatures if improperly applied."

◆ *Clear polyethylene* speeds soil warming, resulting in soil temperatures two or three times greater than under dark or reflective mulches. Clear plastic need not be applied to a perfectly smooth seedbed to be effective. In cool growing areas, clear mulch works well for heat-loving crops like eggplant and melons. It also is effective in light-colored soils which warm up slower and absorb less heat than dense, dark soils. Clear mulches do not block sunlight, and weeds will flourish. If you don't want to use a herbicide, stay away from clear plastic unless you have the time and growing-season length to go through the exacting steps of solarization for a six- to 12-week period.

Color For Special Uses

Aggressive research and testing by the agricultural plastics industry has brought new mulch options that provide multiple benefits not available in either the black or clear plastics alone.

◆ *A brown mulch*, developed in Israel and currently imported by PolyWest and C.D.K. International, produces temperatures significantly higher than black mulch but not quite as high as clear mulch. Weed control is excellent. AL-OR Brown, as it is called, incorporates the qualities of both black and clear mulches but will not scorch plant tissue as black plastic does.

◆ *A green plastic* (IRT-76), which was born, bred and researched in the United States, is another new option. Researchers at the University of New Hampshire found that IRT-76 generated heat much like clear plastic and suppressed weeds like black plastic. IRT-76 is manufactured by AEP Industries of South Hackensack, N.J.

◆ *White-on-white*, another specialty mulch produced by AEP, is a double-layered, co-extruded mulch for use in areas where high soil temperatures have a *negative* effect on production. This material reflects sunlight *and* insulates the soil. Light does not penetrate this product. Weed control is good.

◆ *White-on-black* performs much the same as white-on-white. Some growers believe the black layer transfers some heat to the soil. Soil-temperature increases are slight, nothing like with black mulch. White-on-black blocks all light for excellent weed control.

Researchers at Clemson University observed that the color of the light a mulch reflects back to a plant can significantly affect a crop's growth and production. Dr. Patrick Hunt, a researcher at USDA's Coastal Research and Education Center in Charleston, S.C., found that bell peppers grown on white mulch produced more than 8,300 pounds of fruit per acre, compared with about 7,000 pounds for peppers grown on black plastic. That's a 16-percent increase. Potatoes grown with white plastic produced 25 percent more than potatoes under black mulch. Diffused light reflected from red mulch increased tomato yields by 20 percent over control plants in black plastic, Hunt found.

Mulches with other colors are currently being tested, not only for plant growth and yield enhancement, but also for insect control.

Sunlight Eases Disposal

Photo-degradable mulch film may be of interest to growers who don't like the idea of stuffing landfills with mulch films or who don't want to pay the cost of removal and dumping fees. Breakup begins after the film has been subjected to ultraviolet light for a set period of time. A degradable film's formulation determines whether it will begin to break down in the early, middle or late season. Day length, sunlight intensity and plant canopy shading also will have an effect on the rate and degree of breakup. Only the parts of the plastic exposed to sunlight for the required time will degrade. But once degradation starts, it will continue even if the material is again covered with soil.

Degradables come mostly in clear or black. "Yield response will be similar to conventional films of the same color," says Dr. Stephan Garrison, a vegetable crops specialist at Rutgers University Research and Development Center in New Jersey. "Weed control with the black degradables is equal to conventional black film up until breakup," he says.

"Degradables can be applied in the same way as conventional types, though some precautions are in order. The planting bed must be perfectly smooth and free from depressions. Anything that can cause physical stress to the film will weaken it at the point of contact, causing it to break up sooner than normal," Garrison says. "Footprints, tire and animal tracks and even under-film irrigation tubing can accelerate break up. If a grower matches the proper film with his climate, crop and cultural practices, he should see good results."

Before laying any mulch film by hand or by machine, be sure your soil contains sufficient moisture. It should be workable but not wet. The planting bed must be level. Protruding stones or soil clods can perforate the film as well as reduce direct soil-to-film contact. This is especially important when opaque and degradable plastics are being used. Remember, opaque (colored) films transmit heat through solar absorption, so they must be *against* the soil for optimum heat transmission. Soil nutrients must be added before you lay plastic film unless they can later be supplied through irrigation lines. Opaque plastics should be applied one to two weeks ahead of planting to warm the soil and to cause weed seeds to die before planting holes are cut.

For more information on plastic mulches, write: American Society for Plasticulture, P.O. Box 860238, St. Augustine, FL 32086. Phone: (904) 829-6041.

Plastic Mulch Suppliers

Degradable Plastic
◆ Plastigone Technologies Inc., Capitol Plaza 1, 10700 N. Kendall Drive, Suite 203, Miami, FL 33176
◆ Biolan Corp., 184 Loomis Court, Princeton, NJ 08540
◆ AgPlast-LecoFilms, 36 Tidemore Ave., Rexdale, Ont. Canada M0W 5H4

Conventional Plastic
◆ Tredegar Film Products, 1100 Boulders Parkway, Richmond, VA 23225
◆ Blako Industries Inc., P.O. Box 179, 10850 Middletown Pike, Dunbridge, OH 43414-0179
◆ Edison Plastics Co., P.O. Box 609, Washington, GA 30673

◆ PolyWest, 1106 Second St., Suite 112, Encinitas, CA 92024
◆ C.D.K. International Corp., 3113 Roswell Road, Suite 204, Marietta, GA 30062
◆ Ken-Bar Inc., P.O. Box 504, Reading, MA 01867-0704
◆ A.E.P. Industries Inc., 125 Phillips Ave., South Hackensack, NJ 07606

Mulch Layers/Removal Equipment
◆ Holland Transplanter Co., 510 E. 16th St., P.O. Box 1527, Holland, MI 49423
◆ Mechanical Transplanter Co., 1150 S.Central Ave., Holland, MI 49423
◆ Market Farm Implement, R.D. 2, Box 206, Friedens, PA 15541
◆ Zimmerman Irrigation Inc., R.D. 3, Box 186, Mifflinburg, PA 17844

Weeder Geese Boost Berry Profits $222/A

Unlike herbicides, they don't leach, drift or worry consumers.

DULUTH, Minn. — In 1989, Joan Weyandt-Fulton made an extra $159 per acre on PYO strawberries by paying her weeding crew chicken feed. Well, actually, it was goose feed.

You see, Weyandt-Fulton used geese to control weeds on half of her 3 acres of strawberries, and compared that to her adjacent 1.5-acre plot where she used herbicides. "The geese reduced the labor I needed for hand weeding by one-third compared to conventional weed control," she reports. "With a late spring and dry weather that year, weed pressure wasn't very heavy."

Weeds *were* heavier in '90, and her geese proved even more valuable. They again reduced labor costs by about 30 percent, and helped Weyandt-Fulton net an extra $286 per acre. That's an impressive two-year average of $222 added profit per acre.

"Weed control is critical for pick-your-own operations," she stresses. "The fields have to be clean so the customers can find the berries. One of my biggest expenses is for hired labor for hand weeding to keep them that way."

Not only do the geese reduce that labor expense, but at the end of the season Weyandt-Fulton recoups supplemental feed costs — and then some — by selling the birds for $10, each, plus the cost of butchering.

To some, the idea that geese can be a practical and profitable way to control weeds may seem a little farfetched. "Even my husband was a little skeptical at first," recalls Weyandt-Fulton. "But by the end of the first season, he wanted to know when we could fence in the rest of the strawberries so we could run the geese on all of them."

Proving Them Wrong

Weyandt-Fulton started experimenting with weeder geese in the mid-'80s. She used Electronet fencing (Premier, Box 89n, Washington, IA 52353) to confine a small flock of 10 to 15 birds to clean up weeds in trouble spots. Problems with herbicides, in part, furthered her interest in the birds.

"Herbicides never work as well as you want them to," she laments. "But my biggest problem is that some can only be bought in 5-pound bags. For a small operation like ours that's a lifetime supply." In addition to being a potential storage and disposal headache, herbicides are prone to leach from Weyandt-Fulton's sandy soils.

But moving the flock and fencing around the field was too labor-intensive. So Weyandt-Fulton obtained a grant from the Minnesota Department of Agriculture's Sustainable Agriculture Demonstration Program to see if fencing a larger area was economical.

To keep out dogs, coyotes and other predators, she built a 32-inch-high perimeter fence with seven strands of high-tensile wire. "People say you

Weyandt-Fulton pauses alongside the 32-inch-high electrified perimeter fence she built to protect weeder geese from predators.

can't use electric fence like this for geese. But I'm out to prove them wrong," she says. She still uses Electronet to control "grazing" within the perimeter fence, in much the same way that other livestock graziers use temporary portable fencing. The geese graze half-acre plots, and are moved to the next plot every two or three days.

Weyandt-Fulton buys day-old goslings in mid-April. They cost from $2.90 to $3.50 apiece at chicken-supply houses and feed stores. She prefers large breeds such as Toulouse, because at season's end they are easier to market than small-framed breeds would be.

She trains the geese to the electric fence when they are 2 to 3 weeks old. It's important to start early, because once the geese are fully feathered they are less sensitive to the shock, she explains. When they are about 5 weeks old, she starts moving the 35- to 40-bird flock into the berry patch. Geese are good natural grazers, and the fast-growing birds fan out across the field and aggressively

feed on weeds.

When the field is clean, Weyandt-Fulton moves the geese to the couple's Christmas tree plantation, where the birds continue to gorge themselves on grass. After renovation of the berry fields, the geese are again turned in to control weeds until fall. In coming years, Weyandt-Fulton also plans to try the geese in some blueberry plantings that she hopes to establish.

"Alternate pasture is important," she observes. "If you leave the geese in a cleaned-up field they'll start sitting on the plants and damage them. That's one reason for starting with goslings when the plants are small. They do less damage."

The geese stay in an adjacent coop at night, and Weyandt-Fulton supplements their grazing with duck grower ration in the evenings. "We try to keep them fat and happy. After all, we're going to sell them at the end of the year. Even with the extra feed, they still have a healthy appetite for weeds," she notes.

Weed Smorgasbord

When it comes to dining on weeds, geese have distinct preferences. They start with grasses, and particularly relish oats and wheat that volunteer from straw mulch. Then they attack broadleaves. "They'll even eat thistles if they're small," observes Weyandt-Fulton. "But they don't care for weeds with hairy leaves, and won't touch wood-sorrel (sheep-sorrel) or wild buckwheat (black bindweed)." Knotweed and white cockle also weren't controlled by the geese. The birds will only attack the strawberries if there's nothing else to eat, she says.

Weyandt-Fulton discovered the first year how important it is to make sure the geese are ready to graze when the weeds are still small. That spring, cold weather delayed fence construction. "By the time I got the geese into the field, some weeds that they would have eaten earlier were more than 3 or 4 inches tall. That increased the hand weeding we had to do," she recalls.

Picking starts in late June or early July at Weyandt-Fulton's Strawberry Ridge Farm. "I pull the birds off three or four days before picking begins. Their droppings disintegrate quickly, enriching the soil. And you can hardly tell they were there," she notes.

As an added benefit, Weyandt-Fulton thinks the birds also might help boost berry sales. "They make me unique. They separate me from other strawberry growers," she says. "They are fun birds with a lot of personality, and the customers love them. They bring their kids and the geese all come running and honking up to the fence when they see people coming."

New Farm *Photos by Craig Cramer*

Honking herbicides entertain a visitor.

Word-of-mouth publicity also makes it easier to sell the birds. "Last year I sold about 25 of the prettiest geese to hobbyists with ponds," she says.

A simple ad in the local pennysaver helps line up Christmas goose sales. "The hardest part of selling them for meat is finding a certified slaughterhouse that can prepare geese properly," she notes. She thinks it would be easy for others to market properly slaughtered geese through their local supermarkets. But, she cautions, "Midwesterners aren't as used to having geese in their diet as Canadians are."

She has these words of counsel for others studying use of geese in berry patches:

◆ **Construct your fence securely before you think about buying your geese.** If improper fencing allows your birds to get out or predators to get in, you can lose your chance to get geese into the fields on time.

◆ **Before selecting your breed, think about how you will market the geese at the season's end.** Will they be sold for meat or for pets? Most geese are too big during their second summer to avoid smashing the strawberries, but the Chinese breed may work for two years due to its smaller frame size.

"Geese are an economical alternative to herbicides," she concludes. "When you add the difficulty of recruiting and training people who are willing to do hand weeding, they are *very* attractive. And if you like raising geese, it's easy."

Geese Beat Herbicides

In the first two years of her project, Joan Weyandt-Fulton netted an average of $222 more per acre per year with weeder geese compared to an herbicide-treated plot.

Costs	$/A		Income and Savings	$/A
Geese	$ 74		Goose sales	$245
Feed	158		Hand-weeding savings	195
Fencing (10-year depreciation)	91		Herbicide savings	130
Miscellaneous	25			
			Total	$570
Total	$348			
			Net	+$222

Chapter 5

TOOLS OF THE TRADE

*How to choose and use the right machinery
for mechanical weed control.*

It was May 1986, and Bob Moore, vice president of sales at Bush Hog in Selma, Ala., was facing a major challenge.

Bush Hog's parent company, Allied Products Corp., had just bought the Lilliston line. With it came the Lilliston rolling cultivator, designed for use in row crops.

But domestic sales of new row-crop cultivators were in the midst of a 50-percent decline from the year before. So Moore decided to do what

most any sensible businessperson would do: "Our plan was to sell off the inventory and let it go," he recalls.

Farmers had other ideas. They responded so enthusiastically to ads for the unit, that, before long, Moore had a hit on his hands. "We've built the volume up," he says. "Sales have increased by a good 300 percent since we took it over."

Moore says part of the increase in sales was due to Bush Hog's aggressive promotion of the culti-

Photo courtesy of Bush Hog

Bush Hog's Lilliston rolling cultivator stirs and mulches soil in one pass, to uproot and cover weeds simultaneously.

vator, something Lilliston didn't do. "But part is also due to a resurgence in interest in this type of product," he stresses.

"We're not anywhere near what we think we can do with it," adds Moore. "Our challenge, now, is to convince people that they need this product in lieu of chemicals or another cultivator."

If recent implement-sales trends are any indication, Moore's biggest competition won't come from chemical companies. It will come mainly from other cultivator manufacturers looking to cash in on farmers' increasing interest in mechanical weed control.

Between 1986 and 1988, domestic sales of new row-crop cultivators shot up by an astounding 150 percent, from 4,110 units to 10,154, according to USDA's "1990 Agricultural Statistics."

By contrast, sales of new moldboard plows dropped by 17 percent, while chisel plows enjoyed a 64-percent increase.

All of this took place at a time when farm numbers dropped by more than 2 percent.

Apparently, farmers have become as interested in cutting herbicide costs as they are in controlling soil erosion.

Farm equipment makers are starting to sit up and take notice. They're introducing a variety of innovative new cultivators, rotary hoes, guidance systems and other implements.

Typically, the new tools are aimed either at improving the speed and accuracy of cultivation, or at making mechanical weed control effective in high-residue conditions. "We're trying to do both," says Mark Miller, ag advertising manager at Hiniker Co. in Mankato, Minn.

The Hiniker 1000 series cultivator, introduced in 1991 at trade shows around the country, is designed for fast cultivation in high-residue fields that aren't under ridge- or no-till systems, says Miller. The unit features a single sweep to tear out weeds between rows without plugging,

Hiniker's new 1000 series row-crop cultivators are designed for high-speed use in heavy residue.

and rotary hoe-type shields that uproot weeds near the row while protecting crops from flying clods.

"It's basically a lighter version of our 5000, except it doesn't have the ridging wings," explains Miller. "I'm sure it won't be long before farmers start welding ridging wings onto it, though," he chuckles.

There's one more important difference between the 1000 and the 5000: price. An 8-row 1000 configured for 30-inch rows retails for $4,893 to $7,553 depending on options, notes Dee Das, of Hiniker's sales department. A model 5000 in the same size will cost you $8,369 to $12,389, he says.

"We're positioning the 1000 directly against the C-tine and S-tine cultivators," explains Miller.

In this chapter, you'll get a close look at some of the other new machines farmers are using to cut herbicide costs. You'll also learn how to make the best use of mechanical weed control tools you probably already have.

Get The Most From Your Field Cultivator
'Ultra-minimum tillage' saves soil and helps control weeds without chemicals.

JIM BENDER

WEEPING WATER, Neb. — Like it or not, some form of conservation tillage will soon become part of your operation — if it hasn't already. But that needn't mean spending $25 or more per acre for herbicides, as is common in most minimum-

till systems. And it needn't mean investing in thousands of dollars worth of new equipment.

The soil-saving tillage system I use on my 642-acre beef and grain farm in eastern Nebraska requires neither of these items. It uses conventional implements for planting and mechanical weed control. And it has permitted me to completely eliminate herbicides since 1980.

I call it "ultra-minimum" tillage.

No Fall Tillage

The system begins with avoiding fall tillage after harvesting corn, milo or soybeans, and delaying spring tillage of stalk fields for as long as possible — usually until late April or early May. I can delay tillage because I include small grains, pasture and hay in my rotation, which reduces my row-crop acreage.

When it's time to start spring tillage, weed growth has reached the point where if it were any heavier, I couldn't destroy it properly with just one tillage operation. The delay extends the period of residue cover, minimizing erosion in winter and early spring.

Postponing spring tillage also lets me destroy a crop of weeds and create a seedbed at the same time. In fact, the longer I wait before first tillage, the fewer the weed-control operations I need to make later in the season.

Late tillage also helps me take advantage of the weathering effect on crop residue. Leaving stalks untouched in the field over winter cuts surface residue by 10 to 30 percent, according to the University of Nebraska (UN) Extension Service. That means I have less residue to manage.

Finally, this schedule adds flexibility to my beef management. My cattle graze stalks through winter, sometimes into April. And the undisturbed stalks have been useful locations for calving, especially during wet periods.

When it's time to till, I prefer to use my field cultivator instead of a disk or some other primary tillage tool. Again, my reasons for this are many. The shanks minimize shredding, cutting and breaking of stalks. And they leave from 50 to 80 percent of the residue on the soil surface — more than any other operation that can simultaneously kill weeds and prepare a seedbed, according to a UN Extension bulletin. A field cultivator also eliminates the erosion-promoting ridges associated with most tandem, and some offset, disks.

Other benefits of field cultivating include lower horsepower requirements, easier maintenance, leveler fields, superior seedbed preparation and greater ground speed. I can generally pull my field cultivator 2 to 3 miles per hour faster than I can pull my 19-foot offset disk.

Making It Work

Two problems must be overcome to make this system work. One is residue management, which is affected not just by how much residue you start with, but also by winter grazing and whether or not your combine has a shredder. The other is excessive plugging during tillage, which is affected by the design of your field cultivator and the existence of soil-saving structures like terraces.

Almost all of my tillage must be done on the contour between terraces in the same direction as

Photo courtesy of Deere & Co.

Field cultivator saves soil and makes herbicides virtually useless in Nebraska farmer Jim Bender's system. Harrow section can be adjusted to reduce downward pressure and minimize plugging.

the rows of the previous year's crop. I plant in 30-inch rows with an average corn population of 19,500 plants per acre and a milo seeding rate of 7 to 10 pounds per acre. I combine some of my crops, and have others custom-harvested. But the combines never use shredders. Instead, after harvest, I generally turn in 25 to 30 beef cows to graze 160- to 320-acre field units.

My field cultivator is a 26½-foot Krause model 1504 equipped with 9- to 11-inch sweeps. The unit is nearly 17 years old, and obviously wasn't designed to work in heavy residue. Its frame is only 56 inches long, which reduces residue clearance between the front and rear rows of shanks.

Current designs are much-improved in this respect. For example, frame length of the Wil-Rich 10 is 90 inches. It's 130 inches on the Case-IH 4600-4800 series, and from 89 to 135 inches on the John Deere 960S.

Despite having to negotiate terrace channels and follow previous rows, my field cultivator has done the job for seven years with very little plugging in corn. I try to perform the operation during the driest part of the day, so the unit doesn't have to deal with a lot of wet residue. Harrow sections on the rear of field cultivators can be adjusted to reduce downward pressure and minimize plugging at that point.

When my field cultivator does plug, I unclog it gradually, scattering stalks over a large area of a field. I do that by slowly raising the unit as I drive ahead or turn around, so that the residue is not dumped in one big pile.

I've had some trouble directly field-cultivating soybean stubble, depending on harvesting conditions the previous fall and the extent of grazing. Subsequent tillage operations usually destroy the residue. If I can plant after just one field-cultivation, much more residue remains on the surface than would be the case with disking.

Milo is my biggest challenge, because of the large amount of residue. I commonly field-cultivate portions of a milo plot where I can drive at an angle to the rows (such as the middle between terraces), then disk what's left. Subsequent tillage operations would be with the field cultivator.

I'll have to continue this procedure until I can use more intensive grazing in milo, or until I get a field cultivator with more clearance between the front and rear rows of shanks.

Pull The Plug On Trash

I field-cultivate a second time (sometimes a third, depending on rainfall) just before planting. My IH Early Riser planter, like the John Deere Max-Emerge, features sharp staggered disk openers that work well in heavy residue. Occasionally, I've had a problem with corn stalks or stalk roots lodging at the furrow-closing wheels. That, in turn, pushes soil and eventually plugs seed flow. I minimize this by planting during the driest part of the day.

The Case-IH 900 series planter has staggered furrow-closing wheels to discourage lodging. It also has adjustable furrow-opening disks that serve the same purpose.

I rotary hoe once (sometimes twice) just before crop emergence or a few days after emergence.

Both heavy corn and heavy milo residue can be difficult to rotary hoe. The problem, especially with corn, is roots lodging between the wheel and support arm of modern, single-row-style hoes.

With milo, my main concern is not so much plugging (unless the residue is mixed with morning glory vines) as it is the risk of poor soil penetration by the hoe spoons. That hasn't happened often, though. And it has never caused me an overall loss of weed control.

Trash deflectors on the hoe's wheel-mount arms help prevent residue from lodging between the support arm and the wheel. These are available from many machinery dealers. Cost would be about $200 for a 21-foot flex-wing rotary hoe.

Another remedy is speed. In heavy residue, I try to run my hoe 10 miles per hour or faster. Old-style hoes, with rows of wheels on axles, seldom plug.

When done properly, rotary hoeing aggressive-ly shreds residue, and is the likely reason I've had few problems with row cultivations later in the season. I row-cultivate once as soon after hoeing as possible, and a second time if there's enough rain to awaken more weeds.

Early crop residue buildup hasn't been a problem, probably because of the broad diversity of crops in my rotation. I commonly rotate from milo or corn to soybeans, and then to wheat, oats, alfalfa and clovers. That provides ample time for heavy residue to break down before my next row crop.

For Me, Herbicides Aren't Key

It is widely assumed that herbicides are the key to effective conservation tillage. My own experience suggests just the opposite. It appears that at some point, large amounts of residue will interfere with herbicide effectiveness.

I grow row crops with more residue cover than you could possibly maintain while still using soil-incorporated herbicides effectively.

While modern field cultivators, planters and rotary hoes can function in heavy residue, herbicides could well be a waste of money in my ultra-minimum tillage system.

For example, suppose a farmer wants to field-cultivate corn or milo stalks and incorporate a

---

'Ultra-Minimum Tillage' At A Glance

1. After Corn Harvest — Combine should not shred stalks. No fall tillage. Delay spring tillage as long as possible, preferably until late April or early to mid-May. A field cultivator (rather than disk or other tillage tool) is preferred to keep maximum residue on soil surface.

2. Before Planting — In preparation for June 1 soybean planting, field-cultivate one more time (twice if necessary). Use planter with rolling disk openers and other features designed to cope with residue.

3. After Planting — Rotary hoe (with trash deflectors) just before crop emergence, or a few days after. A second hoeing may be required, depending on rainfall.

4. After Emergence — Cultivate with row-crop cultivator as soon as possible after rotary hoeing. No special adjustments needed. Cultivate a second time if rainfall awakens a heavy, new population of weeds.

herbicide at the same time. The sprayer booms at the front of the field cultivator would mostly spray on undisturbed residue and new weed growth.

As the cultivator's shanks stir soil, most of the sprayed residue is disturbed, but placed right back onto the soil surface. The result would be good soil protection but uncertain herbicide incorporation. Residue simply can't remain on the surface (which is the conservation objective) and also be incorporated into the soil at the same time (which it seems would be necessary to make good soil contact with the herbicide sprayed on the residue).

Maybe the herbicide could be incorporated with a later tillage operation. Or, a pre-emergence herbicide could be used. But the point remains that the more residue left on the soil surface, the greater the risk of herbicides not working the way they should.

No-till is another option, of course. But that's for farmers willing to tolerate high chemical costs and the risk that carryover chemicals will damage next year's crops. I'd prefer not to base my planting decisions on last year's spray schedule.

Keep Cultivators On The Straight And Narrow

High-tech guidance systems make weeding faster, easier.

Born of the accuracy needed by ridge-till farmers, cultivation guidance systems are making life harder on weeds and easier on drivers. New technology uses electronics, hydraulics and microcomputers to automatically keep cultivators hugging the row. Experts say that with these new systems, farmers can take full advantage of breaks in the weather by cultivating up to twice as many acres — in half the time. Another benefit is savings of up to 84 percent in herbicide use.

Adding a few miles per hour can make a big difference when speeds are in the single digits. Dr. Jerry D. Doll, Extension weed scientist at the University of Wisconsin, reported in 1990 that doubling speed from 3 mph to 6 mph with a six-row cultivator in 30-inch rows boosts estimated acres covered per hour from 5.45 to 10.91. On 100 acres, the change would cut by half the time needed for cultivation — from 18.3 to 9.2 hours, Doll says.

"You can put in longer hours. That can be worth quite a bit if you're fighting weather," says farmer Allyn Hagensick, of Hampton, Iowa. "I've already run at night. You can do that and trust it to work."

Hagensick, who also sells planters, cultivators and guidance systems, says used systems are showing up on the market for 50 to 70 percent of the cost of new, and lease arrangements let new units out for about $900 a year. "If it saves you 1 bushel of corn per acre on 450 acres, it has paid its way," he says of leasing.

It also means bigger savings on herbicides. "When we went with 100 percent reliance on her-

bicides, some people thought we didn't need cultivation anymore," says Elbert Dickey, Extension specialist in agricultural engineering at the University of Nebraska. "But now, even in no-till, farmers are going to herbicide banding *with* cultivation — and saving money. Guidance systems come into play regardless of ridge-till, no-till or conventional farming."

That's just the beginning. "As we continue to go to conservation tillage and to limit chemical use, you'll see an increased use of guidance systems," predicts Bobby Grisso, a colleague of Dickey's. One thing is sure: There are more cultivators to be guided. The U.S. Census Bureau reports 51 percent *more* cultivators were sold in 1989 than in 1985, paced by gains of 110 percent in 6- and 7-row models and of 144 percent for 8-row and larger units.

Saves Plants, Saves Time

By ensuring precision cultivation down to the inch, the systems reduce cultivator blight, cut field time and decrease the driving skills needed to do the job. "Lots of farmers want to buy them for 'Dad' to get back on the cultivator," says Ralph Baillie, inventor of the Cat Whiskers steering indicator and president of Tri-R Innovations in Gibson City, Ill. With a guidance system, less-skilled operators of any age who can turn the tractor around at the end of the row can handle the weed-control passes.

Plant-sensing wands and furrow-following weights are the two ways the systems "see" where they are supposed to go. In the first approach,

Crop-sensing wands, like those used in the steering indicator on Tri-R Innovations' Cat Whiskers, keep cultivator guidance systems in line.

when crop height is ideal — 8-inch corn or 4-inch soybeans — metal or plastic feeler wands suspended ahead of the cultivator drag along the soil surface at the base of the crop row. Pressure against the wands activates cultivator adjustments hydraulically. However, most manufacturers now use a more-responsive electronic sensor to interpret wand movement for the system.

But what about when crops are immature? Or when last year's corn stalks are protruding along this year's row? Or when weeds are as stiff as the corn? A small-packed furrow laid down by a marker at planting serves as a track for other guides that keep a cultivator on track as surely as a high-speed passenger train follows its rails.

Most of the leading systems work on one of two mechanical principles: 1) a laterally sliding interface between hitch and cultivator that compensates for tractor movement, or 2) a pivoting center hitch that steers implements that have stabilizing rear coulters.

84% Less Herbicide

Reducing tractor-seat time is only part of the reason guidance systems are showing up on more farms. "The push is to less and less herbicide. People from Denmark have to go to zero. In Ontario, Canada, there is a tiered-reduction program year to year," says Jay Groelz of Lincoln Creek Manufacturing.

Keeping cultivators running closer to the row allows a narrower band of herbicide over the row. While a 15-inch band on 30-inch rows offers a 50-percent savings from the broadcast herbicide rate, cutting back to a 6-inch band on 36-inch rows

would squeeze the chemical application down to only *16 percent* of broadcast. A band that narrow may be technically possible, but 8-inch bands will be the goal for spray-stingy producers. Ten-inch bands, once considered radically narrow, will be fairly common, Groelz predicts.

"Ridge-till people need to keep their rows centered up nicely. Once they began using guidance systems, their neighbors saw how nice the rows looked, and it snowballed from there," says Jim Tuttle, an engineer at Sukup Co. in Sheffield, Iowa. "Regardless of farm size, people are noticing a payback in the reduction of crop losses." The amount of savings is difficult to measure, with the greatest benefit going to the least attentive operators.

However, even careful drivers who never get drowsy lose some stalks. Fleischer Manufacturing Sales Manager Dale Kumpf estimates that manual driving results in stand reduction of 1 to 5 percent, including damage done by root pruning.

The bigger the acreage and cultivators, the quicker the payback on a guidance system. Higher ground speed allows more acres to be covered during critical weed-growth times between showers. And, with larger machinery, pinpoint accuracy has much greater benefits if a swerve off center scoops out plants in 12 rows rather than four.

Is A Guidance System Right For You?

List prices for 1991 ranged from $3,450 to $5,200 for active cultivation guidance systems. To calculate whether a system makes sense for your farm, check these factors:

He Loves RoboCrop Cultivating

"I don't want to be without it anymore," says Lloyd Johnson of Gibson City, Ill., who farmed for 44 years before buying a Robotic Driver in 1987 from Tri-R Innovations to steer his tractor while cultivating. "I thought it was kind of stupid at first, but it's tremendous for cultivating. It takes off a lot of pressure so I can pay much more attention to the quality of job I'm doing.

"You can put in quite a few hours without tiring, and you can up the speed to the limit," he adds. "In a couple years, you can pay for it in the corn it saves. Without it, a lot of the time you are cutting roots."

The Robotic Driver uses three sensors, a dash-mounted microprocessor and a small rubber tire pressed against the steering wheel to actually steer the tractor while the driver keeps a closer eye on cultivator plugging, hydraulics and rocks. A timer sounds an alarm near a row's end.

It is one of a handful of automatic pilot systems available to help farmers cultivate closer and faster than ever before. Prices for these systems range from about $3,200 to $4,500. ("Passive" guidance systems, which require the tractor driver to do the steering, retail for less than $1,000.) Here is a list of suppliers:

◆ **Tri-R Innovations Inc.**, 628 South Sangamon, Gibson City, IL 60936. Phone: (217) 784-8495.
◆ **Pathfinder Systems**, Box 605, Lexington, NE 68850. Phone: (308) 324-6363.
◆ **Sigmanetics Inc.**, 1000-Q Detroit Ave., Concord, CA 94518. Phone: (415) 789-2255.
◆**ElectroDyne Corp.**, 3355 Juanita Dr., Denison, TX 75020. Phone: (214) 465-1342.

Small rubber tire pressed against the steering wheel relays steering commands from sensors on Tri-R Innovations' Robotic Driver.

◆ **Can you start banding herbicides, or narrow the size band you already use?** Going from 15 inches to 10 inches can save an estimated $3 to $4 per acre.
◆ **How much do you value relief from the stress of critical driving hour after hour?** "Most guys tell themselves they are saving money, but the stress relief is 75 percent of it," says Todd Wetherell, of Wetherell Manufacturing.
◆ **How much will improved crop survival mean?** Even a 2-percent yield improvement in 150-bushel corn can return more than $5 per acre. One potato grower said his $4,000 unit paid for itself in one year, on 160 acres, because of the protection it provided by not exposing potatoes to sunlight.
◆ **Is your most skilled tractor driver needed elsewhere during cultivation times?**
◆ **How many years will it take for the investment to earn its keep?**
◆ **What kind of warranty is provided?** Ask about extended warranties on electronic controls.

"After 10 hours of cultivating without a guidance system, I would be worn out and grouchy," Nebraska professor Dickey admits. The systems are like a tractor cab, he says. "They are not necessary in all circumstances, but they sure make life easier at the end of the day. Farmers who have them really like them."

'Keep The Guy Running'

Maintenance is low, manufacturers claim, due to the dependability of electronics relative to mechanical systems. Limited moving parts, heavy-duty construction and replaceable wands keep down-time low. Soil conditions and degree of use determine how fast the wands wear down, but a new set of two costs $10 to $25. Some units come with two sets. Replacement of electronic controls, if needed, often means just plugging in a new circuit board for $50 to $70.

"The key is, you'd better keep the guy running. You only can cultivate about three weeks out of the year," says Howard Rink, of HR Manufacturing. "We will send out a loaner electronic part right away, and pick up the pieces after the season." Rink says some HR Navigator units that have worked 4,000 acres could be "painted up and sold for new." Out of the more than 1,800 Navigators sold since its introduction in 1988, "I don't know of any that are not functioning," he says.

"These aren't like lawnmowers," Todd Wetherell cautions. "You don't just take them home and start down the field. It takes some calibrating, adjusting and getting used to. Don't expect miracles in the first 40 acres." Other manufacturers agree that initial set-up assistance constitutes the bulk of their service requests.

"Nobody plants without a planter monitor,"
says Randy Rink. "Somewhere down the road, nobody will cultivate without a guidance system."

Pivoting Guidance Systems Right For Ridges

In the early '80s, advances in crop-sensing systems attracted the attention of ridge-till pioneer Mathew "Bud" Fleischer. He saw the potential of the new technology to help keep his Buffalo line of cultivators on the row. In 1987, Buffalo unveiled its guidance system, "The Scout," with a patented center-pivot movement on a 2.5-inch-thick hitch pin. Meanwhile, self-taught engineer Gene Schmidt, now president of Sunco Products, developed his Acura Trak A/T. Introduced in 1986, he says it's the first pivoting system to use quick-hitch attachment.

In '91, Sunco's Acura Trak T/T joined the Scout and Sukup's Auto Guide in the electronic-over-hydraulic pivot hitch category. All three brands feature dual hydraulic cylinders on a quick-hitch frame, outboard electronic sensors mounted on the toolbar where the operator can watch them, and self-centering action when cultivators are raised.

When pivoting systems are in use, sway bars are removed or turned up. This allows full side movement of three-point hitch lift arms that laterally slant the tool bar. The pressure pushing against the cultivator's rear coulters steers it back in line with the row. All three brands offer controls for steering the implement from the cab, and manual override switches for operating in rough field conditions.

◆ **Acura Trak T/T, A/T**
   Cost: Model T/T, $4,250; Model A/T, $3,985; marker weights, $126
   Contact: Sunco Marketing, P.O. Box 2036, North Platte, NE 69103
   Phone: (308) 532-2146

The Acura Trak design doesn't use a center hitch-pin. Instead, it has vertical cylinders inside castings attached to crank arms to accomplish the tool-bar steering.

Sunco Marketing began selling the all-hydraulic A/T model in 1987 and now has 220 dealers in 16 states. Its new Model T/T has an in-cab control box with two LED bars showing wand and implement position. The implement indicator moves into the red zone and a buzzer sounds if the crop is being damaged. A sensitivity dial gives the operator control over how great a change in row position is needed to move the implement. Other features include a new "Soft-Shift" valve for smoother movement and PTO-driven implement capability.

◆ **Sukup Auto Guide**
   Cost: $4,250
   Contact: Sukup Mfg. Co., Sheffield, IA 50475
   Phone: (515) 892-4629

Since '89, Sukup has offered its Auto Guide, equipped with a power top link to adjust the pitch of the unit on-the-go and to make hitching easier. Its cab control box has a sensitivity control and uses a sweep dial to monitor the hitch's deviation from center position.

Sukup has changed its wand arrangement from the standard mid-row suspension of two outward-reaching feelers sensing two rows. By suspending the wands over a single row, switching them to point inward to center on the row and increasing the angle at which the wands travel, the Auto Guide achieves greater sensitivity, says Sukup engineer Jim Tuttle. The system will deliver about 80-percent accuracy on even 3-inch-tall corn and beans, and will tend to hold the cultivator during skips in the row — a situation that can give two-row wand systems trouble.

Photos courtesy of Sukup Mfg. Co.

Several companies use cab-mounted control boxes that show implement movement relative to the row, monitor system functions and allow adjustments. Sukup's Auto Guide system has a remote switch for changing to manual operation in unusual field conditions.

Sensing from a single row in small crops is an option with the Auto Guide from Sukup Mfg. Co. Wands, shown here suspended on a remote toolbar mount, convert to standard outward configuration for two-row sensing.

Tuttle says accuracy drops when wands are operated closer to the ground to rub on the short plants, allowing soil clods to make contact.

Drive-in replaceable spring steel bushings at all wear points were introduced by Sukup in 1991. An adapter hitch is available for pull-type planters and a chain sensor provides guidance for conventional planters.

◆ **Buffalo Scout**
Cost: Scout, $3,895; marker sled, $140; marker weights, $140
Contact: Fleischer Mfg. Inc., P.O. Box 848, Columbus, NE 68602-0848
Phone: (402) 564-3244

The Scout's balanced wand assembly will not drift on hilly fields, and responds to only 2 ounces of pressure from small plants. Its frame is compatible with Category II and Category III hitches. Row guidance weights allow the Scout to follow a marker disk in conventional conditions.

This New Unit Doesn't Pivot or Slide

A computerized microprocessor and a proportional hydraulic control valve form the core of two unique guidance systems from Orthman Manufacturing. The Nebraska company pioneered the wand probe technology now used industrywide.

◆ **Orthman Tracker MP III**
Cost: Tracker MP III, $5,200; Swinger, $3,775
Contact: Orthman Mfg. Inc., P.O. Box B, Lexington, NE 68850
Phone: (800) 658-3270

New in '91 is Orthman's Swinger, which pioneers a new guidance system movement mechanism that is neither pivot nor slide. It applies force against the tractor's lower tug bars of the three-point hitch to swing in their normal arc. A "pause" command allows an operator to freeze the implement position to even out squiggles in the row.

Engineer Joe Michaels says Orthman introduced the Tracker MP III in 1989, a decade after the company entered the guidance system business. The unit continues to use one or more pivoting 27-inch coulters positioned behind the implement to steer it. About half the buyers of the Tracker MP III use wands for sensing in row-crop cultivation, with the balance about evenly divided between a furrow/guide weight approach and guide tires on ridges for use with planters.

Switches in the control box adjust how the system reacts to probe signals. The operator can choose how fast the steering disks move, how far the disks react to a given action on the probe (steering toward alignment sharply or gradually), and signal averaging frequency (which determines whether the system responds to each deviation of the probe or to averages of probe signals for intervals of up to 2.5 seconds). The microprocessor provides self-diagnosis and automatic calibration, decreasing the operator involvement needed on the earlier Tracker II.

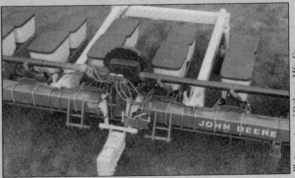

Photo courtesy of Orthman Mfg. Co.

Steering discs behind the implement are operated by a microprocessor in the Tracker MP III from Orthman Mfg. Co. Other types of guidance systems attach in front to position the implement by sliding, pivoting or moving tug bars.

Side Shifters Let Tractor Move

Side-shift models don't steer the implement in the same sense that pivoting systems do, says Randy Rink, vice president of HR Manufacturing. With sway bars locked, the front of side-shifting units moves with the tractor while the rear, sliding part moves with the implement.

"The unit doesn't really move the cultivator, but adjusts the relationship to accommodate tractor drift. The cultivator never moves sideways — it's the tractor that's wandering around," says Rink.

◆ **HR Mfg. Navigator**
Cost: $4,295 to $4,995
Contact: HR Mfg. Co., Rt. 1, Box 71, Pender, NE 68047
Phone: (402) 385-3220

The Navigator from HR Manufacturing handles loads up to 10,000 pounds. It uses a 20-inch-stroke hydraulic cylinder and cam followers for smooth motion. A three-year warranty on hydraulic and electronic components and a free second set of sensing wands were offered in '91.

There are two models. The wider one is recommended for tractors with more than 180 hp, especially with 12-row or larger ridge-till implements. Two custom-made sizes also are available, one for Category IV hitches and one for tractors with 46-inch tires.

An optional automatic slope control adjusts the Navigator upward against the grade to keep soil from rolling downhill into the row. An optional planter-mounted marker attachment and cultivator marker ball combination helps accuracy in guess rows, high-residue conditions or young crops.

◆ **Wetherell Guide Hitch**
Cost: Guide Hitch, $3,890; marker, $295; ball probe, $119

Contact: Wetherell Mfg. Co., Cleghorn, IA 51014
Phone: (712) 436-2266

Todd Wetherell says his firm chose the sliding design for its guidance system so it could be used with all major types of cultivators — S-tine, C-shank and no-till types. The Wetherell Guide Hitch, introduced in 1989, comes with parking stands for easy storage and concentrates all its controls on the guidance system, allowing quick changing between cultivators. It comes in either an open (early IH) or closed (John Deere) hydraulic system.

Also available is a planter marker and guide weight system for cultivating corn shorter than 8 inches, the recommended height for best guidance system performance.

◆ **Lincoln Creek Guide**
Cost: The Guide — pivot-type, $3,450; side-shift type, $3,800; Crab Steer, $700
Contact: Lincoln Creek Mfg., Rt. 1, Box 41, Highway 34, Phillips, NE 68865
Phone: (402) 886-2483

Lincoln Creek Mfg., which has been in the cultivator guidance business since 1984, builds "The Guide" in both pivoting and sliding models, and introduced its Case Crab Steer in '91.

The Crab Steer hooks directly into the advanced hydraulics of a Case 4690 tractor, "tying into the brains of the tractor, making the rear wheels steerable," explains Lincoln's Jay Groelz. The tractor is a four-wheel-drive, straight-frame model. Also new in '91 for the company was a single-row sensing arrangement.

The Guide's side-shift model works for drawbar implements, while the pivot model is designed for implements with heavy rear coulters. Groelz says the company offers in-house engineering to accommodate custom applications.

Farm Machine Shop Home Of First Wands

ELSIE, Neb. — Lynn Flaming suspected his sandy, rolling soil would be a real challenge for the double-disk groove designed to navigate his new cultivator guidance system. And his fears came true one year in the early 1980s.

Washouts in Flaming's corn fields had made it impossible for his guidance system's probe weights to track the grooves. His 12-row cultivator was drifting from the row, despite the Orthman pivoting rear-disk steering system that was supposed to keep it running true.

So Flaming went back to his farm shop to put together something that would allow the guidance system to work.

"Farmers are inherent tinkerers. I don't think I ever bought a piece of machinery I didn't improve," he recalls.

His solution closely resembles the standard crop-probe device now used on all row-crop guidance systems, varied and altered by each maker without patent restriction. Although he had never seen anything like it, Flaming downplays the inventiveness of his idea—bending ⅜-inch rods into plant-sensing wands, then attaching them where the Orthman groove-following weights had been. "I don't know if there are ever any really new ideas. Isn't everything kind of an evolutionary process?"

What evolved for him was a combination of the wands *and* the groove-weights, which worked better for him than either probe device by itself. Orthman engineers visited his shop and took photos of his innovation. Company founder Henry Orthman already was at work on a wand crop sensor because washed-out furrows were common in spring '82 due to several downpours. The company was the first to market wands, offering an initial version that very spring in conjunction with a furrow wheel to redeem the season for its customers. A refined wand offered in '83 has not been changed substantially since then by the company.

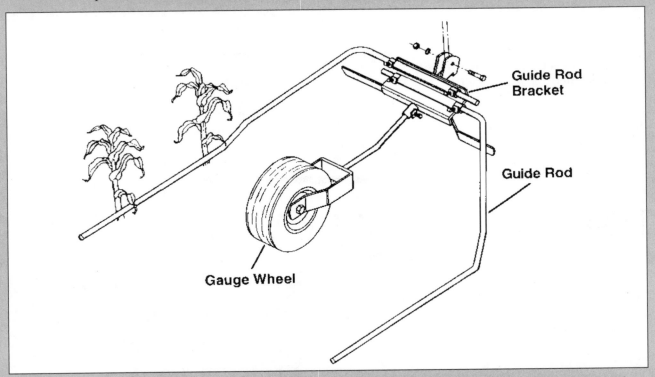

Guide Rod Bracket

Guide Rod

Gauge Wheel

From the archives of Orthman Mfg. Inc., this June 1982 drawing shows the company's first attempt at using probe wands to sense machine movement directly off of a growing crop.

It's All Done With Mirrors

You don't have to spend thousands of dollars for a high-tech guidance system to keep your cultivator on track. For less than $200, you can equip your tractor with mirrors that will let you know at a glance whether or not you're straying off course.

"I pull my disk hillers in to just 5 inches. If you're going to cultivate that close, you've got to have mirrors," says Dick Thompson, a Rodale Institute on-farm research cooperator who ridge-tills corn and soybeans without herbicides on his 300-acre farm in Boone, Iowa.

To get a clear view of inside rows while cultivating, Thompson mounted "Culti-Vision" mirrors on both sides of his tractor frame behind the front wheels. A single mirror will do. But Thompson finds that shifting his eyes back and forth between the two mirrors helps minimize fatigue and strain. Some farmers even mount lights on the cultivator to illuminate the rows visible in the mirrors, making it possible to cultivate after dark.

Without mirrors, tractor drivers inadvertently tend to move the steering wheel when they turn around to check their position, says Ken Klingler. That's why his father, Jerome, developed the 15-by 11-inch mirrors. More than 10,000 have been sold in the last 16 years.

The mirrors come with a mounting bracket that attaches to 99 percent of all tractor models with just one or two bolts. Also featured are doors

Tractor-mounted "Culti-Vision" mirrors let Dick Thompson control weeds mechanically within 2½ inches of the row. Note image of disk hillers reflected in mirror.

New Farm *Photo by Craig Cramer*

to protect the mirrors while you're driving on gravel roads. List price is $89.95 each, plus shipping. Write: Klingler Mfg. Co., Rt. 1, Box 186A, New Ulm, MN 56073. Phone: (507) 354-8735.

Turn Up The Heat On Weeds
Flame 'cultivation' is cheap, effective and safe.

WELLS, Minn. — For more than a decade, brothers George, Don and Ray Yokiel have banded a post-emergence corn "herbicide" that costs just $2.50 an acre per application. It kills both broadleaves and grasses, and it leaves no residue to damage following crops or taint groundwater.

This "herbicide" doesn't need rain for activation, and can be applied when the soil is too wet to cultivate. "Our test strips every year have shown a 4- to 13-bushel yield increase over where we didn't use it—even when there wasn't any difference in weed pressure," says George. "And it's so cheap, we even use it to run our tractors."

But don't look for the Yokiels' miracle herbi-

New Farm *Photo by Mitch Mandel*

cide at your local chemical dealer. Unless, of course, your dealer also happens to sell liquefied propane (LP) gas. You see, the Yokiels don't poison their in-row weeds. They sear them with nearly invisible flames from LP-gas burners mounted on their cultivator.

"Flame-weed control has proven effectiveness, and is economical compared to herbicides," says Ron Jones, a crop consultant who started working with flame weeding in the early '80s. He now works with Thermal Weed Control Systems Inc. (TWC), a fledgling firm that had 30 of its newly developed flame weeders on farms in 1989. "It's safe, as easy to use as most mechanical cultivators, and it controls weeds where they do the most damage: in the row."

This simple technology can do more than just control weeds in corn. It's also been used for decades to kill weeds and insects in alfalfa. In Europe, flaming controls weeds in high-value crops like carrots and onions. And Jones reports flaming is also used for brush control and as a dessicant for potatoes, an insecticide to control Colorado potato beetle, a fungicide for mint production and a herbicide for orchards and blueberries.

Herbicide Nightmare

Flaming isn't new. The first flame weeder in the United States was patented in 1856. Flamers fueled by kerosene and diesel oil were used with horse-drawn cultivators at the turn of the century, according to Jones. Butane- and propane-fired flamers were common in the '40s and '50s, until the advent of selective herbicides. "Herbicides were a miracle for farmers," says Jones. "But then that miracle turned into a nightmare. Now we have herbicide-resistant weeds, carryover problems, herbicide failure and groundwater contamination. Farmers know they are going to have fewer chemical options in the future. That's why they're rediscovering flaming."

Herbicide failure in 1978 was what got the Yokiels interested in flaming. "Rain carried our herbicide too deep. And it was too wet to get in and cultivate," recalls George. Fortunately, the brothers remembered that, back in the '60s, a local LP supplier was promoting flame weeding. After a little detective work, they tracked down the old demonstration unit hidden behind some brush in the corner of a storage yard. It was a '50s-vintage Afco flame weeder manufactured in Little Rock, Ark., originally designed to kill weeds in cotton.

"We didn't have any literature or know anything about how to use it. But we got it working," says Ray. "By that time, the weeds were 2 feet tall. We drove slow and burned a lot of propane.

At first, it didn't look like the flamer did anything."

After a few days, the flamed weeds started to die and fall over. "We left an 8-row check strip that we didn't flame. And by the end of the year, it looked like one of those herbicide ads showing what happens if you don't use their product," jokes Ray.

The Yokiels then removed the burners from the original unit and added them to their 8-row Danish-tine cultivator. "The original Afco unit didn't have any shovels. We figured as long as we were making a pass flaming, we might as well cultivate, too," recalls George.

Burners were staggered on either side of the row, and set to blow through the row. Setting them opposite each other would have created turbulence, causing the flames to boil up and damage the crop, explains Ray. Staggered 4-inch shovels run ahead of the burners, killing weeds between the rows.

Gas pressure and ground speed are used to control the heat. "What's important is the residence time in the flames. It needs to be long enough to kill the weeds without damaging the corn," says Ray. Jones estimates that time to be about one-tenth of a second for small weeds with the 2,000 F to 2,200 F flame on the TWC flamer he works with. The Yokiels adjust burners at dusk when the almost colorless flame is easier to see.

No Recipes

Just enough heat is applied to expand water in the weeds and rupture cell walls. An hour or so later, weeds turn a dull green. In three or four days, they are brown and dead. Flaming is most effective on grasses, but broadleaf weeds up to 2 to 6 inches don't pose much of a problem, either, notes George. Flaming girdles pigweeds with pencil-sized stems. "Small thistles can't handle the heat, either," he observes.

Hot, dry and windy days are best for flaming. "If the plants are wet from rain or a heavy dew, it's a waste of time and you might as well go home," notes Ray. The burners are powerful enough that they aren't affected much by wind. "But if you've got a tail wind, it can get uncomfortably hot on the tractor, if you don't have a cab," he adds.

Like cultivation, flaming is as much an art as a science. "There aren't any set recipes," says George. "Sometimes we cultivate twice and flame twice. Sometimes we cultivate three times and flame once. You have to see what you've got in the way of weeds, first."

The Yokiels no longer use herbicides. They seldom rotary hoe. But occasionally, they harrow corn just before emergence, if there is heavy weed

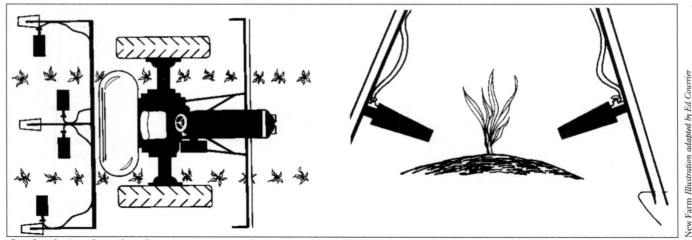

New Farm Illustration adapted by Ed Courier

Overhead view shows how burners are staggered on either side of the row and set to blow through the row, just long enough to zap weeds but not harm crops.

pressure. If conditions are right, they like to cultivate with shields — but no flame — when the corn is in the two-leaf stage, about 4 to 5 inches tall. "That early cultivation loosens the soil and discourages later weeds," says George, whose average corn yield in 1989 was 140 bushels per acre. "We also plant a little later so the corn gets up faster and gets ahead of the weeds."

The brothers flamed about 350 acres of corn between them in 1989. They say the best time to flame is when weeds are small and tender and the corn is about 8 to 10 inches tall. They set the burners to get in under corn leaves and avoid damaging the crop. If they burn a second time, they like to do it two or three days before layby. "That stresses the weeds and gives us a better kill on the final cultivation," says George. "We also add wings to the cultivator shovels at layby to throw soil into the row, so it almost looks like it's ridged."

The Yokiels haven't tried flaming their soybeans. "You'd need a smaller orifice on the burners and less flame. You'd also have to wait until the beans are about 10 inches tall," says George. "And if you haven't got the weeds under control by then, you're in bad shape."

Tinkering with the flaming system was no problem for the Yokiels. They run all of their tractors on propane, so they are familiar with LP hardware and safety precautions. They've even adapted an old anhydrous tank to haul LP for their flamer. "People are afraid of LP. But it's a lot less dangerous than anhydrous," says George. "You just have to have some common sense, like putting a slam valve on the tractor, so you can shut off the tank immediately if you have an emergency."

'Getting A Jump On Weeds'

"It takes more time and management than her-

bicides," Jones notes of flaming. "Once weeds are more than 2 inches tall, they're tougher to kill with the flamer. So when it's time to flame, you can't put it off. Those that are committed to it like it. But if you're too busy with the cows or making hay, you may have problems."

The TWC unit Jones works with is equipped with Lilliston rolling cultivator gangs that run in front of the burners. "I don't want to sound like a salesman, but the Lilliston is a good match for flaming," he says. "It's more flexible than most cultivators. You can go in early and not cover the plants, and cultivate later without pruning roots. It also mulches down the trash so it doesn't interfere with flaming." To clear residue out of the row under high-residue conditions, Jones suggests mounting sweeps on the planter.

He also recommends an early flaming before the corn is about 1½ to 2 inches tall, while the plant's growing point is still below the soil surface. For this pass, he sets the Lilliston gangs to throw soil away from the row. "With the gangs set to throw out, we're not putting weed seeds, clods and trash back into the row," he observes.

"That early flaming is critical to open up the soil and kill early weeds while they're still small," he continues. "We travel about 5½ mph. Most cultivators can't run that fast that early. The corn looks like it was nipped by frost for two or three days, and that scares a lot of farmers. But then it bounces right back and jumps out in front of the weeds."

Jones suggests flaming again when corn is 6 to 8 inches tall, this time with the Lilliston gangs set to throw soil back into the row. "When the corn is about 4 inches, it's an awkward time to flame. It's extremely difficult to do without damaging the crop," he warns.

Corn can be flamed at layby, if needed. Timing is usually less critical, as the larger corn plants can stand more heat. If weeds have grown larger than 2 inches tall, ground speed and burners can be adjusted to hit weeds a little harder. Another advantage of flaming is that you can cultivate farther from the row at layby to avoid root pruning, notes Jones.

TWC sells flaming units that mount on various cultivators, as well as a skid model that can be used to flame without cultivating. The firm also is developing a trailing model for potato vine dessication. The cost of all burners, tanks, hoses and

fittings needed to convert a 6-row Lilliston is about $3,000 f.o.b. A 6-row unit can cover 45 to 75 acres a day and burns 4.5 to 7.5 gallons of LP gas per acre.

Write: Thermal Weed Control Systems Inc., 3403 Highway 93, Eau Claire, WI 54701. Phone: (715) 839- 7242. Alfalfa flamers and other flaming hardware are available from: Flame Engineering Inc., W. Highway 4, P.O. Box 577, LaCrosse, KS 67548. Phone: (800) 255-2469. In Kansas: (913) 222-2873.

From Plowing To Ridge-Till For $1,000

These farmers built a soil- and money-saving ridge planter for one-third the cost of buying new.

SALISBURY, Mo. — Ron Harmon vividly recalls the fall day in '85 when he and his dad, Willard, visited a local machinery dealer to check out ridge-till conversion kits for his planter. "They wanted about $500 per row unit," he says. "For me, that meant $3,000, and that was more than I was willing to spend for something I wasn't even sure was going to work under our conditions."

But the kit's price isn't all that stuck in Ron's mind. Before he left the dealer's shop, he had constructed a mental blueprint of the assembly. And by March '86, he had converted his 1978 John Deere 7000 conventional row planter into a ridge-till planter for just $1,000 — an investment that paid him back at a rate of $10 per acre.

The Harmons, who raise hogs and grow 900 acres of cash grains in central Missouri, became interested in ridge-tillage as a way to cut herbicide costs and reduce the number of trips across the field. "Other aspects of ridge-tillage were also attractive to us," says Ron. "We are on a gumbo, white clay riverbottom soil, which is very heavy and really retains the water. The idea of making ridges that would dry out quicker for spring planting made good sense to us.

"Far too often, we're forced into working the soil before it should be," he adds. "An old saying in Missouri is, 'There's only one good time to work gumbo: Sunday at noon.' Anything that helped us get around working those wet soils deserves a serious look."

But before investing $3,000 in that "serious look," they decided to heed another famous Missouri maxim: 'Show Me.'

Sweep Swap Saves $2,000

Adapting their six-row Lilliston rolling cultivator to build ridges was fairly simple. "We just purchased some wings, and they bolted right onto the back of the shanks," says Ron.

Modifying their planter to clean off the ridge tops and drop seeds at the proper depth was the hard part. Their first step was finding an inexpensive, six-row cultivator whose frame would serve as the ridge-cleaning unit. "I bought a used International cultivator for $75," says Ron. "I'm not sure which model it was, because the paint had rusted off. We think it was manufactured in the late '60s or early '70s. The model isn't so important when choosing the right cultivator as is the tool bar and the main frame. They have to be in good shape."

Next came swapping the cultivator's original sweeps for the tools needed to work on the residue-covered ridges. "Luckily, I was able to locate a retired salesman of Buffalo ridge-till equipment," Ron says. "He sold me six depth wheels, coulters and scrapers for $250, and six used sweeps for $100. I figured that with the parts, bearings, scrap metal and welding costs, the total was just under $1,000 — less than a third of buying a new kit in '86.

"When we fitted the main frame of the cultivator to the planter, we saw that the tool bar would be too far away to give us the kind of control we needed to keep it on the ridge," Ron explains. "Reversing the frame, and shortening both ends of the square shaft that the cultivator shanks and rubber wheel were attached to, gave us the stability we needed. Also, without reversing the frame,

New Farm Photos by Ken McNamara

Ron (right) and Willard Harmon use this six-row Buffalo ridge-till cultivator to give their modified Lilliston a helping hand. "We had too many acres to get it all cultivated and ridged (with one cultivator) at the right time," says Ron.

we would have had to add about 4 feet onto the tongue in order to be able to turn within a reasonable amount of space."

To attach the depth wheels and coulters to the front of the cultivator, they used metal pieces for the arms, fitted in an arrangement similar to what Ron had seen on other ridge-till planters.

For the ridge-cleaning sweep, they were able to use the cultivator's original shank, but needed to move the attachment forward about 16 inches toward the depth wheel. But because the original shovels were too small for ridge-cleaning, Ron needed a way to attach larger sweeps. "We bolted the larger ridge sweep directly onto the cultivator shovel. This way, everything remains easy to adjust," he explains. "We can still move the shank up and down, and can change the angle of the sweep when needed."

The Harmons felt they might also want to use their planter conventionally, so they devised a way

to lift the ridge-cleaning unit — coulters, depth wheels and sweeps — without affecting the planter. This was accomplished by adding another hydraulic cylinder near the original planter cylinder, and attaching it to the front end of the cultivator's main frame. "We lift it not only when planting conventionally, but also at each end row. It is really a handy feature to have," Ron says.

Ridges Save Flooded Crops

The Harmons spent almost the entire winter of '85-'86 working on the project, and were ready to call it quits more than once. "It was discouraging at times," Ron says. "But we had gone too far to turn back. We were determined to see it through."

They would work on just one of the six ridge-cleaning and planting mechanisms until they thought it was right. Then they'd run it under field conditions and bring it back inside for adjustments. When they finally perfected one, they used it as a model for the remaining five.

The result: a conventional row-crop planter with ridge-cleaning units mounted in front.

The Harmons had hoped to use the machine on all of their roughly 840 row-crop acres in '86. They built ridges the previous year with the modified Lilliston cultivator. "But the fall of 1985 was awfully wet, and we rutted up some of our fields to the point where we felt we had to till them conventionally," says Ron.

They ended up with usable ridges on about half of their 460 acres of soybeans, and on 350 of their 375 acres of corn. "This gave us a good comparison between the two tillage systems," Ron says.

The sweeps on the homemade ridge-planter scraped off about a 6-inch strip of soil, one-half inch deep, from the top of the ridge. And like most ridge-till farmers, the Harmons cultivated once when the plants were 4 to 6 inches tall, then built ridges at layby.

"It was a good year for seeing the value of ridges," says Ron. "Right after second cultivation, when we had just finished build-

The Harmons built their ridge-cleaning unit for about one-third the cost of a new ridge-till conversion kit. The device lifts out of the way for conventional planting.

ing the ridges, we had a real flood. There is no doubt in my mind that, without those ridges, we would have lost the crops in all of our lower fields.

"In fact, a number of farmers in our area had to replant," he adds. "The plants on our ridges stayed out of the water longer and dried out faster. There wasn't even a difference in crop yield between the lower fields and our higher ground.

"Although I don't have real accurate data, we got about 40 bushels of beans per acre on the ridges and a bit less than that on conventional. The beans on the ridges just looked better all growing season, both when it was too wet and too dry." Corn yields were identical in both systems — about 131 bushels. "We were pretty amazed," Ron says.

Less Spray, Fewer Weeds

The savings amazed them even more. "Input costs were about $10 per acre less with ridges," Ron notes. "Eliminating the plowing and disking saved us both time and money. Also, by just spraying over the ridge at planting, I cut my herbicide cost by more than half."

Rotary hoeing, or an extra cultivation, might eliminate the need for herbicides, he adds. But for now, the Harmons feel their combination of chemicals and cold steel is paying off just fine. "We used to put on $8 to $10 (worth of herbicides) an acre for soybeans and $5 to $6 for corn," Ron says. Now, his herbicide costs are half that or less, he says.

Ron had planned to ridge-till all of his crops, eventually. He even bought a used Buffalo ridge-till cultivator in 1986, to give the modified Lilliston a helping hand with cultivation and ridge-building.

But despite his early success with ridge-till, Ron has since switched back to minimum- and no-till practices on most of his ground. "We found more and more that the ridges stayed too hard in spring, and we had to cut off the top 2 or 3 inches to get to the moisture," he explains. "The soil doesn't have much organic matter. That may be one reason our ridges didn't get mellow in spring."

Little else has changed about his weed-control practices, though. Ron still relies on the modified Lilliston and the used Buffalo to help control weeds with fewer chemicals. And he still uses the Buffalo to build ridges on about 60 acres of what he calls "tough, gumbo-like ground."

Compared with the Lilliston, Ron says the Buffalo does a better job building ridges. But he has no regrets about the time and money he spent building his homemade ridging equipment. "I think it's a real good way to learn what ridging is all about," he stresses. "And, you can do it in a cheap way until you find out whether or not ridging will work in your situation."

He's Making Herbicides Obsolete
With tools that control weeds in crop rows, not just between them.

OROSI, Calif. — His furrowers and guide wheels will help your cultivator do its job quickly and accurately, without mirrors on your tractor frame or microchips in your cab.

His spring-hoe weeders, a set of tapered, finger-like blades mounted on a bracket suspended from a tool bar, will uproot in-row weeds you wouldn't think of trying to reach with a normal cultivator.

And his rotary brush rake, a pinwheel-shaped series of cables with weed-scraping teeth on the ends, will clean around tree and vine crops better and cheaper than an army of fieldhands with hoes.

He is Paul Bezzerides, president and co-founder of Bezzerides Bros. Inc. And when this octogenarian holder of 18 patents says, "I can build a machine that'll do that," it's good news for farmers. That's because he has spent much of the past four decades designing mechanical solutions to chemical problems.

"It costs a lot of money to spray, and they're taking a lot of chemicals away," says Bezzerides, who designs, builds and sells his equipment out of a tin-roofed, former tomato-packing shed in California's San Joaquin Valley. "What we've got is what I feel every farmer needs in order to farm without chemicals."

Not every farmer knows that, yet. But Bezzerides isn't worried. "When we first came out with the spring-hoe weeders in the mid-'60s, our distributor told us it would take 10 years for them to catch on," he recalls. "It took even longer than that.

"It took so long because farmers are set in their ways," he explains, his familiar straw fedora bobbing forward for emphasis. "They're dubious and it takes them a long time to change. Labor was cheap. Then chemicals came along and they were cheap.

"We didn't use herbicides at all," adds Bezzerides, who spent his youth growing vegetables and citrus crops with his parents. "Our weed control was all hand-work, and I thought we could do it easier and do it better."

Farming has changed a lot since then. But the need for safe, efficient weed control is stronger than ever. And so is the demand for Bezzerides' equipment. In '89, he marketed to field-crop, fruit and vegetable growers in 23 states and at least two foreign countries, and his yearly sales totaled $250,000.

Sales of the spring-hoe weeders ($75 a pair), which averaged 500 units a year in the '70s, have doubled. And Bezzerides' vine and tree weeders, which sell for $348 a pair and work much like the spring-hoe weeders, have become the mechanical weed control tool of choice among Western orchardists. "They like the way it works, rather than going to chemicals, which are getting more expensive," observes Ron Twinn of Meyer West, which distributes Bezzerides' machinery in California and Arizona. "Nothing is as economical and efficient. People know the vine and tree weeder by name."

Meet Needs, Not Markets

Rather than adding high-tech bells and whistles to tools that are already on the market — and then trying to sell them with slicker ads and shinier paint — Bezzerides takes a more direct approach: He observes and listens to farmers, then builds machinery to meet their unique needs. "Something comes up that's a problem, and you try to find the answer," he says matter-of-factly.

It's a habit he learned early in life. The son of Turkish immigrants who began farming in central California around the turn of the century, Bezzerides has grown everything from olives and oranges to cucumbers and cotton.

Each enterprise presented new cost-cutting challenges. And typically, each cost-cutting challenge gave Bezzerides and his brother Art an idea for a new machine. "We developed most of the tools together," says Bezzerides.

Mechanical Herbicide Band

The Bezzerides brothers left farming in the mid-'70s, and Art passed away a few years later. By then, making and selling their in-row weed control tools had become a full-time business. And

Bezzerides was well on his way to establishing a custom-cultivating sideline that now helps California farmers cut herbicide costs on thousands of acres of cotton, bush beans and other row crops.

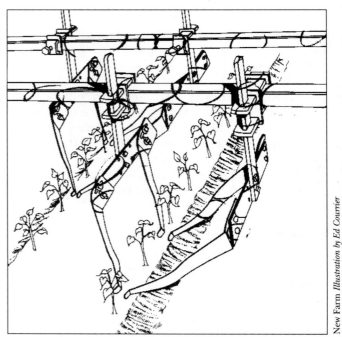

Bezzerides' spring-hoe weeders gently lift soil and uproot weeds within 1 or 2 inches of crops.

Key to both enterprises was — and still is — the spring-hoe weeder, which Bezzerides designed in the early '60s for use on the family farm. The device consists of spring steel blades bolted in pairs to left- and right-hand brackets.

The blades are about 16 inches long, and travel just below the soil surface at a 45-degree angle to the row. As the tractor moves forward, blades vibrate beneath the soil, mulching and uprooting weeds within inches of plants. "We used it in our fall cabbage and our insecticide dealer came by and asked, 'What did you do?'" recalls Bezzerides.

What he had done was create a mechanical device capable of controlling weeds not just between crop rows — but *in* them.

That's been one of Bezzerides' main goals ever since. In fact, of his six patented tools that are actually on the market, all but one — the brush rake — were designed solely for improving in-row mechanical weed control. "Most cultivating is from row to row," observes Bezzerides. "We specialize in getting weeds in the row, because that's where the problem is."

One way to accomplish that is by stirring the soil underground within inches of crop plants, explains Bezzerides. "When you mulch the ground on each side of the plant in an uneven pattern...you break the soil underneath the surface of the ground and don't hurt the plant at

New Farm *Illustration by Ed Courrier*

all."

That's the main mode of action for his spring-hoe and vine and tree weeders. Both rely on flat-running blades that penetrate soil just 1 or 2 inches deep, gently lifting and uprooting weeds. The main difference between them is the blades, themselves. The row-crop weeder has curved blades forged from just one piece of steel for more flexibility.

The vine and tree weeder has straight blades, each consisting of five leaves of spring steel bolted together like a sandwich. The longest blade is 30 inches. Those that follow become gradually shorter, giving the assembly both flexibility and added strength. Blades taper from 4 inches wide at the bracket end to about 1 inch wide at the business end, where optional caster wheels can be installed for smoother action against vines and tree trunks.

Results 'Fantastic'

Bezzerides' torsion weeders also make use of the underground soil-stirring principle. These thin sticks of spring steel are angled to probe just beneath the soil for small weeds within inches of young plants. They're designed for use early in the season. "The spring-hoe weeder is too aggressive to use on young plants," says Bezzerides. "But the torsion weeder will flex up and down, and won't move a lot of soil."

Just after perfecting his torsion, spring-hoe and vine and tree weeders, Bezzerides developed what

New Farm *Photo by Mike Brusko*

Bezzerides' ground-driven rotary brush rake uproots small weeds around trees and vines, and sweeps prunings into row middles for easy cleanup.

may be the oddest-looking weed weapon in his arsenal: his "spyders." They look like a crude attempt to turn a small disk blade into a rotary hoe wheel, with the teeth (actually fingers) alternately bent inward and outward. But they offer the advantages of two tools at once. They're sturdy enough to mulch and aerate heavy soil, like a disk. But the staggered teeth, like the spinning spoons on a rotary hoe, leave behind few, if any, clumps.

Rounding out Bezzerides' weed-control catalog are:
◆ **Spinners**, which uproot weeds while aerating crusted soil.
◆ **Thinners**, which are identical to spinners, except they have small blades on the end for precisely removing larger plants.
◆ **Cultivator-guidance system**, which uses a small furrower-sweep to create a track for specially angled guide wheels.

Farmers typically mount two or more of Bezzerides' tools on the same toolbar. For example, a spyder-torsion weeder tandem helped New York farmers Dick Prochazka and Lynn Lyndes control weeds with no herbicides whatsoever in several acres of broccoli, onions and celery in '88. "It worked OK on large weeds up to 8 inches tall, but it was fantastic on smaller weeds — even in stony ground," they say. "It looked just like someone used a hoe or pulled weeds by hand."

The brush rake and vine and tree weeder make an effective combination, too. "The vine and tree weeder will leave trash right around the vine where the brush rake sweeps it away," says Bezzerides.

But the rake can be a money-saving weed control weapon in its own right. Farmer Ed Bradley used one of the $8,000 units in his 400 acres of wine and table grapes near Delano, Calif, in '88. "It will sure help us make the decision whether to cut out herbicides," he says. "If I had to do by hand what I just did with this machine, it would have cost me $12,000. Running the brush rake on 80 acres cost me maybe $200 or $300."

Bezzerides has grown accustomed to such testimonials. One reason is his great confidence in his machinery, but another is that he simply isn't satisfied until his customers are. And if that means traveling to a farm to help adjust or modify one of his tools, so be it. "As they go along and find different problems, it forces you to find ways to solve them," he says.

Ideas To Spare

With such a broad lineup of practical, innovative tools, you'd think Bezzerides would need a team of lawyers just to handle all the buyout requests from large machinery firms. But that hasn't been the case. "I have approached different manufacturers. They want big-ticket items and they don't want to bother with my stuff," says Bezzerides, whose tools seldom retail for more than $100 to $500 per row.

"It's not necessarily wanting to be small," he

adds. "I'm looking for a manufacturer. I'd like to have somebody come in and say, 'Let's go, we'll push this thing worldwide.'"

For now, Bezzerides Bros. Inc. remains a home-grown business, with family members handling most everything from bookkeeping to marketing.

Bezzerides' main role — in case you haven't guessed — is chief tinkerer and designer. It's a chore he tackles with the energy of someone a fraction of his age. "Sometimes he'll be thinking about something at 1 or 2 o'clock in the morning and go out in the shop until 4 or 5, then come back in and get a few more hours of sleep," says his wife, Marana.

When he wakes up, Bezzerides might start writing some promotional material, or head out with his grandson to help a customer adjust one of his machines in a field of cotton.

But more likely he'll go back to the shop and start sketching, bending, twisting and welding — until last night's dream becomes either a practical new tool or an addition to the scrap heap.

"I've never evaluated anything formally," he says. "If it's something that's needed, and would save a lot of money and help them do away with chemicals ... that is where I've been working, and that's where I see the need for things to be done."

Get The Most From Your Rotary Hoe

And trim your herbicide bill at the same time, with these farmer-proven tips.

JIM BENDER

WEEPING WATER, Neb. — I haven't used herbicides on my 642-acre farm since 1980. And while many aspects of my non-chemical weed control program have changed over the years, at least one has remained constant: my dependence on my 31-foot Hiniker rotary hoe.

I can't imagine controlling weeds without this tool. Crop rotation helps disrupt weed life cycles, and timely cultivations are a good weapon against larger weeds. But anyone who relies on mechanical weed control knows that destroying competition early is essential. By controlling weeds before they can gain a foothold, my rotary hoe does just that, and keeps my weed control costs to as little as $6 per acre.

It hasn't always been that way. My neighbors used to tell me teasingly that rotary hoeing promotes weeds, and for awhile, I was tempted to believe them. But if the past decade has taught me anything, it's that I didn't know much about rotary hoeing during those early days. To be successful at it requires great attention to detail. Improper equipment, operating mistakes and bad timing are the biggest enemies of good weed control with a rotary hoe.

Let's take a look at each of these issues separately, and see how they can combine to offer low-cost weed control with various tillage systems and conservation structures.

The first thing I recommend is using the widest

hoe possible for your terrain and horsepower. Farmers often use 90-horsepower tractors to pull 14-foot rotary hoes, when a tractor that size could easily pull a 20- or 30-foot hoe.

The maximum hoe size for your tractor depends on how fast you hoe. Hoeing speed is usually from 7 to 13 mph. According to Jim Garthe, an agricultural engineer at Pennsylvania State University, you need about 1 PTO horsepower per foot of hoe at the slower speed, and about 2.5 hp per foot at the higher speed. A rule I like to follow: If you can't find a satisfactory way to hold the front end of your tractor down, or if you can't get up to speed without excessive clutch slippage, you need a smaller hoe or a more powerful tractor.

Naturally, the larger the hoe, the higher the price. A 16-foot hoe sells new for about $3,000, but you can expect to spend about $12,000 for a 41-footer with wings. It's possible to find used 16-foot hoes in good condition for about $1,000.

Why opt for the larger hoe? One reason is timeliness. Only a farmer who's never relied on rotary hoeing could fail to appreciate the frustration of having 100 acres of newly planted soybeans to hoe and hearing rain forecast for the rest of the week. With my 30-foot hoe, I can do the job properly in a day. Not so with a smaller one.

Another consideration is soil compaction. A larger hoe reduces the weight per unit of soil

Rotary hoeing early keeps weeds from gaining a foothold.

area, and creates fewer wheel tracks, where compacted soil makes it difficult for hoe wheels to penetrate and do their job. Likewise, a larger hoe reduces the number of total turns on turn rows, resulting in less stress to crops planted there. I usually hoe twice, but I sometimes hoe the same field three times in one season. So, minimizing turn-row stress is vital.

Finally, a larger hoe can be easier to hold in place on the backslopes of steep terraces. That's because the wider the hoe, the more likely the tractor's position will be down off the steepest part of the backslope.

Wings Add Options

I'd also suggest your hoe have folding wings, with gauge wheels and separate hydraulics for each wing. For example, a 21-foot hoe usually can be purchased with a rigid tool bar, or with a 12-foot center and two folding wings. Unless you have time to unhitch and rehitch for traveling on a road, you'd be better off with the latter.

Another advantage of folding wings is that they maximize field options, especially if you plant on terraces or contours with point rows. After hoeing one of these point rows, you'll find that some unhoed spaces will be narrower than the hoe. By raising the wings and using just the center section, you can hoe fewer delicate, small plants twice in a short period of time. In fact, folding wings with gauge wheels are a virtual necessity in hilly, terraced fields, because they enable the unit

to flex and conform to contours and terraces.

No matter what size hoe you own, there are several things you can do to improve — and extend — its performance. One is to avoid turning the tractor around, or turning the front wheels sharply, until the hoe has been raised off the ground. Failure to do so can result in bent or broken wheel teeth, stressed wheel bearings and bent mounting arms.

The weight of a large hoe, or of a smaller one on a tractor that's not equipped with much ballast, can make turning around an effort. That increases wear on the brakes and front tires. You can avoid this problem by backing around, which pushes the hoe's weight toward the tractor.

Still, if your hoe is 28 feet wide or more, turning around in all but the flattest fields results in gouged humps, waterway edges and terraces, all of which cause considerable damage to hoe ends. I solve this problem by routinely raising the wings about 5 percent before each turn. To avoid damaging the inner wheels of the wings, I always raise and lower the wings while the hoe's center section is in the raised position.

A very wide hoe in a raised position may rock against its mounting arms if the tractor is driven at an angle across changes in a field's terrain, such as a waterway or terrace channel. That puts stress on the rear end of the tractor. Remedies I've used include slowing down, driving straight into depressions or — if the hoe is already rocking — gently setting it down to stop the motion.

Spread Planting Dates

Hoe wheels are shaped like little spades. They do their work by penetrating soil and flicking it backward as the wheel rolls on. Not surprisingly, this action is most effective at higher speeds. I generally travel about 13 miles per hour in established crops, but I have to slow down to 7 mph on very small, delicate crops. The important thing is to start and stop abruptly, so that the ends of fields are hoed effectively.

I believe it is best to hoe turn rows, first. That way, they are hoed before you've packed them by repeated turns. If you have waterways in a field, it's best to hoe their borders first, too. That compensates for the times you'll need to stop and start at waterways when you're hoeing the rest of the field.

Preferred hoeing weather is hot, sunny and windy. Ideally, a rotary hoe should be used during the hottest part of the day, when exposed weed roots are stressed the most. Weed kill is always less effective if you have to hoe during the evening hours, because cooler weather gives the plants more time to recover.

That calls for some preparation, beginning with spreading out planting dates. If weed growth is at the same stage on too much acreage, your opportunities for timely hoeing are greatly reduced. I try to plant all of my 10 to 100 acres of sorghum around June 1, so that warm soil will promote fast emergence. I plant my 100 to 200 acres of soybeans between June 1 and June 15 (a field every two or three days) for the same reason. The planting date for my 50 acres of corn is determined mostly by the yield and drydown characteristics of the hybrid.

Corn and sorghum may be hoed until the spike stage breaks into the first two leaves, while beans may be hoed until the hook is about to break through the soil. I've hoed all three crops successfully before emergence, but I generally wait until three days after planting, to permit weed germination.

My biggest complaint about pre-emergence hoeing is that it commits me to two additional hoeings: one shortly after emergence, and another about a week or so later. Each hoeing kills a new crop of emerging weeds, but also contributes to surface compaction. By the third pass through a field, my silt-loam clay soil is often too compacted for the hoe to work properly.

By planting later when soil has warmed, you'll give your crops a jump on weeds, and you can reduce the need to hoe before the crop is up. Generally, though, I've had success with pre-emergence hoeing. It's a great way to get ahead of weeds when rain is in the forecast.

Timing Critical

The biggest danger in early postemergence hoeing is covering up the crop. That's something to keep in mind if you ridge-plant, or if the field you're hoeing is on a hillside.

On level ground, damage to young plants is seldom excessive. You may want to hoe a test strip and then count exactly what your seedling loss is. Mine is seldom more than 2 percent (it's never as bad as it looks from the tractor). One way I minimize seedling losses from hoeing is to increase my soybean and sorghum planting rates by about 10 percent. The extra seed cost is minimal — roughly $1 per acre.

I don't increase my corn planting rate, though. My farm is located on the western edge of the Corn Belt, and since moisture is frequently low I don't worry about losing a few corn plants to hoe damage. If your rainfall is dependable, you may want to increase your corn planting rate to compensate for the loss.

I can usually hoe corn and beans a second time three or four days after they emerge, provided I reduce my ground speed. Sorghum is a different matter. It's much more susceptible to damage just after emergence. I try to wait until the crop is at least 3 inches tall before the second hoeing. That may take up to a week, which gives me extra incentive to do a pre-emergence hoeing in sorghum.

When corn and sorghum have reached a height of 6 inches or so, they can usually withstand a more aggressive hoeing at about 13 mph. Of course, crop losses on turn rows increase as the plants grow larger. Once I can push soil into the row without damaging plants, I turn the weed control duties over to the cultivator.

Even if your goal isn't to eliminate herbicides completely, a rotary hoe can still reduce your need for them. It also can help you get the most effective weed control from the herbicides you do use. For example, it's a good tool for combating crusting problems and for incorporating pre-emergence herbicides when rains don't arrive to do that for you. And if pre-emerge herbicides fail completely, hoeing can rescue the crop at far less expense than another spraying can.

What To Look For In A Rotary Hoe

◆ *Should be hitch-mounted* (two- or three-point) rather than pull-type, which can't be raised. This makes transport easier, reduces turn-row stress, permits direct backing and aids in unclogging trash.

◆ *Should be equipped with trash deflectors,* steel bands on each mounting arm that prevent trash from accumulating between the mounting arm and hoe wheel. These are especially useful in minimum- and no-till systems. If a wheel is stuck with trash while traveling over a row, it will tear out a portion of that row — crops and all.

◆ *Wheel bearings should be mounted with bolts rather than rivets.* Rivets make it more difficult to change bearings in the field.

◆ *Pressure on hoe wheels should be adjustable* (will vary from 15 to 50 pounds or so per wheel), to accommodate varying field conditions.

◆ *Hoe width must match your row spacings.* For example, a 160-inch hoe is designed for four, 41-inch rows. Since your tractor must drive between rows, you couldn't use such a unit on 30-inch rows. You'd end up skipping a strip, or hoeing a row a second time on the return pass.

'This Hoe's For Sale'

Rotary hoeing isn't a good option on his farm.

TOM CULP

LEXINGTON, Ohio — One of our long-range business objectives is to operate a profitable farm utilizing sustainable methods as much as possible. Now that I've quit using insecticides because of effective crop rotation, I'm working to cut down herbicide use. I experimented in '89 and '90 with intensive cultivation in an effort to trim weed-control costs and still harvest profitable yields. However, my experience with the rotary hoe after those two years was disappointing. I'm still trying to cut herbicides, but my rotary hoe is for sale.

Soils on our farm are predominantly silt loam with organic matter content ranging from 1.9 to 2.7 percent. Fields are rolling enough that I use a side-hill combine. Tillage is primarily chisel plow with some moldboard plowing and some no-till. Our basic rotation is corn-soybeans-corn-soybeans-wheat. Soybeans are solid-seeded with a rye/hairy vetch winter cover crop, and the wheat is spring-planted, interseeded with medium red clover. Our typical residue cover after planting is 35 to 45 percent, except where sod is moldboard-plowed. Fifty percent of our crop acreage is corn, 30 percent soybeans and 20 percent wheat.

To reduce or eliminate herbicides and maintain acceptable weed control, I had two choices. The most desirable for me was to substitute cultivation for pre-emerge herbicides I had been using. The second was to reduce herbicide application rates as much as possible.

I decided to dedicate 26 acres (corn, soybeans and sweet corn) in 1989 and 9 acres (corn and sweet corn) in 1990 to a cultivation system. In corn, this meant three passes with the rotary hoe — one pre-emerge and two post-emerge. In comparison, we also included some 30-inch-row soybeans, which got the same treatment as the corn.

Since 1987, I've experimented with cutting herbicides across the rest of our row-crop acreage by gradually reducing application rates below labeled rates to find how low I can go and have the weed control I need. I still broadcast pre-emerge herbicides after planting. Banding would also cut herbicide use, but I haven't tried it, due to equipment limitations.

New Hoe, No Experience

Before buying a rotary hoe to accompany our six-row Danish tine cultivator, we talked to several rotary hoe users, looked at several hoes at farm shows and read all we could find on the subject. Three contenders emerged from our search: John Deere (standard model), Case IH (standard and high-clearance models) and M&W (high-clearance model). With the high levels of surface residue I prefer, I wanted a high-clearance model, primarily on the basis of fellow Rodale on-farm research cooperator Dick Thompson's experiences in Iowa. Neither our local dealer nor the area Case IH rep was able to find out enough

Need a good, used rotary hoe? Call Tom Culp.

New Farm *Photos by T.L. Gettings*

about their high-clearance model to permit an evaluation. As a result, we bought the 15-foot M&W MT 1815 rotary hoe in early 1989 for $3,000.

Buying a hoe was one thing. Figuring how to make it work its best was another. Because there are few rotary hoe users in our area, I had to rely on the instructions which came with the hoe and whatever I could find to read. Operating instructions suggested that I "hook it up, level it and travel 7 to 8 mph."

Other publications helped with information on when to hoe and supported common-sense operating techniques, such as not turning when the hoe is still in the ground and using caution on side slopes. However, we could find no advice on how deep to run the hoe, how fast, how to hoe when the field is too wet but the weeds are at white-shoot stage, how to keep from covering emerged corn plants or how to react to the ever-present rocks. We had to learn all these practical techniques in the school of hard knocks.

Hitting The Fields

Armed with what knowledge we had, we hit the fields in the wet spring of 1989. Our initial plan was to hoe our corn about four days after planting to kill any weed shoots which developed after pre-plant tillage. We had increased our planting depth from 1.5 to 2 inches to accommodate cultivation. However, it rained immediately after planting. We were forced to wait five and one-half days before hoeing the first time. The soil was still too wet. We ran the hoe at full depth (about 2 inches) at about 8 mph. So far so good.

Rains kept us from returning to the field until the corn was at the three-leaf stage and the weeds had sprouted. We realized that an aggressive hoeing was needed to kill as many weeds as possible, but we didn't know how the corn would take it. No information was available about this situation, so we did our best. We ran the hoe full depth at about 8 mph, which took out a lot of weeds and didn't seem to damage corn excessively, although it did cover many leaves with soil. Perhaps, if the rain had let up, this would not have been a problem. However, continued rain matted the soil down and prevented further cultivation.

With a combination of soil-covered plants and cold, wet conditions, enough corn plants died that we had to replant 80 percent of that field. Our other field survived much better because we ran slower — at about 3 mph — for the second hoeing when the corn was at three-leaf stage. Two cultivations followed in both fields, the final one when corn was about 18 inches tall.

Weed control *between the rows* was good, but late-season weeds reached significant levels *in the row*. Our 1989 corn yields were 65.2 bushels per acre for cultivated fields (including the replanted field of 10 acres) and 90.7 bushels per acre for low-rate herbicide fields.

The difference in yield was much greater than the difference in weeds. I don't know why so many more bushels of corn came off the herbicide-treated field, but I know it was not entirely due to weed control, because weed counts were not significantly different between the fields. Overall yields were far below our previous five-year average of 124 bushels per acre for corn. Extreme weather conditions have dragged yields below that figure for the past three years.

Beans Did Better

Thankfully, our soybeans fared better. The weather window allowed us to hoe about four days after planting, as we had hoped. Our next hoeing should have been in about five days, judging by the weed shoots. However, when we tried to hoe, we broke off too many bean plants that had emerged but had not yet developed a true leaf. We had to wait until the beans reached first-leaf stage to keep the damage down. Our second hoeing was done at full depth (2 inches) but at about 3 mph to minimize soybean damage. We hoed a third time at the first trifoliate leaf at full depth at 8 mph.

Rowed beans were also cultivated twice at later growth stages. Weed control was good in solid-seeded beans, which made up 80 percent of the trial. Only a slight amount of foxtail was present. The rowed beans were clean. Our 1989 soybean yields were 30.9 bushels per acre for cultivated fields and 32.2 bushels per acre for low-rate herbicide fields.

High Hopes For '90

With a year's experience, we entered the 1990 crop season with better expectations and a better weather pattern. We had decided that if the wet weather returned, we would broadcast herbicides as needed. We also knew we needed to do a better job removing weeds within corn rows.

We planted our corn early under good conditions. Cooperative weather permitted three rotary hoeings: the first at four days after planting (8 mph); the second at two-leaf stage about seven days later (3 mph); and the third about four days later (5 mph). All hoeings were done 2 inches deep on dry soil when soil was in excellent condi-

tion, with good results. Two cultivations followed at appropriate intervals, with the last when corn was 18 inches tall. Weed control was very good.

In sweet corn following soybeans (in 1989's cultivation trials), significant levels of late-season in-row weeds were present. Our 1990 corn yields were 73.0 bushels per acre for cultivated fields and 81.3 bushels per acre for low-rate herbicide fields.

Wet weather returned immediately after planting soybeans, so we chose to apply pre-emerge herbicides. Soybean yields in 1990 were 45.6 bushels per acre for low-rate herbicide fields.

Herbicide System

Our normal weed control practice is to broadcast tank-mixed pre-emergence broadleaf and grass herbicides, using a pickup sprayer with 50-foot booms immediately after planting. Since the late '80s, we have been systematically reducing application rates below label rates, seeking the threshold where weed control is unacceptable. For us, this is the point where economic crop loss occurs. We tolerate some weeds and don't demand clean fields.

Research indicates that the effective window for herbicides is from planting to canopy closure. After canopy closure, shading suppresses weed

Ohio farmer Tom Culp bought a 15-foot M&W minimum-till rotary hoe to diversify his weed-control strategy. The unit's use of extended rear-wheel arms offsets front and rear wheels, providing self-cleaning action in high residue.

Putting Cultivation To The Test

For Culp's 2-year test, low-rate herbicide treatments cost less than mechanical weed control.

| | CULTIVATION $/A (estimate)[1] | | | HERBICIDE $/A (actual)[2] | | | |
| | CORN | SOYBEANS | | CORN | | SOYBEANS | |
	'89/'90	'89/'90		'89	'90	'89	'90
Hoe (3x)	$15	$15	Material	$9.85	$12.88	$19.80	$22.19
Cult. (2x)	10	10	Application	3.00	3.00	3.00	3.00
Totals	**25**	**25**	**Totals**	**12.85**	**15.88**	**22.80**	**25.19**

1. *Estimate $5 per acre per cultivation pass, Ohio State University, "Custom Rates Guide," 1990. Culp notes field size and shape, flatness of terrain, labor cost and width of cultivation tool cause the actual cost to vary from farm to farm.*
2. *Culp Farms enterprise accounting, 1990. Herbicide cost difference due to 1989 pre-season discounts.*

growth adequately for most early season weeds, but may not control late-season weeds such as lambsquarter and red-root pigweed.

In corn, we use Bicep 6L at 0.5 gallon per acre in 28 percent nitrogen. This is 16 percent less than the label rate of 0.6 gallon per acre for our soil type. For soybeans, we use 1.25 pints of Linex 4L and 2.0 pints of Dual 8E in water—reductions of the label rates for our soil type of 16 percent and 20 percent, respectively, from label rates of 1.5 pints and 2.5 pints.

I've found that if I provide a carrier pH of around 6.0, I can reduce rates even further. Our water pH averages 6.8 and the 28 percent N averages 7.0. I use acetic acid (vinegar) to reduce pH.

My figures also show that some herbicide formulations using the same active ingredient provide better weed control *per unit* than others. For example, Linex 4L at 1.25 pints per acre provides identical weed control to Lorox L 4L at 2.0 pints per acre. We continue to pursue rate reductions. Weed control remains very good.

To determine the economics of the two herbicide-reducing alternatives, I compared the costs of cultivation and our reduced-rate spray programs. We knew the charges for the herbicides, but we had to do some figuring to establish our cost for cultivation. Our actual costs were incurred on too few acres to be meaningful. Ohio State University has established a cost of $5 per acre for both rotary hoeing and for cultivat-

ing of row crops. This price includes equipment, labor and fuel, amortized over machine life. The table shows the costs of each alternative on my farm.

Compaction Concerns

In our soil type, rotary hoeing and cultivation appear to cause excessive compaction in wheel rows (two rows out of six). We first noticed this compaction in 1989, but we attributed most of it to the wet soil conditions that year. In 1990, compaction was again evident even with dry soil, particularly during the rotary-hoeing interval. After we hoed, water stood in the wheel tracks for long periods while none stood on top of the ground in other rows.

To check one result of compaction, we measured earthworm populations. We found 25 percent fewer earthworms in wheel-track rows than in other rows. In our cultivation system, wheel tracks cover 17 percent of the field area. Wheel tracks in our herbicide system cover only 5 percent of the field. While it's hard to put dollars to this soil damage, I'm sure it's significant in the long term.

An additional cultivation-related cost is the yield reduction in soybeans in our area when they are planted in rows (to accommodate cultivation) rather than solid-seeded. OSU data indicates that 30-inch-row beans average 10 percent lower yields. Our farm trials agree. The yield drop cost us $24 per acre, based on our 42-bushel average.

Further, we have not yet been able to consistently remove late-season weeds from the rows. It appears that more effective rotary hoeing is helpful, but better cultivation techniques are needed to ensure consistency. Because I work off the farm during the day, I don't have much time to cultivate, especially during the hottest part of the day when it would do the most good.

I haven't given up on cultivation, but I'm concentrating instead on my reduced-herbicide program because it cuts my costs, causes less soil compaction and fits my schedule better. Overall, it appears at this writing to offer a better balance for us.

Editor's Note: *Tom and Marilyn Culp farm 400 acres of grain, 3 acres of vegetables and produce 400 hogs per year. They are members of the Rodale Institute's On-Farm Research Network. Tom also works as a traffic engineer for the Ohio Department of Transportation.*

'This Hoe's For Keeps'
It helps him save $20 per acre on herbicides.

DON ELSTON

GROVER HILL, Ohio — Where I come from, almost every farm has a rotary hoe of some description. With very flat ground, poor drainage and soil that is 65 percent clay, crusting is a real problem. By making my hoes more aggressive and changing the way I treat my soil, I've come a long way in weed control the past 15 years.

Because of our soils, I use the hoe as much for crop emergence as for weed control. Even at that, it pays its way as a weed fighter. I figure it works ideally two years out of 10, gets shut out by weather about as often, and is usable to some degree in the other six years of the decade. Its effectiveness in the swing years depends on the management of the operator and the weed-attacking quality of the hoe.

With the advent of effective post-emergence herbicides, more often than not, the hoe lets me pocket the $20 per acre that I figure it costs me to spray. Cultivation expenses in this region are about $1 per acre. I could rent a rig for $30 per hour, and cover 30 acres in that time.

Consider 1990. My first beans went in May 1, solid-seeded in 7-inch rows the day after a pass with a Danish-tine/rolling basket finishing tool. My hoe was ready to go, but the weather the next several weeks was cold and wet. When weeds passed the stage they could be controlled with hoeing and cultivation, I used a rescue treatment of Pursuit at the label rate. It worked beautifully.

The last of my 400 acres of soybeans went in exactly a month later. Conditions were suitable for the rotary hoe. Two trips each with the hoe and cultivator left me a clean enough field. Fields planted in the interim had various levels of culti-vation and rotary hoe attention, depending on timing. Yields were about the same across the board.

Don't get the idea my success with the rotary hoe came with my first year on the farm. It came with time, experience and some hard knocks. By the late 1960s, I had sold my limited livestock holdings of earlier years and decided to specialize in crop production. We farmed more than 1,000 Paulding County acres in northwestern Ohio near the Indiana border. I was using a John Deere six-section pull-type rotary hoe. To get soil penetration, we had to use two or three homemade 80-pound cement weights on each gang. Most farmers made railroad iron sleds just to move those cumbersome "state of the art" rotary hoes of the '60s.

I admit, the industry improved things with the heavier section rotary hoes mounted on a three-point hitch. We tried an IH 21-foot model, and it really would dig better than our first hoe. But — and there always seems to be a "but" — it was so heavy and it extended so far back that it took a tractor of at least 110 hp just to lift it.

By 1975, implement companies introduced toolbar-mounted models with spring-loaded arms. These lightweight machines seemed to be the answer to weeding and soil crusting. (A half-inch of rain just after planting is all it takes to keep our soybeans from pushing through.) In the late '70s, I bought a used 21-foot John Deere 400, attached new wheels and confidently waited for spring.

Too Hard To Hoe

Our first attempt at hoeing with this rig was a

disaster. Even with the new wheels, it just pecked little holes in the soil. It didn't even penetrate the crust, which was up to 1.25 inches thick. I was sick. I thought I would go back to the heavy old IH hoe, which we had kept in storage. But it also merely poked the surface. I realized it was time to stop and think about what was going on with my entire farm operation.

There were other signs things were not well. Our soil no longer had earthworms in it. Its structure was getting poorer and poorer. Absorption had become so restricted that even moderate rains would leave puddles in the field rather than soak in. While many farmers blamed the weather, I wondered if the answer wasn't in how I was treating my soil. In talking with farmers who were taking their soil seriously, I saw that it is a living entity and that I was violating some basic concepts. Unless I started to manage it in a way that promoted life, I was convinced that it would eventually become non-productive.

I started to search many farm magazines for articles to show me how to farm in a new way that would promote bacteria, worms and healthy soil. After a friend loaned me a copy of *The New Farm*, I subscribed right away. It's still at the top of my list of farm magazines. In its pages, I read an ad for Ho-Bits replacement spoons made by Manufarm Specialties Ltd. in Canada.

Conversations with folks at Manufarm convinced me of two points: 1) A rotary hoe wheel is made like a three-sided center punch. After a season or so it wears down too fast and becomes a compaction tool. 2) Our soil was simply getting too low in organic matter content and needed minimum-tillage treatment if it was going to come back. My goal was to keep organic matter partially exposed and mixed into only the top 3 inches of soil where 90 percent of the soil life is located.

Thinking Like A Weed

I didn't grasp what difference the shape of the wheel points would make until I thought like a weed facing the business end of a rotary hoe. I asked myself, "Which would I have a better chance of dodging if I was a half-inch tall — a pointed-wheel that disturbs only 10 percent of the soil, or wheels tipped with sharpened knives that stir up 50 to 60 percent of my home turf?"

It was 1976 when we began to cut back on tillage. After several crop seasons, soil was noticeably softer and had better tilth. We began to see worms return. To help them out, we began to inoculate our fields with live bacteria on a regular basis. Soil tests showed fields which had readings of 2 percent organic matter in 1976 improved to 4 percent by 1986. Along the way, we learned it takes at least 3 percent organic matter for soil bacteria to survive.

How a rotary hoe performs in a field can be a good test of the soil health and type. I could see

Let it fly! Extra-sharp replacement teeth make Ohio farmer Don Elston's rotary hoe more effective at uprooting weeds and breaking up hard-crusted soil.

my fields changing from year to year, with more penetration and soil disruption. Some of the fellows who were still moldboard plowing would take their rotary hoes out to the fields, make a few rounds then quit. The crust from the turned-up lower layers just didn't have the tilth to crumble sufficiently.

But when I sold my 21-foot John Deere hoe to a neighbor who farmed organically, it was *my fields* that looked like parking lots by comparison. He bought a tool that wasn't getting the results I wanted, and he loved it. When I visited his farm, I saw soil that was soft and spongy — the result of careful organic soil management for 11 or 12 years.

For a five-county area from Fort Wayne to Lima, farmers worry about compaction because of our soil types. I don't think my cultivation adds appreciably to the problem for several reasons. We use controlled traffic. The planter, hoe and cultivator move in the same rows, each taking a 30-foot swath. The sprayer is twice that wide.

We hoe with a 10,000-pound tractor moving at 10 mph exerting only minor pulling pressure on the soil — not nearly as much as the planter. The tractor is that big because the hoe is really doing something to the soil. Lots of guys pull bigger hoes with smaller tractors, but examination of the soil surface after they've gone shows why — little penetration, little effect. The rooster-tailing effect of the Ho-Bits brings soil full-circle and makes it kind of gritty being the driver, but I guess that's part of the price of success.

I believe compaction *does* cut down yields in solid beans, but I don't see that problem in my fields. Also, I think some of the layered subsoil tightness that occurs really isn't caused by downward tire pressure. Rather, it is a settling effect of smaller particles that repeatedly get sifted in excessive tillage. I noted this condition on my farm when I was using a heavy-duty disk for a peri-

Barbara and Don Elston find attention to soil life makes a big difference above and below the ground on their northwestern Ohio farm.

od of time. We've since gone to using a chisel plow with sweeps that drags a heavy leveling bar as our primary tillage piece. Keeping the surface level seems to encourage microbial life in the soil better than lots of jagged clods.

10,000 Acres And Holding

Our current rotary hoe is a 30-foot John Deere 400 we bought used five years ago and equipped with Ho-Bits. These spoons are made of steel which is two-thirds harder than the original malleable iron tips. They allow good welding and wear two to three times longer than the standard factory-issue iron.

Our machine has 10,000 acres on it and the tips look good. We use it as much as possible. What really makes it work is timing. We've never hurt a crop by being too early or too quick with it. Most often my problem is being a day late. I like to keep my nose close to the soil, using my pocket knife to check for foxtail in the white.

Deeper-digging hoe points extend the length of time the tool can be used. Grass is one of the easiest weeds to remove with a hoe, if you get it early. Sometimes, though, foxtail will be up an inch before you can get into the field. With sharp bits, I can dig down three-fourths of an inch and pluck those developing roots out. In my soil, regular bits wouldn't stand a chance.

Just A Tool

Even with the extra aggressiveness I get from my still-sharp tips, I believe the window for optimum rotary hoe operation is fairly narrow. There is a limit to what any tool can do for a farmer. All too often, we buy a new piece of equipment and hope that it will be the answer to all our problems. Now and then, something technical comes along which *can* make a big difference. More often, we succeed by being agricultural artists who make it our life to understand what is happening in our soil — one of creation's most-perfect gifts.

Soil husbandry should be the first line of defense in a weed control program that includes:
◆ A healthy, living soil that is high in organic matter
◆ Mechanical primary tillage that promotes life
◆ Mechanical secondary tillage to germinate the seed
◆ Post-planting tillage to stop weeds before they become weeds
◆ As a last resort, use of post-emergent herbicides, where needed, for specific weed problems

After farming for 37 years, Barb and I believe that farmers need a re-education in the art of recycling all organic matter in the best way possible. Recycling provides both nutrients and habitat for several species of earthworms to proliferate. We've got good numbers now on gray and red worms. Anybody know how we can encourage more nightcrawlers?

Editor's Note: *Don and Barb Elston farm 700 acres of corn, soybeans and wheat. They have 80 acres that are certified organic for production of clear-hilum soybeans.*

Redesigning The Rotary Hoe

Although the basic tool remains the same — 16 small spades on spinning wheels about 21 inches in diameter, attached by spring-loaded arms to a toolbar — equipment makers are fine-tuning the rotary hoe. They're trying to meet increasing farmer demands for machines that work well with fewer herbicides and more crop residue. Here is a look at some of the changes.

M&W Handles Heavy Trash

M&W Gear's 15-foot minimum-till hoe.

M&W Gear introduced the first minimum-tillage rotary hoe in 1981. To accommodate high-residue field surfaces, M&W extended the curved arms used on trailing rear wheels. The design provides greater space between the wheels to prevent clogging and keep wheels clean.

The wheel rows are spaced so teeth on each wheel in one row pass between the teeth of the two wheels in the other row. Any residue caught between two wheels is immediately kicked out by the wheel in the opposite row. M&W introduced 41-foot folding hoes in conventional and minimum-tillage models in 1991.

The company offers hoes on rigid frames (15-foot and 21-foot units only) and on hydraulic folding frames from 15 feet to 41 feet wide in minimum-tillage and conventional versions. In 1991, prices were $2,995 to $9,150 for conventional hoes 15 to 30 feet, and $3,895 to $11,250 for minimum-tillage hoes in the same widths. Write: M&W Gear Co., Route 47 South, Gibson City, IL 60936. Phone: (217) 784-4261.

Yetter Designed For Ridges

In 1991, Yetter introduced a new hoe designed for ridge-tillage. The 3700 Series hoe features five-wheel gangs that engage the planted ridge surface while leaving the ridge middles undisturbed. Keeping hoe wheels out of the residue allows the soil cover to remain in place and prevents wheels from plugging. Fewer gangs makes the hoe lighter and more responsive.

Tension springs on all Yetter hoes, which feature one wheel per arm, may be unhooked to permit arms to be raised for hoeing taller crops. Hoes can accommodate row spaces up to 40 inches without adjustment.

Prices in 1991 started at $2,938 for Yetter's 12-foot model and peaked at $11,986 for its 41-foot folding model. Rigid hoes from Yetter go up to 34 feet wide, while the winged models start at 21 feet wide. Ridge-till models are relatively less expensive for the same width because they use fewer wheels. Price range in '91 was $2,285 for the 15-foot model to $8,865 for the 41-foot model. Write: Yetter Mfg. Co. Inc., Colchester, IL 62326-0358. Phone: (800) 447-5777.

Yetter's new hoe set for ridge tillage.

Case's Minimum-Tillage Hoe

Case IH added minimum-tillage hoes to its line with the introduction of its 181 series in 1988. Like M&W Gear, Case added space between the forward and trailing single-wheel arms. The result is better trash flow between front and back wheels. The minimum-tillage model, which also works for no-till, accounted for 60 percent of Case's rotary hoe sales.

Teeth on the new series are steel rather than cast iron. On sharp impact, steel teeth may bend rather than break. But they can be bent back into position. Teeth are replaceable on the steel-tooth wheels.

Case offers eight sizes from 15 to 41 feet wide, half folding and half rigid, in both standard and minimum-tillage versions. In 1991, prices ranged from $3,246 ($3,674 min-till) for the 15-foot rigid model to $11,987 ($13,349 min-till) for the 41-foot folding model. Write: J.I. Case, 700 State St., Racine, WI 53404. Phone: (414) 636-6011.

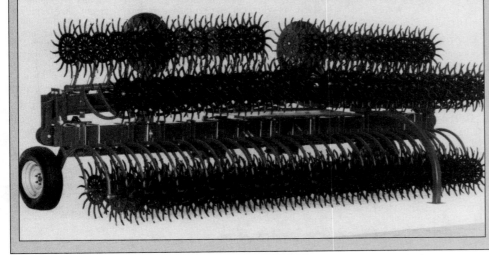

Case IH's 41-foot minimum-till model.

Deere's Weather-Beaters

John Deere continues to offer its traditional hoe, which has two wheels per arm. A secondary arm connects each pair of hoe wheels, acting as a walking beam.

Tom Bueker, John Deere product support manager for tillage systems, says sales of the tools were up slightly in '90 from the previous year. He says weather conditions in a given year may have as big an effect on rotary hoe sales as other factors. If rain causes crusting in soybean regions, or sustained winds threaten soybeans at the vulnerable trifoliate stage, rotary hoe sales may experience a local surge.

Deere rotary hoe prices for '90 ranged from $3,400 for the 15-foot rigid model to $12,170 for the 41-foot folding model. Rigid hoes come in four widths between 15 feet and 30 feet, while folding series entries come in three sizes from 28 feet to 41 feet. Write: Deere and Co., John Deere Rd., Moline, IL 61265. Phone: (309) 765-4714.

Deere hoe with two wheels per arm.

Sharpening The Attack On Weeds

WHEATLEY, Ont. — Jim Tulen farmed enough in 1980 to know that a major shortcoming of a rotary hoe in sandy soils was the frequent need for new wheels — or new machines — just because the soil-shattering points were too worn to work. He and his brother Jack decided to do something about it. "We thought it was an absolute waste to have to deal with a rotary hoe every second year," he says.

Using a special high-grade steel, they designed add-on bits that met their goals of extended wear and longer like-new performance. They form ⅛-inch steel into an elongated,

Ho-Bit replacement spoons give new life to worn rotary hoe points. A mounting jig positions the bit against the wheel for precise welding.

contoured spoon shape that is 2⅜ inches long and ¾ inch wide. Sample spoons are available.

Jim says the Ho-Bits are self-sharpening and effective as long as there is pitch left on the wheel arm. Longevity depends on use and abrasiveness of soil type, but Jim says the product usually lasts about three times as long as standard rotary hoe tips. The projection, thinness and width of the spoons greatly increase aggressiveness due to their soil-lifting action.

A set of 16 spoons sells for $12. Initial success brought discounting of replacement wheels, which are usually available now in the United States for less than $24 — half the price of most replacement wheels when Ho-Bits came out in 1982. Attaching Ho-Bits requires good welding skills. Ho-Bit distributors often rent a production mounting jig which holds the spoons precisely in place at the proper pitch. Good welders can refit five wheels an hour. The jigs are available for $60 each.

Write: Manufarm Specialties Ltd., Rt. 1, Wheatley, Ontario N0P 2P0, Canada. Phone: (519) 825-7354.

Stretch Your Hoe & Cut Your Costs

NEWELL, Iowa — Ever wish you could cover twice as much ground with your rotary hoe? Or spend half as much money hoeing your current acreage?

It's possible if you're a ridge-tiller like Harlan Grau. He took the 24 hoe wheels from a four-row John Deere rotary hoe and mounted them in gangs of three onto an eight-row Buffalo tool bar.

Result: an eight-row unit that gives Grau the weed-killing benefits of rotary hoeing right where he needs it most. "The cultivator will take out anything between the rows," says Grau, who grows about 800 acres of corn and beans. "Where you need the rotary hoe is to help control weeds in the row. So we set up the hoe so it would just run right on top of the ridges, where we need it."

New Farm Photo by Craig Cramer

Iowa ridge-tiller Harlan Grau stretched a 4-row rotary hoe into an 8-row tool designed to run just on ridge tops.

This Bean Bar Has Teeth

DEARBORN, Mo. — When they were young, Howard Boydston's three sons took care of the volunteer corn and other tall weeds in the soybeans on the family's 1,100-acre farm.

"They chopped 'em out with hoes," Boydston recalls. "But then the boys grew up, went off to the military and the like, and I didn't have enough help. I used all the chemicals they had, plus cultivation. But herbicides don't always work. No matter what you do, you still have volunteers come up.

"I thought there had to be something better," he continues. "I wanted something where I could sit on my fanny and still control the weeds, so I came up with this apparatus." What Boydston invented is a machine that really does allow him to control weeds while sitting down. To help minimize costs and pollution, it uses no herbicides. To keep labor needs low, it only requires one tractor driver, rather than the two to four people who usually ride the front of bean buggies with individual spray guns.

Off With Their Heads!

What is it? A 15-foot combine cutter bar mounted on the front of a tractor. With the flick of a lever, the bar can be raised or lowered so that it passes just above row crops, cutting the tops off weeds in its path. "It doesn't matter how high (maximum 5 feet) or how low you go, the cutter bar stays level with the ground. It's not like with a combine, where it points up and down," Boydston says.

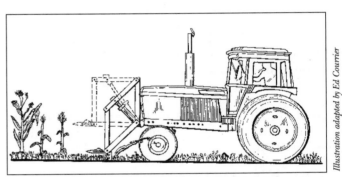

Illustration adapted by Ed Courrier

Side view shows hinged, quadrangular metal frame supporting Boydston's cutter bar. The bar can be raised hydraulically as high as 5 feet. Boydston spent about $2,500 to build the device, but he feels it could be mass-produced for $1,500 apiece.

The cutter bar is supported by a hinged, quadrangular metal mounting frame that is raised or lowered by a hydraulic cylinder attached to the front of the tractor. Boydston got the idea for such a device in the early '70s. He built a wooden prototype and obtained a patent on the design in 1981. But it wasn't until '86 that Boydston went into a neighbor's welding shop for about three days and built a working model of his invention.

"The hardest part was figuring out something that would run for the least amount of machinery," explains Boydston. To power the cutter bar as simply and inexpensively as possible, he ran hoses to a hydraulic motor mounted on the left end of the bar next to the drive unit. An old tractor-wheel weight was placed at the opposite end to balance the bar. The bar, itself, is braced with reinforced quarter-inch angle iron.

"After I got it where it would run, the soybeans were pretty well filled-out in the neighbor's field. I didn't want to take it in there and cause more damage than it was worth. So I took it down the road to a patch of weeds. I also mowed some cornstalks in the garden. It *does* work!" Boydston

declares.

Several people have contacted Boydston about manufacturing his machine. With the high cost of herbicides, increasing concern over pollution and continuing state and federal crackdowns on farm chemicals, Boydston believes, "It won't be long until everybody has one."

Clean Bean Machine
Topper slices weeds, not beans.

DAKOTA CITY, Neb. — Instead of resorting to herbicides to tidy up his low-input beans, Vincent Kramper invented a soybean "topper" — a 10-foot-wide weed clipper that slices off volunteer corn and tall weeds just above the tops of the beans.

"Weeds in soybeans have always been a problem. Some people use chemicals, but I hardly use any at all," says Kramper, who grows 1,000 acres of corn, soybeans, alfalfa and oats. "I figured I needed something to cut them off. It stops the weeds from going into seed."

The topper has five 30-inch steel blades that turn at about 700 rpm. It mounts easily on a 3-point hitch. For safety, the blades are surrounded by iron framework. Each blade is equipped with a slip clutch.

Cuts High Or Low

"If the weeds aren't very thick, you can move along in fourth gear at a quick pace. But if they're thick, you better slow down," he says. "I use it only on my soybeans once a year, but some people also use it on milo. You can really use it on any crop that doesn't grow higher than 4 feet. That's about as high as you're going to get on a 3-point hitch. It can be used as low as 1 foot off the ground.

"I don't care what the coffee-shop talk is. I go by what goes into the bank," Kramper says of his reliance on rotation, tillage and the topper for weed control.

Besides, the topper has become a profitable sideline. After his initial investment of $500 six years ago, Kramper now manufactures the toppers himself and sells them for about $1,100 each.

"I haven't had any complaints, but I've heard that some customers are still using chemicals," says Kramper. "I suppose that's their decision. I foresee the day coming where many chemicals will be banned. The time is coming that we'll be using more machines like this."

For more information on the topper, write: Soybean Topper, c/o Vincent Kramper, R.R. 1, Box 338, Dakota City, NE 68731. Phone: (402) 987-3560.

Slick Wick Wipes Out Weeds

RUSHMORE, Minn. — "Bean buggies and walking the beans are a thing of the past," says farmer Darwin Reyne. "Our 'Weed Attack' system is the wave of the future, because it uses a minimum of herbicide and no extra trips across the field."

And when Reyne says minimum, he means *minimum*. His over-the-row wicks require just 1 gallon of Roundup and 2 gallons of water to control in-row weed escapes on *300 acres*. "Plus, there's no physical contact with the chemical as in hand-

spraying while walking or riding on bean bars," he adds.

The wipers consist of a 16-inch long, ⅝-inch-diameter rope wick mounted on a fully adjustable 24-inch-long arm. The units are mounted on the cultivator to ride just above the crop row. A 12-volt pump is switched on to recharge the wicks as needed through ¼-inch-diameter tubing. Herbicide is held in a 3-gallon tank, enough to cover 100 to 300 acres without stopping to refill.

Reyne cultivates his ridge-tilled soybeans twice with an eight-row Buffalo cultivator equipped with the wipers. The cultivator is also rigged so he can spot-spray low-growing weeds in the row, when necessary.

"Large, conventional wipers are a lot more expensive and use three or four times as much chemical," Reyne points out. "Plus they require an extra trip over the field."

Reyne began testing his Weed Attack wick system on his own and neighboring farms in '85. Now he has a growing business making and selling the product. "I feel I'm ready to challenge any weed-control system. I use very little chemical, and I'll be done a lot sooner, too," he says.

Cost is $31.50 per row unit, including mounting brackets, metering device and all necessary fittings and tubing. Electrical components, pump, valve and tank cost an additional $110. Reyne makes brackets for Deere, IH, Buffalo, Hiniker and all Danish-tine model cultivators. Write: Darwin Reyne, Rt. 1, Rushmore, MN 56168. Phone: (507) 478-4213 or 478-4437.

New Machine 'Prevents' Weeds

FARGO, N.D. — If inventor Art Fossum has his way, you'll soon be able to cut your herbicide bill and harvest weed seeds for livestock feed while you harvest your grain.

Since the mid-'80s, Fossum has been perfecting a device that attaches to the back of combines and harvests weed seeds that would otherwise pass through and reinfest the field. "This is the best way of keeping weeds out of the field," he says. "My hope is that it will help those farmers who are trying to eliminate herbicides. They'll benefit the most."

North Dakota State University (NDSU) research shows weed-seed screenings can make excellent feed. "Screenings run 14 to 16 percent protein. And they're pretty high in energy — 70 to 75 percent TDN — making them similar to oats," says Vern Anderson, NDSU livestock specialist.

Simple To Build

"It's a very simple machine. Anyone could build one," says Fossum. Material coming off the combine's chaffer is fed into the weed-seed harvester's chute. A drag chain carries it over a vibrating screen, which separates weed seeds from straw. A continuous auger moves the seed into a 65-bushel bin.

In field tests, Fossum found that the harvester works best separating light-seeded weeds such as pigeongrass, wild oats and kochia. Depending on weed pressure, it might take anywhere from one round to an hour or more to fill the bin with weed seed. "You can definitely see the difference the next year. A lot fewer weeds come up," he observes.

Fossum's invention was inspired by his experiences as a thresher when he was younger. "In those days, we stacked the straw and the weed seeds and burned them," he recalls. He has built two prototypes of the machine and is working to find someone to manufacture and market it.

For more information, write: Art Fossum, 1034 North 15th St., Fargo, ND 58102. Phone: (701) 235-0833.

Appendix
Groups That Can Help

Reading about controlling weeds with fewer chemicals is one thing. But seeing is believing. One of the best ways to boost your non-chemical weed-control confidence is to attend field days and workshops in your area that feature farmers who use some of the practices you've just read about in this book.

A good place to start is with the nearest Rodale Institute On-Farm Research Network cooperator. The Institute has networks in the Midwest, Mid-South and Mid-Atlantic regions. For information about workshops and field days, write: Field Days, Rodale Institute, 222 Main St., Emmaus, PA 18098.

Field days are also held each summer at the Rodale Institute Research Center (RIRC) in southeastern Pennsylvania. Write: Field Days, RIRC, 911 Siegfriedale Rd., Kutztown, PA 19530.

Many regional nonprofit groups also sponsor field days and workshops. Check the following list for those near you.

Some state departments of agriculture and land grant universities also sponsor on-farm and experiment station field days that may be of interest. We've listed some that specifically focus on controlling weeds with fewer chemicals. Also listed are organizations that can provide additional information.

National

Alternative Farming Systems Information Center
National Agricultural Library
Room 304
10301 Baltimore Blvd.
Beltsville, MD 20705
(301) 344-3724

Appropriate Technology Transfer for Rural Areas (ATTRA)
P.O. Box 3657
Fayetteville, AR 72702
(800) 346-9140

Bio-Dynamic Farming and Gardening Association
P.O. Box 550
Kimberton, PA 19442
(215) 935-7797

Committee for Sustainable Agriculture
P.O. Box 1300
Colfax, CA 95713
(916) 346-2777

Institute for Alternative Agriculture
9200 Edmonston Rd., Suite 117
Greenbelt, MD 20770
(301) 441-8777

National Coalition for Alternatives to Pesticides
701 E St. S.E.
Suite 200
Washington, DC 20003
(202) 543-5450

Organic Crop Improvement Association
3185 Twp. Rd. 179
Bellefontaine, OH 43311
(513) 592-4983

Rodale Institute
222 Main St.
Emmaus, PA 18098
(215) 967-5171

Rodale Institute Research Center
911 Siegfriedale Rd.
Kutztown, PA 19530
(215) 683-6383

USDA Sustainable Agriculture Research and Education Program
Dr. Paul F. O'Connell
USDA/CSRS
Aerospace Bldg.
901 D St. S.W.
Washington, DC 20251
(202) 447-2860

Midwest

Alternative Energy Resources Organization
44 North Last Chance Gulch
Helena, MT 59601
(406) 443-7272

American Farmland Trust
407 S. Dearborn, #1550
Chicago, IL 60605
(312) 427-2943

Center for Rural Affairs
P.O. Box 405
Walthill, NE 68067
(402) 846-5428
and:
P.O. Box 736
Hartington, NE 68739
(402) 254-6893.

Farm Alliance of Rural Missouri
P.O. Box 1094
Jefferson City, MO 65102
(314) 636-6005

Farm Verified Organic
R.R.1, Box 40A
Medina, ND 58467
(701) 486-3578 or -3579

Illinois Sustainable Agriculture Society
Box 500
Rochester, IL 62563
(217) 498-7422

Indiana Sustainable Agriculture Association
1145 Krannert Building
Room 621
Purdue University
West Lafayette, IN 47907-1145
(812) 939-2813

Iowa Natural Heritage Foundation
505 5th Ave.
Des Moines, IA 50309
(515) 288-1846

Kansas Rural Center
304 Pratt Rd.
Whiting, KS 66552
(913) 873-3431

The Land Institute
2440 E. Water Well Rd.
Salina, KS 67401
(913) 823-5376

Land Stewardship Project
P.O. Box 130
Lewiston, MN 55952
(507) 523-3366
and:
103 West Nichols Ave.
Montevideo, MN 56265
(612) 269-2105

Leopold Center for Sustainable Agriculture
Agronomy Hall
Iowa State University
Ames, IA 50011
(515) 294-3711

Michael Fields Agricultural Institute
3293 Main St.
East Troy, WI 53120
(414) 642-3303

Michigan Agricultural Stewardship Association
c/o Tom Guthrie
7301 Milo Rd.
Delton, MI 49046
(616) 623-2261 or -2255

Minnesota Department of Agriculture
Energy and Sustainable Agriculture Project
90 W. Plato Blvd.
St. Paul, MN 55107
(612) 297-5599

University of Minnesota
Sustainable Agriculture Working Group
Department of Agronomy
411 Borlaug Hall
1991 Buford Circle
St. Paul, MN 55108
(612) 625-0220

Nebraska Sustainable Agriculture Society
P.O. Box 736
Hartington, NE 68739
(402) 254-2289

Sustainable Agriculture Center
University of Nebraska-Lincoln
Chuck Francis
222 Keim Hall
Lincoln, NE 68583-0910
(402) 472-1581

Northern Plains Sustainable Agriculture Society
Susanne Retka Schill
R.R. 1, Box 36
Maida, ND 58255
(701) 256-2424

Ohio Ecological Food and Farm Association
65 Plymouth St.
Plymouth, OH 44865
(419) 687-7665

Practical Farmers of Iowa
Rick Exner
2104 Agronomy Hall
Iowa State University
Ames, IA 50011
(515) 294-1923

South Dakota Sustainable Agriculture Society
Box 214
Rosholt, SD 57260
(605) 537-4308

Wisconsin Rural Development Center
1406 Highway 18-151 East
Mount Horeb, WI 53572
(608) 437-5971

Wisconsin Sustainable Agriculture Program
Department of Agriculture, Trade
& Consumer Protection
P.O. Box 8911
Madison, WI 53708
(608) 267-3318

Northeast

Finger Lakes Organic Growers Cooperative Inc.
P.O. Box 549
Trumansburg, NY 14886
(607) 387-3333

Maine Organic Farmers & Gardeners Association
Box 2176
Augusta, ME 04330
(207) 622-3118

**Natural Organic Farmers Association
  of Connecticut**
Rt. 2, Box 229
Durham, CT 06422
(203) 888-9280

**Natural Organic Farmers Association
  of New Hampshire**
C/O White Farm
150 Clinton St.
Concord, NH 03301
(603) 648-2521

**Natural Organic Farmers Association
  of New Jersey**
R.D. 1, Box 263A
Pennington, NJ 08534
(201) 932-9394

**Natural Organic Farmers Association
  of Massachusetts**
Julie Rawson or Jack Kittredge
R.D. 2, Sheldon Rd.
Barre, MA 01005
(508) 355-2853

**Natural Organic Farmers Association
  of Vermont**
15 Barre St.
Montpelier, VT 05602
(802) 247-3979

**Natural Organic Farmers Association
  of New York**
P.O. Box 454
Ithaca, NY 14851
(607) 648-5557

**Natural Organic Farmers Association
  of Rhode Island**
89 Country Dr.
Charlestown, RI 02813
(401) 364-9930

New Alchemy Institute
237 Hatchville Rd.
East Falmouth, MA 02536
(508) 564-6301

Western New York Crop Management Association
   Cooperative Inc.
21 South Grove St.
East Aurora, NY 14052
(716) 655-4353

South

Arkansas/Oklahoma Sustainable
   Agriculture Network
Dr. Gail Lee
Arkansas Cooperative Extension Service
P.O. Box 391
Little Rock, AR 72203
(501) 671-2173

Carolina Farm Stewardship Association
115 W. Main St.
Carrboro, NC 27510
(919) 968-1030

Community Farm Alliance of Kentucky
200 Short St.
Berea, KY 40403
(606) 986-7400

Kerr Center for Sustainable Agriculture
P.O. Box 588
Poteau, OK 74953
(918) 647-9123

Mississippi Organic Growers Association
Tom Dana
Rt. 1, Box 442
Lumberton, MS 39455
(601) 796-4406

Ozark Small Farm Viability Project
Larry Williams
P.O. Box 205
Greers Ferry, AR 72067
(501) 825-7500

Tennessee Land Stewardship Association
Jim Joiner
Rt. 1
Liberty, TN 37095
(615) 563-2353

Virginia Association of Biological Farmers
Box 252
Flint Hill, VA 22627
(703) 885-3590

West

BioIntegral Resource Center
P.O. Box 7414
Berkeley, CA 94707
(415) 524-2567

California Action Network
P.O. Box 464
Davis, CA 95617
(916) 756-8518

California Association of Family Farmers
Box 363
Davis, CA 95617
(916) 756-7420

California Certified Organic Farmers
P.O. Box 8136
Santa Cruz, CA 95061
(408) 423-2263

Demeter Education Foundation
4214 National Ave.
Burbank, CA 91505
(818) 843-5521

Northwest Coalition for Alternatives to Pesticides
P.O. Box 1393
Eugene, OR 97440
(503) 344-5044

Oregon Tilth
P.O. Box 218
Tualitin, OR 97062
(503) 691-2514

Organic Farming Research Foundation
P.O. Box 440
Santa Cruz, CA 95061
(408) 426-6606

Palouse-Clearwater Environmental Institute
P.O. Box 8582
129 W. Third St., Suite 28
Moscow, ID 83843
(208) 882-1444

Progressive Farmers of the Inland Northwest
Bob Klicker
R.D. 4, Box 236
Walla Walla, WA 99362
(509) 525-2494

**Sustainable Agriculture Research
    and Education Program**
c/o Agronomy and Range Science Department
University of California
Davis, CA 95616
(916) 752-7557

Washington Tilth
c/o Anne Schwartz
1219 East Sauk Rd.
Concrete, WA 98237
(206) 853-8449

Canada

Canadian Organic Growers
Box 6408
Station "J"
Ottawa, Ontario, Canada K2A 3Y6

**Centre de Developpement D'Agrobiologie
    du Quebec**
224 Rue Principale
Ste. Elizabeth-de-Warwick
Quebec, Canada J0A 1M0
(819) 358-3850

Ecological Agriculture Projects
Box 191
Macdonald College
Ste. Anne de Bellevue
Quebec, Canada H9X 1C0
(514) 398-7771

**Resource Efficient Agricultural Production
    (REAP-Canada)**
Roger Samson
P.O. Box 125
21111 Lakeshore Rd.
Ste. Anne de Bellevue
Quebec, Canada H9X 1C0
(514) 398-7743

Index

D

E

F

G

H

T

V